Sway of the Ottoman Empire
on English Identity in the
Long Eighteenth Century

Brill's Studies in Intellectual History

VOLUME 209

The titles published in this series are listed at brill.nl/bsih

Sway of the Ottoman Empire on English Identity in the Long Eighteenth Century

By

Emily M.N. Kugler

BRILL

LEIDEN • BOSTON
2012

Cover illustration: Frontispiece from *The life and surprizing adventures of Don Antonio de Trezzanio*, by Muhammad ibn Abd al-Malik Ibn Tufayl (d. 1185), London: printed for H. Serjeant, at the Star, without Temple-Bar, [1761]. ©British Library. This text is an abridged and as the title implies, altered translation of *Hayy Ibn Yaqzan* published after the period of translations discussed in this book.

This book is printed on acid-free paper.

Library of Congress Cataloging-in-Publication Data

Kugler, Emily M. N.
  Sway of the Ottoman Empire on English identity in the long eighteenth century / by Emily M.N. Kugler.
    p. cm. — (Brill's studies in intellectual history, ISSN 0920-8607 ; v. 209)
  Includes bibliographical references and index.
  ISBN 978-90-04-21422-4 (hardback : acid-free paper) 1. England—Civilization—18th century. 2. National characteristics, English—History—18th century. 3. Turkey—History—Ottoman Empire, 1288–1918—Public opinion. 4. Turkey—Foreign public opinion, British. 5. Public opinion—Great Britain. 6. Imperialism—History—18th century. 7. Great Britain—History—18th century. I. Title.

  DA485.K84 2012
  303.48'24105609033—dc23

                                                                          2011048132

ISSN 0920-8607
ISBN 978 90 04 21422 4 (hardback)
ISBN 978 90 04 22543 5 (e-book)

Copyright 2012 by Koninklijke Brill NV, Leiden, The Netherlands.
Koninklijke Brill NV incorporates the imprints Brill, Global Oriental, Hotei Publishing, IDC Publishers, Martinus Nijhoff Publishers and VSP.

MIX
Paper from
responsible sources
FSC
www.fsc.org   FSC® C004472

PRINTED BY DRUKKERIJ WILCO B.V. - AMERSFOORT, THE NETHERLANDS

For T.K.

CONTENTS

ACKNOWLEDGEMENTS

I wish to express my gratitude to the many people and institutions that supported this project. My thanks first go to the editors at Brill for their patience and guidance, particularly Rosanna Woensdregt, Assistant Editor History and Sociology, and Marti Huetink, Senior Acquisitions Editor History and Sociology. Thanks are also due to EJ Eckert for her help editing this project.

The early seeds were sown for this book during my undergraduate years at Scripps College. When fellow alumna hear about my research, they often reply, "How very Scripps." Its interdisciplinary and transnational approach to the humanities tempted me away from pre-law into the study of literature. The theoretical tools learned there still serve me today. I would not have thought to become an academic without the examples of professors such as Mark Katz, Preethi De Silva, or the late Michael Harper. During this time, I also had the good fortune to take a class with Claremont McKenna College's Audrey Bilger, who introduced me to a version of eighteenth century that made me abandon literature of the millennial United States as my primary focus. She continues to the standard by which I judge myself a teacher and scholar.

The actual research that led me to this subject began during my doctoral program the University of California, San Diego's Literature Department. I first began writing on Aphra Behn in a seminar on masculine sensibility with Jordanna Rosenberg, read of medieval models of race through the guidance of Lisa Lampert-Weissig, and grappled with Samuel Johnson's eccentric vision of the Oriental under Nina Zhiri's supervision. The staff, particularly, Ana Minvielle, was an invaluable resource in helping me find funding for my early career, including a year-long fellowship that allowed me to complete my dissertation. The UCSD community continues to help my research as an academic. I'd especially like to thank Kathryn Shevelow and Rosemary Marangoly George, for their support and guidance. Warm thanks also go to Marcel Hénaff, Lisa Lampert-Weissig, Cynthia Truant, Sarah Johnson, Steve Cox, and the late Masao Miyoshi for their generous feedback and advice.

Completing this project was made possible by the intellectual and emotional support of my colleagues in Colby College's English Department, as well as the material support of its administration. Anindyo Roy and William Orchard provided excellent sources of knowledge in the last phases of this project. It is remarkable how much academic employment aids scholarship. It provides access to libraries and academic databases, but more importantly, it fosters scholastic communities that make new research possible. I am grateful to Deans and English department chairs at the institutions where I have studied and worked, as well as to those at other universities, who adopted me into their communities and granted me access to their resources: San Diego State University's William A. Nericcio, University of San Diego's Sister Mary Hotz, and Roger Williams University's Dianne Comiskey and the Assistant Dean of Humanities and Performing arts, Roberta Adams.

I am also grateful for the feedback of colleagues at conferences, especially at the annual meetings of the American Society for Eighteenth-Century Studies in 2007–2010. The audience at the 2007 German Society for Eighteenth-Century Studies panel chaired by Stefanie Stockhorst greatly helped me clarify the ideas that would become the second chapter of this book. The bibliography shows how much I have benefited from the new work presented at these meetings.

This research was made possible by librarians and other staff members at the British Library, Bodleian Library, Brown University's John D. Rockefeller, Jr. Library, The Huntington Library in San Marino, California, Colby College's Miller Library, San Diego State University's Love Library, UCSD Mandeville Special Collections, The Victoria and Albert Museum's Theatre and Performance Archives at the Blythe House in Kensington Olympia, and particularly, UCSD Social Sciences and Humanities Library, whose Rob Melton still generously responds to all the queries I send.

In both tangible and intangible ways, my friends and family have helped create this book. My parents, David and Nancy Patterson raised me with the belief that I deserved a university education; my sister, Rosemeri, possesses the ability to be equally at ease with Classical Greek as she is with computer programming, which never ceases to prove useful or astonish me; my in-laws, Jacek José and Cheryl Kugler, for reading several drafts, even though my humanities background rarely overlapped with their respective expertises in political science or library science; my grandmother, Meri Nitta, who taught me that every 'truth' has a historical origin in the fictions of those with power; and most of all, Tadeusz Kugler, for always being prepared to read a paragraph, hear an idea, and honestly evaluate everything I brought to him.

THE 'OTHER' ENGLAND:
OTTOMAN INFLUENCE ON ENGLISH IDENTITY

During the eighteenth century a significant shift occurred in England's perceptions of its position in relation to the rest of the world. It is difficult to underestimate the magnitude of the changes in England from its small colonial attempts in the seventeenth century to its global empire of the nineteenth. For example, consider the stark differences between England's statuses in 1750 to 1850. During this time the population of the British Isles tripled and the political turmoil experienced in other European nations was largely avoided.[1] But most of all, England transitioned from its paltry colonies bordered and often threatened by other European powers, such as the French, Spanish, and Ottomans, to a vast global empire. Maya Jasanoff provides a sense of the huge scope of the nineteenth-century British Empire that was made possible by the late eighteenth-century 'swing to the East':

> The British Empire in 1850 encompassed a quarter of the globe, stretching from Ottawa to Auckland, Capetown to Calcutta, Singapore to Spanish Town. One in five people in the world was Queen Victoria's subject; many millions more (in Argentina or Portugal, for instance) lived in states bankrolled and indirectly steered by Britain.[2]

At the beginning of the eighteenth century, however, this future as the nearly undisputed imperial power of the nineteenth century could not be known.

Examining the eighteenth century as the fulcrum point of this change, my book explores shifting views of race and national identity in England through the lens of it representations of an established empire of the era, the Ottomans. During the nineteenth century, English representations of the 'Orient' would position the British Empire as more powerful than 'Eastern' states, such as India and Egypt. In English texts during the periods leading up to and throughout the eighteenth

---

[1] Maya Jasanoff, *Edge of Empire: Lives, Culture, and Conquest in the East, 1750–1850* (New York: Knopf, 2005), 5.

[2] Ibid., 6.

century, the Ottomans are not portrayed as powerless, decaying, or passive. Instead, the Ottoman Empire represented a powerful force that influenced European politics, culture, and self-image. The Ottoman Empire existed from 1299 to 1922, with the height of its power is widely seen as occurring in the sixteenth and seventeenth centuries. Its territories stretched from the Middle East to Southeastern Europe and North Africa. In the latter, it held Algiers, Tunis, Tripoli, Alexandria and Cairo. It encompassed the Red Sea and stretched to the Caspian. It possessed sites central to Western European mythology, such as Athens, Jerusalem, and Constantinople, later renamed Istanbul. In many ways, it was also a European power. Belgrade, Budapest, and most of the Balkans were Ottoman territories. Its influence reached even further. Examining the emergence of abolition in Islamic empires, William Gervase Clarence-Smith uses slavery as a means of showing the scale of the Ottoman Empire's reach in the sixteenth century:

> Ensconced in Maghibi ports under Moroccan or Ottoman suzerainty, Barbary corsairs culled people from as far as the Newfoundland Banks and Iceland.... The Ottomans took the Balkans and penetrated into Central Europe, only being checked at the gates of Vienna in 1529, and again in 1683. Crimean Tatars, Ottoman vassals, sacked Moscow outside of the Kremlin walls in 1571, and assiduously 'harvested' Christians.[3]

In Early Modern studies, many scholars are currently reassessing the role of the Ottomans in shaping England's relations with other nations. Goran V. Stanivukovic, for example, reminds us that the famous English defeat of the Spanish Armada in 1588 was made possible by Ottoman engagement with Spanish fleets in the Mediterranean, which prevented their full force from reaching England.[4] The Ottoman Empire, he points out, were "the only real empire in the sixteenth-century Mediterranean, [and] it was the obvious entity for England to engage with, if it was to battle the older maritime powers, particularly Spain, Italy, and France, for dominance on the seas and in the markets."[5] From the sixteenth to the early eighteenth century, the

---

[3] William Gervase Clarence-Smith, *Islam and the Abolition of Slavery* (Oxford: Oxford University Press, 2006), 8.

[4] I find this ironically similar to Britain near the end of the eighteenth century. Its naval superiority was countered in the American War by the French helping North American colonist divide up British military forces by engaging them globally.

[5] Goran V. Stanivukovic, "Introduction: Beyond the Olive Trees: Remapping the Mediterranean World in Early Modern English Writings," in *Remapping the Medi-*

Ottoman Empire dictated terms of European travel and trade in the Mediterranean, occupied sections of central and eastern Europe, and was enmeshed in the culture and politics of Europe.

This book holds that although imperial ambitions existed prior to England's rise to power in the nineteenth century, these ambitions functioned as part of fantasies emerging from a sense of cultural, economic, and martial inferiority when compared to other imperial powers, such as the Ottoman Empire. Regions later seen as Oriental 'Others' dominated by a European 'Self' were perceived as powerful, active forces capable of overwhelming and redefining English identity.[6] For me, the Ottomans' North African holdings are of particular interest, as they demonstrate a shift in the region's representations: Oriental Ottoman-inflected princes and warriors become associated with European enslavement of Africans. Excellent historical work can be found on this period. Though the work of these scholars forms the context for my argument, the focus of this book is less on the factual reality of international relations, trade, and politics. Instead, I use literary texts and their reception in spaces outside of official political power. I am interested in what kind of narratives were created at this time to explain, influence, and interpret England's relationship to the rest of the world.

By focusing on texts dealing with the Ottomans, I argue that we can observe the turning point in public perceptions, the moments when English subjects began to believe British imperial power was a reality rather than an aspiration. This book charts a transition in English cultural representations of itself, the Ottomans, and the relationship of these representations to shifts in transnational power relationships: as England grows into the center of power for the British Empire, its

---

terranean World in Early Modern English Writings (New York: Palgrave Macmillan, 2007), 5.

[6] While it is debatable when the concepts of 'English' or 'British' identity emerged, I am defining English identity here as coming out of a progressive movement away from older connections, namely to the Catholic continent. This trend includes the break made by Henry VIII and Elizabeth I with the Catholic Church; the emergence of England as part of an empire through both its colonial holdings and its creation of a United Kingdom beginning with the Acts of Union between England and Scotland in 1706 and 1707; and the limitations of monarchal power through the Civil War and the creation of a constitutionally limited monarchy in 1688. Through these events, 'Englishness' began to take on a religious and political meaning distinct from the populace's view of the rest of Europe.

self-representations become more powerful while its representations of the Ottoman Empire become less threatening and influential.

At the end of the eighteenth century and dawn of the nineteenth, old racial models that focus more on rank and religion are increasingly replaced by biological ones. More confident in England's position as the central power of the British Empire, audiences turned to cultural representations that were less concerned with anxieties over a loss of identity to older powers such as the Ottomans and instead more focused on debates over what responsibilities Britain possesses as a dominant world power. The majority of this work challenges concepts of an ahistorically powerful England and shows both that the intermingling of Islamic and English Protestant identity was a recurring theme of the eighteenth century, and that this cultural mixing was a topic of debate and anxiety in the English cultural imagination.

The New Orientalism: Challenges to Old Paradigms in Early Modern Studies

The ideological frameworks producing scholarship on 'Western' encounters with and representations of the 'East' underwent significant change during the last decades of the twentieth century. Arguably one of the most influential texts in the creation of this scholastic shift, Edward Said's 1978 *Orientalism* described an oppressive Western colonizing subject and an oppressed Oriental subjugated object. This text not only analyzed way colonial relations were represented: it challenged they way acceptance of or blindness to these representations reproduced political and cultural oppression. By creating a binary between Orient and Occident, European colonizers could justify their oppression of these other cultures by representing themselves in positive characteristics in opposition to those assigned to their subjects: if the "Oriental is irrational, depraved (fallen), childlike, 'different,'" then the European can emerge as "rational, virtuous, mature, 'normal.'"[7] The European is set up as the Subject who gives meaning to the Orient as Object: "[W]hat gave the Oriental's world its intelligibility and identity was not the result of his own efforts but rather the whole complex series of knowledgeable manipulations by which the Orient was

---

[7] Edward Said, *Orientalism* (1978) (New York: Vintage Books, 1994), 40.

identified by the West."[8] Separate from any cultural or political reality existing in North Africa, the Middle East, and Asia, the Orient stands in for a system of ideas that negatively define Europe:

> Knowledge of the Orient, because [it is] generated out of strength, in a sense *creates* the Orient, the Oriental, and his world.... [The] Oriental is depicted as something one judges (as in a court of law), something one studies and depicts (as in a curriculum), something one disciplines (as in a school or prison), something one illustrates (as in a zoological manual). The point is that in each of these cases the Oriental is *contained* and *represented* by dominated frameworks.[9]

While Said does not dwell on the active role the Oriental subjects had in creating the objects that represented them—native informants, for example, acting as translators and guides or booksellers providing European scholars with local texts and artifacts—he does provide a key to understanding representations of the East and how they fit into the cultural logic of Europe.

European imperial power over the Orient, he argues, resulted in a static, often monolithic idea of the 'Orient' as an absolute Other, who is passive, feminine, and incapable of progress in the modern sense of the word. Said points to cultural representations as part of the foundation and justification of future colonialism: "To say simply that Orientalism was a rationalization of colonial rule is to ignore the extent to which colonial rule was justified in advance by Orientalism, rather than after the fact."[10] Part of this justification of European colonization of the Orient centers on scholarly projects as part of "growing systematic knowledge in Europe about the Orient," which was

> reinforced by the colonial encounter as well as by the widespread interest in the alien and unusual, exploited by the developing sciences of ethnology, comparative anatomy, philology, and history; furthermore, to this systematic knowledge was added a sizable body of literature produced by novelists, poets, translators, and gifted travelers.[11]

After the advent of Orientalism, Said believes that Europe

> was always in a position of strength, not to say domination. There is no way of putting this euphemistically...the essential relationship, on

---

[8] Ibid., 40.
[9] Ibid., 40.
[10] Ibid., 39.
[11] Ibid., 39, 40.

> political, cultural, and even religious grounds, was seen—in the West,
> which is what concerns us here—to be one between a strong and a weak
> partner.[12]

Yet historically, this is inaccurate when applied to European-Ottoman interactions before the nineteenth century. As Said's work focuses almost exclusively from the post-Napoleonic period onward, it should not be seen as a project focused on the past. If read within the context of Said's trilogy of *Orientalism, The Question of Palestine* (1979) and *Covering Islam* (1981), it primarily focuses on representations of the Middle East in the twentieth century, a period when Europeans possessed more power in international relations.

During the last decade of the twentieth century, the concept of Orientalism prior to the nineteenth century has been complicated by an examination of Early Modern England's relationship with Islamic nations, especially with the Ottoman Empire. Scholars have challenged applications of Said's Orientalism onto Early Modern English culture. The work of Nabil Matar—a prolific and influential scholar of European, particularly British, interactions with Arabic cultures—questions previous interpretations of Oriental representations. His *Islam in Britain, 1558–1685* (1998) presents the seventeenth century as a point of origin for racist ideology that would later justify English imperialism in the Near East. Focusing on the issue of apostasy in English thought, Matar argues that initially negative portrayals of Islamic peoples emerged from English insecurities in the face of Ottoman might. Plays depicting Christian converts to Islam punished and sermons fantasizing about the conversion of Muslims to Christianity are read as evidence of fears that the allure of Islam would sway English subjects away from Crown and Church. His subsequent work expands on this thesis by broadening the geographic scope and diversifying the cultural perspectives examined. *Turks, Moors and Englishmen in the Age of Discovery* (1999) presented a 'Renaissance Triangle' that linked English attitudes toward Islam to its dealings in the Mediterranean and Americas. The third installment of this first 'trilogy,' *Britain and Barbary, 1589–1689* (2005), continues to argue that the role of the Ottoman-controlled Mediterranean played as important a role than the more frequently recognized influences of Ireland and the Americas on shaping English identity. His second trilogy—*In the Lands of*

---

[12] Ibid., 40.

the Christians (2003), *Europe through Arab Eyes, 1578–1727* (2009), and *Britain and the Islamic World, 1558–1713* (2010), co-authored by Gerald MacLean—focuses on Arab portrayals of Europe.

Matar's groundbreaking work presents the seventeenth century as the turning point in English-Ottoman relations, frequently citing the rise of British naval forces as fundamentally changing the power relations between the rising empire and its predecessor. Similarly, other scholars position the early eighteenth century as a conclusion to the shift in political power. Gerald MacLean's *The Rise of Oriental Travel: English Visitors to the Ottoman Empire, 1580–1720* (2004), for example, contends that prior to the eighteenth century "English attitudes towards the Ottoman Empire in the early modern period were not as uniformly hostile or as fearful as we have often been lead to believe" and "that for many English people at the time, life within the Islamic Mediterranean offered an enormously attractive alternative to life in the British Isles."[13] His 2007 *Looking East: English Writing and the Ottoman Empire Before 1800* holds that we must look at a pre-colonial period where "English attitudes toward the Ottoman Empire can be better characterized by a discursive formation that I call 'imperial envy.'"[14] Within this mindset, the Ottoman represented both a model for imperial imitation as well as a source of anxiety over the potential threat of a foreign imperial force:

> To the pious among the English, the Ottoman Empire was at once the great enemy and scourge of Christendom, yet to the commercially minded it was also the fabulously wealthy and magnificent court from which the sultan ruled over three continents with his great and powerful army.[15]

Similarly, Daniel Vitkus analyzes Early Modern English plays on the assumption that its authors and audience viewed the Islamic holdings in the Mediterranean from "a vantage point of awe and deference (and sometimes envy)…from a position of inferiority" and that "English subjects were well aware that the metropolitan centers of wealth,

---

[13] Gerald MacLean, *The Rise of Oriental Travel: English Visitors to the Ottoman Empire, 1580–1720* (New York: Palgrave Macmillan, 2004), xiii, xiv.

[14] Gerald MacLean, *Looking East: English Writing and the Ottoman Empire Before 1800* (New York: Palgrave Macmillan, 2007), 20.

[15] Ibid., p. 21.

culture, [and] civilization...were located in the Mediterranean."[16] By contrast, "London was on the periphery of Europe and far from the Mediterranean Sea,...which had been home to the empires that really counted—Rome, Byzantium, then the empire of the Turks." By controlling large sections of the Mediterranean, the Ottoman Empire was perceived as the heir to both the region's "imperial history (from Alexander the Great to Suleiman the Great)" as well as its role, "for Christians, [as] the religious center[s] of the world." Jerusalem and Constantinople "were now ruled, however, by the Turks."[17] While he contends that Early Modern theatrical representations "helped to introduce a model of contact and engagement with foreign peoples that prepared the way for empire," his discussion of English representations of Islam upsets today's concepts of Occident-Orient power dynamics.[18]

This growing body of scholarship dealing with theatrical depictions of the Ottoman that do not adhere to Said's Orientalism frequently cuts off as the eighteenth century begins. Bridget Orr's *Empire on the English Stage, 1660–1714* (2001), Richmond Barbour's *Before Orientalism: London's Theatre of the East, 1576–1626* (2003), and Linda McJannet's *The Sultan Speaks: Dialogue in English Plays and Histories about the Ottoman Turks* (2006) all build off Matar's presentation of Early Modern England's insecurity about its imperial prospects, and pinpoint the seventeenth century as an end of an era when dealings with a more powerful Ottoman Mediterranean shaped English identity.[19]

---

[16] Daniel Vitkus, *Turning Turk: English Theater and the Multicultural Mediterranean, 1570–1630* (New York: Palgrave Macmillan, 2003), 31.

[17] Ibid., 31.

[18] Ibid., 198.

[19] Orr's work on the Ottoman influence also intersects with a larger movement that questions the stability and acceptance of an English Empire in the Early Modern and Restoration eras. In recent work on the transition out of the Commonwealth into the 1688 constitutional monarchy, Gary De Krey highlights the sense of instability surrounding these early colonial ventures: "The English colonial domain was nevertheless still in its infancy, and it was challenged by French competition as well as that of the Dutch. Settlement in the North American colonies remained scattered, for instance, with fewer than 60,000 colonists, and the New Englanders had hitherto accepted little direction from England. The growth of English Overseas trade, especially of its colonial trade, would accelerate noticeable during the Restoration.... In time,...the English would overtake their Dutch and French trading rivals. Anglican royalists of the 1660s could not foresee these results, however" (*Restoration and Revolution in Britain: A Political History of the Era of Charles II and the Glorious Revolution* [New

Rethinking the Ottoman Influence in English Studies

Building on the work of these scholars, I apply their examination of Early Modern English culture to the eighteenth century. Although the political reality of English-Ottoman relations may have shifted militarily, culturally it took longer for either side to grasp this new power dynamic. An illusory view of Ottoman Empire's power persisted into the eighteenth century. Ann Thomson, for example, points out that Europeans saw a stable imperial outpost in the North African Ottoman holdings, when in fact

> regencies, under the nominal control of the Sultan in Constantinople, were ruled by the Turkish militia, which was completely separate from the rest of the population, who had no influence over or say in the government. The policy of these states was largely independent of their nominal overlord and they behaved to a certain extent as independent states, which caused the Europeans difficulties in their relations with them.[20]

In addition to the lack of uniform rule throughout the Barbary, Matar adds that by the seventeenth century "there were already infrastructural and economic weaknesses in the Ottomans' Empire, [but] they were not yet widely evident to the average Christian/Briton."[21] In the cultural artifacts of plays, translations, and prose fiction, the growing realization of Ottoman decline is delayed, and we can see the Ottoman influence continuing to shape English identity into the mid-eighteenth century. Examining these texts for the appearance of the gradual realization of a stable English empire also reveals how images of Ottoman might were replaced with those of Oriental decay or African servitude.

I position the long eighteenth century as a pivotal moment where England's perception of its position in the world shifts. This is the period where the pre-colonial awe of more powerful empires such as the Ottomans transforms the imperial mastery explored by Said. Prior

---

York: Oxford University Press, 2007], 49–50). Similarly Jonathan Scott's examination of empire and republicanism during the mid-seventeenth century emphasizes unstable present and unclear future of English colonialism (*Commonwealth Principles: Republican Writing of the English Revolution* [Cambridge: Cambridge University Press, 2004]).

[20] Ann Thomson, *Barbary and Enlightenment: European Attitudes Towards the Maghreb in the 18th Century* (New York: E.J. Brill, 1987), 11.

[21] Nabil Matar, *Islam in Britain, 1558–1685* (Cambridge: Cambridge University Press, 1998), 16.

to and during the eighteenth century, the Ottoman world, especially its Mediterranean territories, possessed a different relationship with and played a different role in the cultural imagination of Europe than other areas of the world. The Ottoman territories of the North African western and central coastlines of present-day Morocco, Algeria, Tunisia, and Libya, referred to as the Barbary Coast or Maghreb during this era, represented to Europeans a space of cultural tradition and imperial stability. Surveying eighteenth-century European perceptions of this region, Ann Thomson argues that

> North Africa was not, in 'civilised' European eyes in the early eighteenth century, a savage region; it was not an area to which Europeans traveled in search of marvels and mysteries, or even in the main to find primitive people, as they went to North America or afterwards to the South Seas. It was not, in short, a land for exploration.[22]

Nor was it "an immediate example of an ancient civilisation from whose philosophy they could learn, as were China or India."[23] Instead, North Africa represented an immediate part of European life through the two "numerous and continuous contacts throughout history,...[making North Africa] an integral part of the Mediterranean civilization" (1). Basing her argument on the historical relationship between Europe and the Mediterranean, Thomson contends that while Europeans perceived North Africans as different from themselves, "[t]he Barbary states were in many ways part of the world that was familiar to Europeans" (2).

This perception remains distinct from Said's concept of an Oriental Other. Instead of comprising an unfamiliar, exotic culture, Thomson contends that the "Barbary states were in many ways part of the world that was familiar to Europeans... [thus they] tend to become invisible to present scholarship, although this does not mean they were not present in European thought" (2). She supports this claim by pointing to areas of study where North Africa is absent and other countries are positioned as the Other: "We never find the North African used as an example in ethnographical, sociological or philosophical works in the eighteenth century. Nor did Barbary exercise the exotic fascination of civilizations like that of China or even of oriental towns like Constantinople" (2). She goes on to argue that by looking "more

---

[22] Thomson, *Barbary and Enlightenment*, 1.
[23] Ibid., 1.

[Handwritten margin note: But what about English? In earlier pages Keҫler asserts that London perceived itself as peripheral to the Med world.]

closely at the way Barbary was perceived," we can then learn "how categories present during the Enlightenment for interpreting the rest of the world made it difficult to find a place for this reason and for the knowledge concerning it" (2). Thomson's insistence on the immediacy of the Islamic world, specifically the Ottoman Mediterranean, in European scholarship is part of the foundation of my own interpretation of eighteenth-century texts. It is vital that this period of history be viewed not only through the global imperialism it set up in the nineteenth century, but in its own historical context when Islamic empires stood as world powers often superior to their European counterparts.

England in particular was not in a position to dominate the 'Orient' until perhaps its eastward colonial swing at the beginning of the nineteenth century. Even though it began to grow as a colonial power throughout the seventeenth and eighteenth centuries, it is important to keep in mind that the precariousness of England's political situation remained: the Tudor period was marked by religious upheaval and uncertain succession, and the Stuart period by regicide and civil war. Even the Hanovers dealt with political unrest throughout their rule. During the period examined in this book, the existence of a British empire—or for that matter, 'Britain' as a unified political entity—was an emerging concept of future aspirations. To emphasize this nascent and unstable imperial phase, I will refer to an 'English' empire. Its insecurities as an empire are seen not just in its dealings with the Ottomans or its incursions into the Americas and Africa. It was also trying to negotiate its relationship with the rest of the British Isles, namely Scotland and Ireland.

Leading up to the Restoration, England was not a powerful international force, but a small, isolated island when compared to more powerful, better-organized world powers, such as the Ottomans. In his examination of Early Modern English portrayals of Islam, Daniel Vitkus reminds his readers that "the 'idea' of empire arose in England long before there was a real, material empire on the ground…like that ruled by Spain, or ancient Rome. Even a [post-1603] 'composite monarchy,' if that is what Jacobean 'Britain' was, does not comprise a fully imperial power that holds sway over a variety of conquered subject people."[24] The discourse surrounding English power is further brought into question when one considers that terms such as 'empire'

---

[24] Vitkus, *Turning Turk*, 6.

at this time do not necessarily carry the same meaning they do today: "For example, after the break with Rome in 1533, Henry VIII began to claim that England was an empire or 'imperium,' meaning that the kingdom of England was an autonomous polity."[25] Orientalism, in the sense that Said uses it, could not exist at this time because England lacked the power to dominate the East. When compared to the Ottomans, England prior to its 'second empire' inhabits a position similar to Said's Other: a 'passive reactor' to the military and cultural incursions of an Islamic 'actor.' When addressing Islamic-Christian relations, English texts frequently cast Muslims in a position of power, while they themselves—or their European counterparts—existed in a subordinate, even oppressed position. I will examine how the alternative view offered by Early Modern scholars can be extended into eighteenth-century studies.

I have divided the book into two halves. Part One examines the portrayal of English insecurities in the face of a more powerful Ottoman Empire. Chapter One offers an overview of anxieties over a loss of English identity through apostasy. Chapter Two incorporates the twelfth-century castaway narrative, *Hayy Ibn Yaqzan*, of Muhammad I. Tufayl into the section's examination of apostasy anxieties. Between 1671 and 1708, the translations of this text intended for English audiences' debate the definition of English religious identity and contest the amount of influence that other cultures, such as the Arabic one represented by I. Tufayl's work, should have in forming it. In the third chapter, I read the narrative of Daniel Defoe's *Robinson Crusoe* (1719) as a meditation on English fears of the loss of identity to a more powerful Ottoman Empire, and not as a celebration of English colonial conquest.

Part Two ties the argument to a classical model of race found within the European romance traditional depictions of Islamic cultures. Expanding its discussion of the representations of Ottomans to more general racial models of the period, Chapter Four examines a racial model of romance that categorizes humanity by rank rather than biology. At the same time that it links the argument to a pre-Early Modern history, it moves the analysis forward into the late eighteenth century's shift toward English imperial confidence. Chapter Five connects the book's argument about an emerging sense of English power

---

[25] Ibid., 200, n. 6.

within an Ottoman context to the rise of William Shakespeare in the
popular imagination as a representative of English cultural greatness.
In particular, it explores the representations of race, religion and class
surrounding eighteenth-century productions of *Othello*. Connecting
English views of transatlantic slavery with English views of the Ottomans, the ambiguous category of 'Moor' was consistently (and in the)
some of the literature surrounding the play, insistently) interpreted as
Turkish, so that the protagonist was shaped by images of a powerful
military and social force rather than by the 'uncivilized' nations from
which slaves were taken as chattel. Chapter Six furthers this discussion
with an examination of the shift of theatrical depictions of the Ottoman Empire into images of the slave trade in the stage adaptations of
Aphra Behn's *Oroonoko* (1688). Throughout the eighteenth century,
the various stage adaptations shift the protagonist's cultural affiliations from Islamic to 'pagan' African, while the prose narrative's use
of romance tropes to support Behn's royalist politics is also replaced,
eventually leading to the narrative's association with the abolition of
the transatlantic slave trade.

Conclusion

The eighteenth century was an era of transition during which England
rose as an empire while the Ottoman Empire declined. While the latter remained influential in the eighteenth century, England and other
European nations were also gaining prominence. By the end of the
nineteenth century, these countries were able to dominate world
politics and eventually dismantle the Ottoman Empire.[26] This shift is
similar to the changing power dynamics we observe today as Euro-
pean-North American power structures are challenged by the 'East'—

---

[26] Tadeusz Kugler and Siddharth Swaminathan argue that owing in part to population growth, countries such as China and India will be able to exert an increasing
amount of influence on world politics:
    China and India are the two rising giants of Asia…[the] sheer size of their popu-
    lations, combined with increasing access to technology and education, leads to
    projections that these developing giants will become contenders for international
    dominance even before they reach the income per capita levels of current devel-
    oped societies"; while "France, England, and Germany *were* great powers" as long
    as "the rest of the world had not yet joined the industrial revolution, they can no
    longer compete with national populations of the size of the United States, Russia,
    China, or India" ("The Politics of Population: India, China, and the Future of the
    World," *International Studies Review* [2006], 582, 590).

China, India, Southeast Asia, and, to a lesser extent, Eastern Europe. The Western rise to power can be traced back to a historical moment when it challenged the older Mediterranean power base. Recent scholarship in economics and political science points to economic, political, and cultural power growing in these Eastern countries. Scholars who use power transition theory place this new trend within a history of multiple cycles of power as a nation that was used to exerting power over less powerful nations loses its ability to influence the lesser powers in a global hierarchy; unable to control the status quo that keeps it in power, the hierarchy alters to fit the preference of the new set-up of world players. Though it declined during the nineteenth century, it remained a force in global politics until its defeat in World War I, after which it was partitioned and placed under the control of France, Britain, Russia, Italy, and Greece. It is key though that we do not view this earlier era through the lens of the nineteenth century.

During this time, the Ottoman Empire represented a powerful political, economic, and cultural force in the Mediterranean and throughout Europe. It is not until its late eighteenth-century 'swing to the East' away from colonial efforts in the Americas toward new ones in Asia that England emerges as successful empire. One of the earlier historians examining this shift, Vincent T. Harlow places the origins of England's nineteenth-century success as a empire in its eighteenth-century imperial failures: "the catastrophe in North America...was followed by a withdrawal of interest on the part of the British people from imperial activity. Humiliated, burdened with debt, and without friends, the State is portrayed as having gone into retreat for ten years."[27] The 'Second Empire' of Britain is founded in the failures of the first: the loss of the North American colonies signaled its decline in the Atlantic, and the government's move into India, a site of future colonial success, was prompted by the failures of the semi-private East India Company.[28]

---

[27] Vincent T. Harlow, *The Founding of the Second British Empire 1763–1793: Volume I: Discover and Revolutions* (London: Longman, 1952), 1. Harlow goes onto point out that "As evidence of the prevailing attitude of negation toward enterprise overseas,...Britain could think of nothing better to do with the new Austral[ian] Continent which had been acquired than to use it for a rubbish-heap, a convenient dumping ground for unwanted criminals."

[28] For a detailed account of this transition from Company to government colony, see Nicolas B. Dirks, *The Scandal of Empire: India and the Creation of Imperial Britain* (Cambridge, MA: Belknap Press of Harvard University Press: 2006).

What about Colley ??

PART ONE

CHAPTER ONE

CAPTIVITY, APOSTASY, AND IMPERIAL ANXIETIES:
ENGLISH FANTASIES AND FEARS OF THE
OTTOMAN INFLUENCE

The long eighteenth century witnessed a shift in England's view of itself as an international power. Its growing sense of confidence as an imperial force paralleled a decline in its views of the Ottoman Empire. Before this shift, the idea of empire in general generated a sense of unease within multiple English subgroups. Under the Stuart dynasty, the English government pushed for a more centralized powerbase that attempted to extend its authority into newly acquired territories. The 1707 Act of Union, for example, attempted to place both Stuart kingdoms (Scotland and England) under an officially unified Crown. In England's favor, the Act would prevent the then-separate kingdom from choosing a different monarch from England in future, which would lead to a loss of English control over the other nation. In the modern sense of empire, England would lose the territory gained by the Stuart ascension to the English throne. Contradicting this fear of losing imperial status, English skeptics of the Act feared that lack of parliamentary power in Scotland could erode the gains made in England to limit monarchal power and promote a more representative form of government that focused domestically on individual rights. Others expressed anxieties that an enlarged empire would financially weaken England. After all, this attempt to further England's imperial ambitions would involve taking on a state near financial ruin due to its failed colonial project, the Darién Scheme (1695–1700).[1]

---

[1] Seeking to counter England's fledgling colonial expansion, William Paterson sought funding from the Company of Scotland to found a Panamanian colony to link the Caribbean to the Pacific. Due to a combination of factors including domestic hostility from the Bank of Scotland and foreign hostility from England, the colony failed, sinking the nation into debt. A collection of contemporary accounts of and correspondence relating to the Darién Scheme is held in the Spencer Collection at Glasgow University. The collections includes accounts by settlers such as Walter Harris's *A Short Vindication of Phil. Scot's Defence of the Scots Abdicating Darien* (1700) and *An Enquiry into the Caledonian Project* (1701), as well as later reactions in Francis Borland's *The History of Darien* (1779). For a historical overview see Douglas

Known today primarily for his novels, Daniel Defoe, acting on behalf of the pro-Union forces, attempted to allay these fears on both the English and the Scottish sides in pamphlets as well as in conversation. In one of the pro-Union works often attributed to him, *The Advantages of Scotland by an Incorporate Union with England* (1706), the joining of crowns is linked more to future imperial prosperity than any present reality. Much of this positive portrayal of England's colonial future is clearly a counterargument to popular misgivings over England's stability as an empire. The pamphlet's main arguments are against Scotland joining an alliance with the Dutch or French. It does not argue that England is necessarily as powerful as these other colonial forces, but instead focuses on geography. It argues that "there's no Security in Foreign League," but that the proximity of England and Scotland would make it easier for them to defend each other: "Besides, are the French on any Terms capable to Propagate or Defend our Trade so as of Course we must be encouraged and defended when one with England?"[2]

The Scottish arguments against a Union demonstrate the lack of imperial status England held in the early 1700s. In *A Short View Of Our Present Trade and Taxes, Compared With What These Taxes May Amount to After The Union* (c.1706), William Black emphasizes the high English taxes that would not be offset by the arguably small colonial profits of English empire:

> I know, it will be said, That England has made great Riches by Trade, and that by this intended Union, we will enjoy the same Advantage of Trade they have, which will evidently enable us to pay all these Taxes. But those, that advance this Topick, should first consider, what Branches of Trade we get from England by this intended Union, more as we had formerly, and they will find we get none but the benefit of their Plantation

---

Watt's *The Price of Scotland: Darien, Union and the Wealth of Nations* (Edinburgh: Luath Press, 2007) and David Armitage's "The Scottish Vision of Empire: Intellectual Origins of the Darien Venture," *A Union for Empire: Political Thought and the British Union of 1707*, ed. J. Robertson (Cambridge: Cambridge University Press, 1995). For a detailed analysis of the financial history of the project, see Alex Murdoch, "Scotland, the Caribbean and the Atlantic World" *Journal of Scottish Historical Studies* 25.2 (2005): 149–51.

[2] Daniel Defoe, *The Advantages of Scotland by an Incorporate Union with England, compar'd with these [sic] of a coalition with the Dutch, or league with France. In answer to a pamphlet, call'd, The advantages of the Act of security, &c.* . . . ([Edinburgh?] 1706), 32.

Trade; and that this branch of Trade will ever afford us a Fond to pay all these Taxes, is what I am confident, none will affirm.[3]

Rather than offering universal growth, he argues that English overseas trade is monopolized by a few government sanctioned properties "that will restrict the Branches of Trade we presently enjoy: So it's still to be found out where our valuable free Trade is to be sought for."[4] The centralized, often London- and Crown-based organization of English overseas trade is presented as an advantage by Defoe in his three-part piece to English audiences, *An Essay at Removing National Prejudices Against a Union With Scotland* (1706): the Union would allow

> that these two Twin Nations may become one United English Empire, resolved into one Form of Government, one Interest, one Body Politick, under one Head, one Administration, one Representative, and strengthened by one United Body of Power; a Power thereby so Encreas'd, and in it self not only Impregnable, but Formidable to the whole World.[5]

Yet it was this centralized, limited access to empire that worried Scottish anti-unionists, as well as English subjects not involved in the debate.

The Union debates highlight existing anxieties within England over the growth of centralized political power as well as overseas expansions of trade and empire that threatened older hierarchies based upon domestic markets. Merchants wishing to enter foreign markets as independent actors found their ambitions curtailed by government-controlled companies. These government entities, such as the Levant and East India Company, laid the framework for future colonial endeavors. Examining English political conflicts at the beginning of the long eighteenth century, Gary De Krey notes divisions within government factions based in part on the belief that the official trading companies to the Levant, Russia, Africa, and the East Indies constituted a monopoly. Only those granted access by the government could benefit from increased global trade.[6] He points out, for example, that the London city leaders personally involved in overseas interests

---

[3] William Black, *A Short View Of Our Present Trade and Taxes, Compared With What These Taxes May Amount to After The Union* ([Edinburgh?] [1706?]), 6.

[4] Ibid., 7.

[5] Daniel Defoe, *An Essay at Removing National Prejudices Against a Union With Scotland* (London, 1706), 4.

[6] Gary De Krey, *A Fractured Society: The Politics of London in the First Age of Party 1688–1715* (Oxford: Oxford University Press, 1985).

fell along party lines: "Almost three in five of the Whigs were active overseas merchants, but this was true of fewer than one-third of the Tories. Whigs greatly exceeded Tories among City leaders drawn from every sector of London's overseas trade." Tories, on the other hand, were more invested in the domestic, for example, in industrial and bank-related arenas.[7] This partisan divide represented conflicting interests within England. Imperial expansion would benefit sectors of the nation seeking out new geographic areas for financial growth, while the other's political power and financial stability of other sectors relied on domestic interest. The latter could be threatened not only by a rise of new wealth from successful overseas investment contesting Tory policy, but the foundations of their power could be undermined by the failure of the overseas companies.

These fears of English imperial ambitions often intersected with fears of an authoritarian monarchy. Bridget Orr, in her work on seventeenth-century theatrical representations of empire, argues that despite monarchal ambitions for imperial expansion, there was "considerable ambivalence about aspirations to empire."[8] In line with De Krey's assessment, she notes that this skepticism fell along party lines, with playwrights such as John Dryden abandoning "idealized representations of empire" when the Stuart regime promoting it began to falter, and that Tory-affiliated writers such as Aphra Behn and Thomas Southerne (both of whom are discussed in Chapter Six) "criticized the emergent empire of trade" after the Whigs overthrew the Tory-favored monarch, James II, in favor of William of Orange. The literary debates that Orr charts contextualize empire within a struggle "between the appetite for a cultural dominance understood to be the accompaniment of great power and the assertion of liberty as the central political and hence cultural characteristic of the English."[9]

I view these conflicting interests as a debate over what constituted national identity. Would English subjectivity represent an imperial power with cultural, political, and financial influence on a global scale? Or would this expansion limit individual liberty in favor of a strong absolutist ruling power capable of managing an empire, similar to that of France and the Ottomans? Underlying this debate is the reality that

---

[7] Ibid., 126.
[8] Bridget Orr, *Empire on the English Stage 1660–1714* (Cambridge: Cambridge University Press, 2001), 9.
[9] Ibid., 10.

English national identity and the type of state England should become was unclear, unstable, and something both sides felt driven to define.

Yet the image of a powerful centralized government ruling multiple territories also held allure for some English subjects. Such a government could perhaps prevent the faction-driving unrest that caused the English Civil Wars and still played a role in post-Restoration England. England's imperial anxieties were twofold and contradictory: a strong, far-reaching empire could offer a stable identity for England and its territories, but it could also gain more control over disempowered minority groups. Reflecting these contradictory anxieties were the popular representations of the Ottoman Empire in the seventeenth and early eighteenth centuries.

As will be discussed in the following chapters, the Ottomans represented a stable and far-reaching empire. By contrast, England seemed vulnerable and unstable. Highlighting this contrast between the Ottoman Empire and England's standings in the world were the dual dangers the former posed to the latter. Not only were English nationals frequently taken captive on the Ottoman-controlled Maghreb or Barbary coastlines of the North African Mediterranean, many of them preferred the life they found there and converted to Islam. The Ottomans represented a state powerful enough to take away England's subjects against their will, and more frightening for some, it offered a new identity alluring enough that many an Englishman was willing to 'turn Turk.'

English Protestant Apostasy in the Ottoman Empire

The anxiety of English subjects taken into Ottoman servitude manifested itself within the popular imagination in several ways. One cultural manifestation played itself out in the London theaters, often reversing the narrative to a Turk captured by English influence and converting. According to Nabil Matar, writings from the Renaissance through the Restoration offered a means to create a world that empowered England and Christianity while denigrating the Ottomans and Islam:

> The way that English dramatists, preachers, theologians and others confronted Islam and Muslims was by fabricating images about them—by arranging protagonists and geography in a manner that was disembodied from history and cultural surroundings. In the imaginatively controlled

environments of the theater and the pulpit, Britons converted the unbe-
lievers, punished the renegades, and condemned the Saracens. As long as
the sphere of action was fabrication, the victory was won by Christians.
Outside that sphere, however, Englishmen and other Britons treated
Islam as a powerful civilization, which they could neither possess nor
ignore.[10]

In seventeenth-century plays such as Thomas Heywood's *The Fair
Maide of the West* (1604–1610), John Mason's *The Turke* (1607), and
Philip Massigner's *The Renegade* (1624), the figure of the Christian
apostate is punished through castration, represented as an exaggera-
tion of religious circumcision.[11] These point to a domestic need to
make the Ottomans seem less alluring, since the reality was that English Protestants were more likely to renounce country and religion
than their Ottoman counterparts.

English-Ottoman negotiations surrounding early overseas ventures
into Ottoman territories emphasize both the martial danger of the
Ottomans capturing English subjects and the cultural danger of the
prisoners' conversion to Islam. The 1580 agreement between Sultan
Murad III and Elizabeth I in *The Interpretation of the Letters, or Privilege of the most Mightie and Musumanlike Emperour Zuldan Murad
Can...* recognizes this reality of English conversions in the stipulations
involving the return of English prisoners:

> any pirates or other free governours of ships trading the Sea shall take
> any Englishman, and shall make sale of him, either beyonde the Sea, or
> on this side of the Sea, the matter shalbe [sic] examined according to
> justice, and if the partie shalbe found to be English, and shall receive the
> holy religion [Islam], then let him freely be discharged, but if he wil still
> remaine a Christian, let him then be restored to the Englishmen, and the
> buyers shall demaund their money again of them who solde the man.[12]

The language of this treaty item recognizes English rights, but in a
limited way. It recognizes that an English subject may prefer the legal
protection offered to an Ottoman subject, and the item is arguably
more concerned with the rights of Murad's people.

---

[10] Nabil Matar, *Islam in Britain, 1558–1685* (Cambridge: Cambridge University
Press, 1998), 20.
[11] For a more detailed analysis of the circumcision motif, see Matar. *Islam in Britain*, 53–54.
[12] Richard Hakluyt, *The Interpretation of the Letters in Hakluyt's The Principal Navigations, Voyages, Traffiques and Discoveries of the English Nation* (Glasgow: Glasgow
University Press, 1904), 188.

Although the letter opens by addressing Elizabeth I as an imperial ruler, "Queene of England, France and Ireland, the most honouable Queene of Christendom" and "graunt to all her subjects in generall, this our favour" of safe passage within the empire, Ottoman power is emphasized by the rarity of this privilege previously given to only the French, the Venetians and the Poles.[13] The existence of those previously taken prisoner also highlights the unequal relationship between the two nations, as there is no request for the return of Ottoman subjects. Other items in the agreement focus on the vulnerability of English subjects in the Ottoman territories. Murad III pledges his subjects will help when English ships are in danger or lost at sea, accept their money in exchange for food, and if English subjects

> shall for trafique sake, either by lande or Sea repaire to our dominions paying our lawfull toll and custome, they shall have quiet passage, and none of our Captaines or governours of the Sea, and shippes, nor any kinde of persons, shall either in their bodies, or in their goods and cattels, any way molest them.[14]

Even added to the earlier promises of free passage and protection, this is still dependent on the good will of the Ottoman representatives encountered. It is up to the Ottomans to dictate both the terms of the agreement as well as its enforcement. The solidity of the Ottoman law contrasts with the storms, pirates, and other misfortunes of fate facing the English in the text. Items eight through seventeen focus on English rights under Ottoman law. These rights include recourse to interpreters, procedures for absent English debtors, wills, blasphemy charges, and return of prisoners taken by the government (as opposed to the item covering pirates discussed above), all of which emphasize the stable power of the Ottomans against the English lack of political, financial, and linguistic power.[15] The letter emphasizes the danger of captivity facing English subjects attempting to expand English overseas influence. Yet the fear running through much of the English literature is not what happens to English debtors in the Maghreb or of the physical dangers posed by a venture to the Ottoman Empire. Instead, it was the fear of apostasy. This anxiety is not rooted in a threat of cohesion, but in the allure of shedding an English identity in favor of an Ottoman one.

---

[13] Ibid., 184–85.
[14] Ibid., 186.
[15] Ibid., 186–88.

The narrative of English captives and Muslim masters concerning fears of domination and a desire for power resonates throughout the two case studies discussed in this first half of this book: the translations of Muhammad Ibn Tufayl's *Hayy Ibn Yaqzan* (1671–1708) and Daniel Defoe's *Robinson Crusoe* (1719). While the former draws more obliquely on late seventeenth and early eighteenth-century debates over apostasy and captivity, Defoe's narrative begins its adventures with an episode of English enslavement in the Ottoman Empire. Set in the mid seventeenth century, Defoe's text would have resonated with the economic uncertainty created by the abductions at the individual, family, community, and national levels. Contrasted to the image of a stable, expanding English nation found in Defoe's political propaganda pieces, such as those in favor of the Act of Union, Robinson Crusoe's predicament is a believable scenario in the early eighteenth century and places it into an older tradition of English portrayals of Islam that should have been familiar to its first readers.

The threat of captivity produced cultural anxieties that undermined a stable sense of national identity as well as creating a material burden on captives' families from loss of a wage-earner. Despite this, a life within the Ottoman Empire also represented an opportunity for social and financial advancement for those who chose to adapt to their new environment. According to Matar, Islamic societies held a strong attraction for English Christians, particularly the poor and illiterate. The desirability for conversion came from the image of Islamic societies as richer, holding more promise of upward mobility (including the belief that a converted slave might be freed sooner than a Christian one). Ottoman Islamic societies were also viewed as culturally close to Christianity. The easy conversion of captives and other English subjects in the Barbary was facilitated by the belief that Protestantism and Islam possessed many similarities: "for many Christians, especially the poor and illiterate, conversion to Islam did not entail a traumatic change from one religion into another." Instead, it was perceived as a move from one sect to another within the same religion similar to the "way that Greek Orthodox Christians viewed their 'conversion' to Anglicanism and Presbyterianism in the nineteenth-century Middle East: as an adoption of a religion which provided them with a sense of imperial power and with prospects for success."[16] In this light, there

---

[16] Matar, *Islam in Britain*, 16.

was a trend of cultural imperialism between North Africa and England, where the latter was in danger of losing the cultural identity of
many of its subjects to the former.

Responding to the phenomenon of English conversions to Islam,
a sense of anxiety permeated English pulpits and communities. The
seventeenth-century English Church voiced wariness about embracing apostates—or even those suspected of it—returning after living in
predominately Islamic countries. Matar argues that the "reason why
the Church and the preachers were so firm against renegades was that
the parents of a returning convert willingly adopted the distinction of
inner faith and outer dissimulation in order to forgive their kinsman."[17]
Renouncing one's religion represented more than just a change of religious identity, but was also deeply connected to national identity:

> In English seventeenth-century thought, the renegade shared the infamy
> of the Machiavellian, Faustian and Moorish villains because he threat-
> ened not just the faith but the idea of England. He was renouncing all
> that defined England to Englishmen, and he was doing so by adopting
> the religiously different culture of Islam.[18]

In an early attempt to understand and prevent apostasy, the late-
sixteenth-century writer Sir Anthony Shirley divided Christian converts to Islam into four categories: those forcibly coerced into apostasy, child converts, "men who converted to Islam in order to end their
slavery," and those who converted through acculturation.[19] Although

---

[17] Ibid., 68.
[18] Ibid., 71.
[19] Qtd. in ibid., 25. Shirley presents child apostates as the most innocent and dangerous of the categories. Matar points out that "such concern for the children was not
a result only of sympathy. A fact well known among travelers was that those children
grew into one of the most fearsome orders within the Turkish army: the Janizzaries
[sic] (the New Soldiers). That the Janizzaries consisted of men who had originally been
Christian could not but appear as ironic to English and Christian observers" (24).
In his 16 September 1704 installment of *A Review of the Affairs of France*, Defoe
chides English subjects desiring a Ottoman victory over Catholic powers in the Battle
of Vienna: "Without Trespass upon their Prudence, I may very well believe, they never
examined what would be the Consequence of 200[,]000 Victorious *Turks*, settled in
Austria and *Vienna*, Garrison'd with 30[,]000 Janizaries [sic]" (238). His reference to
Janissaries implicitly points to his underlying fear of Turkish invasion: despite the
historical reality of Ottoman religious tolerance, Defoe fears that a non-Christian con-
queror will do more damage than a Christian one. The Janissaries foreshadow Defoe's
prediction that the fall of Catholic Vienna would lead to the forced conversion of
Protestant Germany and then the rest of Europe. If viewed alongside *Robinson Crusoe*,
the protagonist's decision to take the child Xury in his escape along with him, later
selling Xury into slavery until he converted to Christianity, could be read as a fantasy

English commentators such as Shirley tended to focus on the categories that involved coercion, accounts of freed captives who had not opted to convert challenged this belief that apostasy resulted from the application of force from rather than the allure of the Ottoman Empire.[20] Instead, it was likely that Shirley's category of conversion through acculturation was more prevalent. The close connections between religious law and civil life in the Ottoman Empire made the distinction between cultural markers such as dress and religious markers such as the Witness difficult to determine, for after hearing "the Witness so frequently from Muslim friends and associates, a Christian might repeat it inadvertently."[21] For commentators such as Shirley, the most frightening aspect of this possibility was perhaps the easy slippage between the labels of English and Ottoman. The lack of a clear moment of decision emphasizes the absence of stable, distinct identities.

Compounding these domestic fears of unstable national identity, the category of Ottoman was itself a racially and culturally instable category within English thought. The various nations, tribes, and cultural groups who practiced Islam were often grouped into one undistinguished mass, referred to interchangeably as Saracens, Moors, Turks, and Arabs. By not recognizing the cultural divisions between Muslims, many failed to distinguish a cohesive cultural identity in the religion at all. As David Vitkus points out, the

> Turks and their 'nation' were often depicted by European writers as a people without a deep-rooted, essential identity of their own. Instead of possessing a long-standing, ethnic position, they were characterized as upstarts, thieves, or as expanding, dangerously absorptive nations of renegades that had come into existence by feeding off other nations.[22]

The view of Islam as an unstable identity colors the views of those uncomfortable with its effects on English: in their eyes, to mix their

---

reversing the progress of a Janissary. Rather than a Christian child converting to Islam and serving Ottoman interests over European ones, Xury will be forced into service to and conversion into Western European Christianity.

[20] Matar, *Islam in Britain*, 25–26.

[21] Ibid., 30.

Shahadah or 'the Witness,' declaring aloud before witnesses that "there is no god but God and Mohammad is his Prophet," is the only requirement for conversion and is one of the five Pillars of Islam.

[22] Daniel Vitkus, *Turning Turk: English Theater and the Multicultural Mediterranean, 1570–1630* (New York: Palgrave, 2003), 16.

beliefs and identity with Islam's not only threatened to change what it meant to be English (which as discussed earlier, was not that well defined to begin with), but it exchanged their current identity for one that was diverse, chaotic, and rootless.

Arabic in the University and Coffeehouse

The anxieties over 'turning Turk' discussed in the factional and fictional narratives of English captivity in Ottoman territories went beyond anxieties about an unstable English identity abroad. Reactions to a perceived Ottoman influence on life in England varied according to the level of empowerment—or disempowerment—found in various subcultures. The English Civil Wars and Commonwealth had sharply divided the nation. It was not simply a matter of Catholics against Protestants or Royalists against Parliamentarians. Similar to the divide between Whigs and Tories on overseas trade, Dissenters contested the role of a central government in dictating individual religion, while those aligned with the Anglican state church sought to control unorthodox incursions into theology, including those promulgated by Islamic texts. What seems a domestic dispute, however, manifested itself in its dealing with the foreign. Particularly, the role of the cultural signs of the Ottomans' influence highlighted and fed into existing fissures in the idea of an English identity.

At the more empowered end of this debate, university studies were invested in studying Arabic language and literature as Classical objects, separate from present-day power struggles. In this way, established institutions (state-run or church-run schools) could control outside influences on its scholars and intellectual labor. This reflects what G.A. Russell terms the "'Arabick' interest" of the seventeenth and eighteenth centuries. This movement, according to Russell, "permeated English society at all levels, to include the court, the clergy the colleges of universities, diplomatic service as well as mercantile companies."[23] At Cambridge and Oxford, knowledge of Arabic was a requirement for the Arts degree. Increased scholarship in the field led to an increase in the collection, translation, and publication of Arabic

---

[23] G.A. Russell, "Introduction: The Seventeenth Century: The Age of 'Arabick'" in *The 'Arabick' Interest of the Natural Philosophers in Seventeenth-Century England*, ed. G.A. Russell (New York: Publisher, 1994), 2.

texts; theologians and political writers across the spectrum turned to these texts to support their arguments.

While the academic nature of the "Arabick interest" may seem to be a phenomenon limited to England's universities and not the everyday lives of most inhabitants, it is important to keep in mind two factors. First, as Ann Thomson points out, "Small as this educated elite was, it is nevertheless the body of knowledge constituted by them that has come down to us and influences to some extent our perceptions of the rest of the world, despite later developments."[24] The views of an elite body of intellectuals were crucial for shaping political policy as well as public perceptions. Second, it would be a mistake to think that only an educated elite was influenced by this contact with the Islamic world. The sailors on merchant ships, the customers throughout England buying products like coffee, all had their everyday life impacted by England's relationship with the East.[25] Embracing the foreign origins of the drink, many coffee houses identified themselves with the 'Turk's Head' on their sign, and their owners began "to adopt Muslim clothes and customs…[and] many woodcuts of the coffee-house showed owners and customers wearing a turban."[26] As Matar points out, there was a sense of anxiety concerning the potential cultural imperialism of the fashionable drink:

> Coffee could be a Muslim agent to entice Englishmen away from their religion and turn them into renegades [i.e., converts]…an anonymous writer declared, [it] a 'Turkish Renegade berry while water was English and loyal: their mix or marriage was the befouling of the latter'…[and that] coffee makes the drinker as 'faithless as a Jew or infidel.'[27]

The image of apostasy occurring through imbibing coffee is found throughout anti-coffee writing, and blurs the line between race and religion: "Those who drank it, some writers indicated, began to look physically like Turks: their complexion changed and they became swarthy and 'Moorish,'" which was presented as applicable "not only to the physical complexion [of the drinker] but to the moral condition

---

[24] Ann Thompson, *Barbary and Enlightenment: European Attitudes towards the Maghreb in the 18th Century* (New York: E.J. Brill, 1987), 1.
[25] Matar, *Islam in Britain*, 111.
[26] Ibid., 166.
[27] Ibid., 112–13.

CAPTIVITY, APOSTASY, AND IMPERIAL ANXIETIES

too."[28] Outward behavior and appearance signal inward qualities such as religious belief, national affiliation, and moral rectitude.

This fear of 'turning Turk' intersects both racially and religiously in the popular broadsheets and pamphlets, which ironically would have been widely circulated within coffeehouses. As its title implies, *A Broad-side against Coffee; Or, the Marriage of the Turk* (1672) positions the beverage as a threat to English identity.[29] The language of the poem represents coffee as an Ottoman force invading and sexually defiling vulnerable, feminine English waters. Despite being judged by the comic poem as "too swarthy for a Nymph [England] so fair" (line 12), coffee "his sails he did for *England* hoist" (line 13). The language of naval invasion characterizes the danger as not just to an internal conversion of the coffee-drinking English subject but to a undermining of the English state as a whole. The fantasy of the Turk turning English is present here as well: coffee is "a kind of Turkish Renegade," perhaps losing his own identity just as much as the English water (line 1). Although this symbolic conversion from bean to beverage when joined to the water destabilizes his sense of self, this decaying identity in turn infects English, not Ottoman, society. Used as a term of contempt rather than a signifying of chattel, coffee is a 'slave' that resists an equal blending of English and Turkish culture. English water meekly complies with the union, while he "must be *beaten* to it" (line 20). Even this change is temporary since "pause but a while, and he is non of he/Which for a truth, and not a story tells,/ *Nor Faith is to be kept with Infidels*" (lines 22–24). The poem represents the marriage of English water and Turkish coffee as a negative one. Alluding to William Shakespeare's *Othello*, "he suspects, and shuns her as a Whore,/ And loves, and kills, like the *Venetian Moor*" (lines 25–26). The imagery of the first half of the poem focuses on the unhappy and ultimately destructive union of an aggressive, masculine, invading Ottoman to a less powerful, feminine English figure, who is "common" but "too good" (line 28) for her Turkish spouse. The humorous references to cuckolding in this section could be seen as a sign of Ottoman weakness, but the killing of English water and the shift in focus to images of an infected English society undermine this. In England, "canting

---

[28] Ibid., 113.
[29] Anon., *A Broadside Against Coffee; Or, the Marriage of the Turk* (London: 1672).

Coffee has his Crew enricht" (line 33) in language reminiscent of high-waymen, pirates, or foreign invaders.

His "Crew" consists of lower orders of English society, who seduce or infect (depending on the language of the line) the upper ranks. First is a Coachman, a transitory figure who circulates the foreign habit of coffee drinking, creating new converts to "*drive on* the trade" (line 36). The transfer of coffee from coachman to quack emphasizes the foreignness of the drink, as it cries in stereotypically accented words, "*Me no good Engalash* [*sic*]!"(line 39). The "Quack" physician capital-izes the un-Englishness of the drink through his foreign lilt: "*Ver boen for de stomach, de Cough, de Physick*" (line 39). The poem's condemna-tion of coffee's influence echoes its earlier fears of an Ottoman figure setting sail for England through its non-military invasion by foreign labor. The Coachman and Quack are presented as non-native English subjects. Similarly, the vehicle to drink coffee is a "Mock *China* bowl" (line 42), which, resembling the coffee it serves, signals English assimi-lation to foreign practices. The English coffee drinkers are described in fallen language. They are "Drunkards" (line 51) who prefer Turkish coffee to native "Posset or Porrige" (line 52) as their cure for excess drinking. Similarly, they lose some of their humanity by becoming like "hungry Dogs" (line 50) or inhabiting a scene "like *Noah's* Ark, the clean and the unclean" (line 54) mixing indiscriminately. Despite this lowliness, fashion spreads the infection of coffee drink so that "he's no Gentleman that drinks it not" (line 56). The final image of coffee shows it infecting both its metaphorical bride, water, as well as English society at large with a kind of venereal disease: "From Bawdy-houses differs thus your hap;/ *They* give their *tails* [genitals], *you* [coffee] give their *tongues* [tastes] a *clap*!/ *Mens humana novitatis avidißima*"(lines 61–63). The combination of greed for novelty and sexual lust with physical hunger in "avidißima" brings together fears of overseas pow-ers and the loss of Englishness as national, racial, and religious identi-ties. It references the fears of English subjects 'turning Turk' in their search for financial gain and class mobility in the Levant as well as in their domestic fashions for foreign customs. For the poem, the lustful drive for the novel and exotic leads to the physical weakening of the English nation states.

Similarly, *The Maidens Complaint Against Coffee; or the Coffee-house Discovered, Besieged, Stormed, Taken, Untyled, and Laid Open to Publick View* (1663) and *The City-Wifes Petition against Coffee* (1700) associate coffee drinking with a loss of English identity to a powerful Ottoman influence. In the first text, Mrs. Troublesome connects the space of the coffeehouse with both the foreignness of the drink with financial instability when she informs her husband, coffee-drinker and usurer Mr. Suck-Soul, "you'l ene make your body as black with this cursed liqueur, as your Soul is with extortion."[30] Linking the usurer's darkening skin due to coffee with his negatively portrayed profession makes the coffeehouse a site of destabilization that will make its frequenters lose both their English identity as they 'turn Turk' and their financial solvency through dealings with unsavory customers. The coffeehouse attracts other destabilizing forces in English society. Frequenting it are a mountebank and apothecary who, like the Quack in *A Broad-side Against Coffee*, prescribe the drink to patients in order to make them more ill.

It is also undermines English marriages by luring men to its almost exclusively male-space. The servant, Joane, proclaims, "the Devil first invented this liquour, on purpose to plague our Sex." Her comic linkage of damnation with coffee is further developed by her companion Dorothy's preference to remain single rather than wed an absent coffee drinker. His damnation through coffee leads to her own, as she evokes the old saying that single women are damned to "lead Apes to Hell."[31] The sexual disruption of English life and spiritual damnation through coffee continues in *The City-Wifes Petition*, which complains that coffee is a "Turkish enchantress," who not only causes men to neglect women sexually, it feminizes them so that there is the danger that they may "usurp" the female "Prerogative of Tatling" or gossip.[32]

Much like the debates surrounding the I. Tufayl translations, the controversy surrounding that staple of Restoration public life, the coffee house, offers a powerful example of the way seemingly domestic concepts were infused with a foreign influence. According to Nabil Matar, whose work focuses upon the impact of Islamic culture on Early Modern England, part of the appeal of coffee after the establishment of the first coffee house in 1652, came from "a number of translations from Arabic [that] were published which described the health advantages

---

[30] Anon., *The Maidens Complain[t] Against Coffee* (London: 1663), 1.
[31] Ibid., 3.
[32] Anon. *The City-Wifes Petition Against Coffee* (London: 1700), 3, 2.

of coffee-drinking."[33] Referred to as the 'Mahometan' or 'Arabian berry,' the drink became intertwined with English Protestant identity as well, with some scholars arguing that "Coffee was the drink of the practitioners of the Protestant work ethic because it stimulated the mind of the drinker, increased his waking hours for productive work and reduced his sexual desire."[34] Yet, by the end of the eighteenth century, coffee could be evoked as a symbol of British nationalism. Following their loss of the American War, England faced the difficulty of what to do with the Black Loyalists who had fought against the colonist. Offered freedom from slavery and gifts of land during the War, these patriots now needed compensation. Meeting with little success in relocating them to Nova Scotia, Canada and to a lesser extent, the British Isles, many were sent to set up a community in Sierra Leone. In accounts attempting to positively depict the settler's progress, the ex-slaves' ability to produce coffee of equal quality to a London coffee house.[35] This is presented as a sign of the settlement's success as well as the 'Englishness' of the inhabitants. These settlers, many born in America and of African descent, represented a new type of British subject, who could live throughout the globe but identified with an empire based in England.

This connection of English daily life and religious beliefs with Islam contained a conundrum. In order to establish a strong link between national and religious identity, English Protestants need to study Arabic in order to have the intellectual means and historic tradition to break away from the rest of Europe. Yet, the pursuit of this goal required the study of Islamic texts, which ran counter to Christian beliefs that Islam was a counterfeit religion. It is important to remember that during the late seventeenth and into the eighteenth century, England was not a powerful, international force, but a small, isolated island when compared to the more powerful, seemingly better-organized Ottoman Empire.

The following chapters of this section explore the anxiety that the allures of the Ottoman Empire would incite apostasy in two case studies. In *Robinson Crusoe*, the fear of 'turning Turk' is clearly aligned with a sense of English colonial inadequacies when compared to

---

[33] Matar, *Islam in Britain*, 113.
[34] Ibid., 113.
[35] Simon Schama, *Rough Crossings: Britain, the Slaves and the American Revolution* (New York: Harper Collins, 2005), 386.

Ottoman imperial might. But this perceived danger of an Ottoman influence destabilizing English identity was not limited to overseas encounters. As an examination of the *Hayy* translations shows, fears of the Ottoman also manifested in more abstract forms surrounding the introduction of non-Christian Arabic texts into English Protestant thought.

CHAPTER TWO

ARABIC CASTAWAYS IN THE HIGH AND LOW CHURCHES:
DEBATING ENGLISH PROTESTANTISM IN THE
SEVENTEENTH-CENTURY IBN TUFAYL TRANSLATIONS

When mentioned at all in twentieth-century English literary scholarship, Andalusian scholar and philosopher Muhammad Ibn Tufayl's twelfth-century narrative *Hayy Ibn Yaqzan* is usually just briefly cited as a precursor to Daniel Defoe's *Robinson Crusoe*, while its use in understanding late seventeenth- and early eighteenth-century English culture through the translations produced from this period lies relatively untapped. The narrative centers on Hayy Ibn Yaqzan (literally, "Alive Son of Awake"), a man raised in isolation on an island by a doe. After his foster mother dies, I. Yaqzan attempts to discover the nature and meaning of existence. He begins with the material world that can be empirically observed—dissecting his foster mother's body to find the source of life, observing the animals and plants around him. Eventually, he turns away from the material to the spiritual through fasting and meditation, which allows him to commune with God. Afterwards, he meets a 'civilized' man, Asâl, who teaches him languages but is more impressed with this 'natural' man's understanding of the divine. They return to Asâl's civilized island to share I. Yaqzan's enlightenment with the population, but the people cannot cope with this new spirituality that depends on individual searching and not hierarchal commands, forcing the pair to retract their beliefs. By examining the translations of *Hayy* in England between 1671 and 1708, one can see the tensions being played out against each other, as one side seeks to contain I. Tufayl's narrative to a secular, academic world and the other seeks to use it to transform social hierarchies in a religious revolution.

While the influence of Islamic cultures can be seen throughout English society, acceptance of this foreign presence in the national imagination varied. For some, it was a way of breaking away from old hierarchies of Church and State while maintaining a kind of link with the past; for others, it challenged their definition of what it meant to be 'English,' threatening to dissolve this newly emerging identity. An example of these tensions can be seen in the debates surrounding the

English translations of I. Tufayl's *Hayy*. By examining how each of the translations contextualized *Hayy* to fit their ideology, we can see a larger debate at play over English identity and the role that foreign, non-Christian influences should have in forming it.

Ottoman Influence on the Lockean Subject

By the late sixteenth century, the Church of England was established as a sign of monarchial authority. As a result, both areas wrestled with issues of who had authority over whom in English society. On one hand, the Anglican Church had disavowed the power of the foreign Pope over English spirituality and made its own monarchs religious and political heads; in this light, obedience to the state could be conflated with obedience to God. On the other hand, more radical forms of Protestantism, such as the kind that helped fuel the English Civil War, advocated a non-hierarchical view of religion. Everyone could have an individual relationship with God. This individualist view spilled into the political arena, as members of these sects viewed political authorities as men like themselves rather than invested with divine authority.

In the seventeenth and eighteenth centuries, concepts of English sovereignty—over one's self and as a political structure—were deeply connected to other areas of study as well. John Locke embodies in many ways the post-Restoration views of man and government. His 1688 *Second Treatise on Government* offers a justification of William and Mary's coup and the expulsion of Mary's father, James II. Locke's insistence that an infringement on individual rights results in a State of War bolsters the new government's argument that the monarchy's power needed to be limited:

> he who would get me into his Power without my consent, would use me as he pleased, when he had got me there, and destroy me too when he had a fancy to it: for no body [*sic*] can desire to *have me in his Absolute Power*, unless it be to compel me by force to that, which is against the Right of my Freedom, *i.e.* to make me a Slave.[1]

Here, the rights of individuals—not the state—are of the utmost importance, with any threat to their freedom acting as a sign of future

---

[1] John Locke, *Two Treatises of Government* (1688), ed. Peter Laslett (New York: The New American Library, 1963), III.17.5–11.

incursions. Without sovereignty over one's own self, one is reduced to being a slave.

In this light, James's conflicts with Parliament and the appearance that he favored the Catholic minority over the Protestant majority become the first steps in the enslavement of the Commonwealth. A good monarch uses his power to maintain the freedom of the Commonwealth, not to exert authority over his subjects. Therefore, Locke may write "to establish the Throne of our Great Restorer, Our present King William," but he places power over the state in the hands of "the People of England, whose love of their Just and Natural Rights, with their Resolution to preserve them, saved the Nation when it was the very brink of Slavery and Ruine."[2] In this treatise as well as other texts such as the *Essay on Human Understanding* in 1671, Locke bases his view of governmental power on a concept of individual self-sovereignty. Society is formed to protect individually owned property. In a way, each man's property is a state over which he is supreme sovereign. The literal government exists to protect a man's rights over his property/kingdom and to prevent a state of war from arising between individuals.

Locke and the post-1688 government's ideological stance is the product of an England that needed to redefine itself against Catholic Europe and as a result turned to Eastern texts and models. As G.A. Russell points out, this was rooted in the desire to find a new source of religious authority. Repudiating Catholic doctrines of apostolic succession, Protestantism's

> reassessment of the traditional concepts of religious authority, the primacy acquired by the Bible as the source of doctrine led to the importance of textual accuracy for theological interpretation...[making it] essential to resurrect the authority of the original texts, not only in Greek, but also in Hebrew.[3]

The study of Hebrew, in turn, required knowledge of Arabic, since Islamic Spain had already produced a "highly developed and systematic study of Arabic grammars and lexicography that had largely arisen in connection with the exegesis of the *Qur'an*" and, like Syriac and

---

[2] Ibid., lines 5–6, 10–14.
[3] G.A. Russell, "Introduction: The Seventeenth Century: The Age of 'Arabick,'" in *The 'Arabick' Interest of the Natural Philosophers in Seventeenth-Century England*, ed., G.A. Russell (New York: E.J. Brill, 1994), 3.

Aramaic, it was seen as a linguistic descendant of Hebrew.[4] In addition, the study of Arabic played a role in defining English Protestantism as different from the other religions of the continent:

> In their concern to differentiate the Church of England from that of
> Rome, as well as from other reformed Churches in Europe, the English
> saw in the Churches of the East a precursor and model.... Arabic was
> seen as a means of establishing communication with these Christians.[5]

This academic interest in Arabic texts produced the translation of
Hayy in 1671, when Edward Pococke the younger published it as
Philosophus Autodidactus, representing the rediscovery of I. Tufayl
by European audiences. Published in Oxford, the text includes both a
copy of an Arabic edition and Pococke's own translation into Latin.[6]
Based upon this version, translations were made into Dutch, German, and English. The influence of the Latin version extends into the
political arena as well: G.A. Russell makes a compelling argument for
its influence on John Locke as he began writing his *Essay on Human
Understanding* in 1671. She bases her argument on the popularity of
Ibn Tufayl's text and its availability to Locke, which is also attested to
by the two English translations into English before 1688 by George
Keith and George Ashwell (discussed later in this chapter), as well as
an anonymous translation into Dutch in 1672, with a second edition
appearing in 1701. Not only was it available in Latin, which Locke
was familiar with and wrote in, but also in his native English as well
as the language of Holland, the country in which he helped organize
the 1688 revolution.[7]

---

[4] Ibid., 4.

[5] Ibid., 5.

[6] This translation is regarded as meticulous to a fault. Twentieth-century scholar
A.S. Fulton outlines the translating dilemma of persevering with the letter or the spirit
of an original. Comparing Pocock's to Simon Ockley's translation, discussed later in
this chapter, Fulton contends, "Pocock's Latin version has all the merits and defects of
a slavish adherence to the letter of Arabic. Ockley's tendency is very much to the other
extreme. His keen relish of the spirit of the original and his aversion from pedantry
reveal themselves repeatedly in the renderings of singular neatness. On the other hand
he often takes liberties with his original which are quite unwarranted." A.S. Fulton,
introduction to *The History of Hayy ibn Yaqzan*, by Muhammad ibn 'Abd al-Malik
ibn Tufayl (London: Chapman and Hall, 1929), 36.

[7] G.A. Russell, "The Impact of the *Philosophus autodidactus*: Pocockes, John Locke
and the Society of Friends," in *The 'Arabick' Interest of the Natural Philosophers in Seventeenth-Century England*, ed. G.A. Russell (New York: E.J. Brill, 1994), 247. Russell
goes on to point out that "Locke's 'Library Catalogue' lists, however, [contain] a
number of works by two leading figures of the Quaker movement, George Keith and

In some significant ways I. Yaqzan shares a similar approach to spirituality as the titular protagonist of English author Daniel Defoe's 1719 *Robinson Crusoe*, which I discuss more fully in the next chapter. In Defoe's novel, the material and spiritual are deeply connected.[8] His material body having been "removed from all the wickedness of the world," sin is removed from Crusoe's spiritual self: in being taken out of a fallen world, he has neither "the lust of the flesh, the lust of the eye, or the pride of life." This aligns him with the original state of I. Yaqzan on his island. Just as I. Yaqzan eventually grows into not just an inhabitant but a ruler of the island, so does Crusoe: "I was lord of the whole manor; or if I pleas'd, I might call myself king, or emperor of the whole country which I had possession of."[9] This falls in line with I. Tufayl and Locke's view that man's natural state is sovereignty over nature. For them, the point is to have rule over oneself with only God as a higher authority. Crusoe's discontent, however, quickly begins to shine through in ways not experienced by I. Tufayl's natural man. In this way, I. Yaqzan is more in line with an English political philosopher like Locke.

Unlike Crusoe, when Tufayl's protagonist tires of his subjection of the animal and plant world, he turns away from the material world toward spiritual contemplation, leading him to a direct experience with God. Through his own use of reason, I. Yaqzan determines not only how to survive, but how to rule his island ethically. Eventually, "confining himself to his Cave, with his head bow'd down, and his Eyes shut, and turning himself altogether from all sensible Things and Corporal Faculties, and bending all his Thoughts and Meditations upon the *necessarily self-existing Being*."[10] He frees himself—with the exception of his reduced basic physical needs—from any desires of the

---

Robert Barclay. Their inclusion may raise questions in the light of Locke's attitude towards Quakers—particularly, his reaction to the dangers of 'enthusiasm,' or reliance on emotional conviction as a basis of truth—but it provides an additional channel for Locke's acquaintance with the Arabic Narrative" (247).

[8] Although Crusoe interprets his arrival on the island as a punishment for his "ORIGINAL SIN" of disobeying his father, he also sees it as a place of spiritual rebirth: "The same day of the year I was born on (viz.) the 30th of September, the same day I had my life so miraculously saved 26 years after, when I was cast on the shore in this island; so that my wicked life and my solitary life, began both on a day." Daniel Defoe, *Robinson Crusoe* (1719), ed. John Richetti (London: Penguin Books, 2001), 154, 106.

[9] Ibid., 102, 102–3.

[10] Muhammad ibn Tufayl, *The Improvement of Human Reason, Exhibited in the Life of Hai ebn Yokdhan*, trans. Simon Ockley (London, 1708), 121–22.

material world. In these meditations, "all dissappear'd and vanish'd and were as they had never been, and amongst these his own Being dissappear'd too, and there remain'd nothing but this ONE, TRUE, Perpetually Self-existant Being."[11] Though I. Yaqzan arguably has less to desire than Crusoe because he lacks the latter's knowledge of the material world, it is through his isolation that I. Tufayl's mystic castaway experiences a much more radical and individual relationship with God than Defoe's. As shown in his relationship with Friday discussed in the next chapter, Crusoe views his religion not as an isolated relationship between himself and God, but a social one among other men. Material associations such as culture, nation, or race do not fetter the conversion of I. Yaqzan. It is a conversion not to a religion but to a mode of existence independent of the human world. This solidity of *Hayy*'s vision of man's ability to master the material world and come to an instinctual understanding of God that sharply contrasts to the insecurities of Defoe's *Robinson Crusoe* discussed in Chapter Three. Although a direct connection between the two castaway narratives cannot be established, a comparison of the two highlights the kind of stability Defoe rejects in his portrayal of English identity abroad and *Hayy*'s universal vision of man naturally ruling creation, which attracted Locke and other Protestant commentators.

For Crusoe, removal from the world leads to the removal of sin but in a darker tone than it does for I. Tufayl's protagonist. The latter presents the inability to exceed one's needs and to be surrounded by a world of plenty as positive—not negative—aspects. Locke, too, presents property as not only positive but as the main cause for forming a society. The "only way whereby any one devests himself of his Natural Liberty, and puts on the bonds of Society is by agreeing with other Men to joyn and unite into a Community...in a secure Enjoyment of their Properties."[12] Crusoe's negative view of property in some ways anticipates Jean-Jacques Rousseau's depictions of natural man and the corruptive force of civilization. Rousseau views natural man as "deprived of any sort of enlightenment...[and] his desires do not go beyond his physical needs; the only good things he knows in the universe are food, a female and repose, and the only evils he fears are pain

---

[11] Ibid., 123.
[12] John Locke, *Two Treatises of Government*, VIII.95.4–9.

and hunger."[13] Though Defoe is less negative toward society, Crusoe's discontent on the island seems to come from the fact that he is not a natural man, that his needs and fears go far beyond the simple physicality Rousseau describes. The idea of property as a burden and potentially corruptive force to mankind is also mirrored in Rousseau, who famously declared that the "first man who, having enclosed a piece of land, thought of saying 'This is mine' and found people simple enough to believe him, was the true founder of civil society."[14] The product of such a society, Crusoe cannot contentedly count his blessings as Locke and I. Tufayl instruct. Instead, he is driven by needs born out of a materialistic world view.

Debating English Protestantism: The Translations of I. Tufayl

Although it is debatable to what extent I. Tufayl's writing influenced Locke's, parallels can be drawn between this Arabic narrative and the political philosophy that shaped English concepts of individual rights in relationship to governance and property. There is also clear evidence that *Hayy* fit into debates over English religious identity. Following the scholarly success of the Pocockes translation, three major English translations were produced between 1674 and 1708. The first of these moved the text from the elite sphere of Latin-literate readership to a decidedly broader one. George Keith, a Quaker, used the text as a means to convey his own religious beliefs to an English public in 1674. The editorial interventions of this version transplant *Hayy* from the realm of the scholarly into the religious identity of England. Keith's translation better reflects the period's overlapping but still distinct readership than the one represented by Locke, that of the Dissenters and Non-conformists.[15]

---

[13] Jean-Jacques Rousseau, *A Discourse on Inequality* (1755), trans. Maurice Cranston. (New York: Penguin Books, 1984), 89.

[14] Ibid., 109.

[15] The labels of Dissenter and Non-conformist once included Catholics as well as anyone else who did not subscribe to the state religion, but evolved to be synonymous with Protestantism (Oxford English Dictionary, 2009). Despite the prejudice of the Anglican Church toward other Protestant sects, the Dissenters chose to side with the State religion, rather than the Roman Catholic/Dissenter alliance for which James II had hoped. See J.R. Jones's *Country and Court*, 236–46, for more on religious alliances surrounding the 1688 coup. In *An Appeal to Honour and Justice*, Daniel Defoe offers an albeit slightly hyperbolic representation of the popular reasoning behind the choice

In the "Advertisement to the Reader" in his translation, Keith presents his Quaker beliefs as compatible with I. Tufayl's work. Both stress the ability of individuals to access divine truth outside of traditional social and political hierarchies. Keith's translation comes at the end of a century during which Dissenters sought independence from the Church of England as well as the monarchical government and class system supporting it. During England's colonial expansion into the Americas in the seventeenth century, dissenting churches were sites of local power disconnected from the hierarchies in England. Michael J. Braddick contends that these non-conformist attitudes were directly connected in the general public with challenges to government authority:

> throughout this period, to deny public gestures of respect was in effect to deny a claim to authority. For example, Quakers were notorious for refusing to remove their hats in the presence of 'superiors.' This has to be understood as a symbolic repudiation of this larger interaction order— the basis of authority recognized by the Quakers was quite different from the authority projected by patriarchal justices.[16]

I. Tufayl's text appealed to dissenters because of its highly individualized stance on religion, particularly its emphasis on prophecy.

Interest in the *Hayy* also reflects the early days of the English reformation where, despite theological differences, English Protestantism attempted to ally itself politically with the Turks against its Catholic adversaries, especially Spain. In her letters to Sultan Murad III, Elizabeth I "emphasized the fact that as a Protestant Christian, she rejected the veneration of idolatrous images which the Pope and the Spanish king practiced."[17] This political alliance became a theological weapon for Catholic powers wishing to discredit England's break from Rome:

> by 1589 there was such a deep conviction on the continent of an Anglo-Turkish alliance that central European Catholics were saying in Istanbul that 'the English lack nothing to make them sound Mussulmans, and

---

of State Church over the Vatican is illustrated: "I told the *Dissenters* I had rather the Church of *England* should pull our Cloaths off by Fines and Forfeitures, than the Papists should fall both upon the *Church* and the *Dissenters*, and pull our Skins off by Fire and Fagot." Daniel Defoe, *An Appeal to Honour and Justice, Tho' it be of his Worst Enemies. By Daniel De Foe. Being a True Account of his Conduct in Publick Affairs* (London, 1715), 52.

[16] Michael J. Braddick, "Civility and Authority," in *The British Atlantic World, 1500–1800*, eds. David Armitage and Michael J. Braddick (New York: Palgrave Macmillan, 2002), 97.

[17] Nabil Matar, *Islam in Britain* (Cambridge: Cambridge University Press, 1998), 123.

need only stretch out a finger to become one with the Turks in outward appearance, in religious observance and in their whole character.'[18]

While this comment is meant to be more a slur on Protestantism than a real theological analysis, it helps to clarify why Dissenters such as Keith felt comfortable using I. Tufayl's text to bolster his own position. Both the tradition of English-Ottoman relations and the compatibility between I. Tufayl's and Dissenter presentations of individual religious authority made the progression from the scholarly Pocockes translation to Keith's religious and politically driven version a logical transition.

In his "Advertisement to the Reader," Keith explains the specific relevance of this twelfth-century Islamic text to his contemporary English audiences:

> I found a great freedom in mind to put it into English for a more general service, as believing it might be profitable unto many; but my particular *motives* which engaged me hereunto was, that I found some good things in it, which were both very savoury and refreshing to me; and indeed there are some sentences in it that I highly approve [...]. These with many other profitable things agreeable to Christian Principles are to be found here.[19]

Keith aligns I. Tufayl's text with a larger Protestant movement that aimed to educate and inform a literate population of believers about theological truths. His reference to the 'freedom' he gains in translating *Hayy* touches on one of his fundamental beliefs as a Quaker: the freedom of the individual to define his own relationship with the Divine outside of the authority of institutionalized hierarchies. His desire to translate the text is based on a faith in an individual reader's ability to discern what is and what is not useful to his religious growth, even if it is found in a non-Christian text. Keith does add a warning to readers not to "receive for certain, everything in this Book," but maintains his stance that "whatever may otherwise be in it, doth not hinder to make good use of the things which are both good and profitable contained

---

[18] Ibid., 124.

[19] George Keith, Advertisement to the Reader in *An Account of Oriental Philosophy* by Muhammad ibn 'Abd al-Malik ibn Tufayl (London: s.n., 1674), ii–iii. Keith does add a warning to readers not to "receive for certain, everything in this Book," but maintains his stance that "whatever may otherwise be in it, doth not hinder to make good use of the things which are both good and profitable contained therein."

therein."[20] That Keith finds an older Islamic text "very savoury and refreshing" as well as "profitable" for the Christian reader signals part of the radicalism found in dissenting movements in their willingness to go against traditional Church (of both England and Rome) definitions of acceptable spiritual sources.

It is not just a break with the traditions of older religious Christian institutions but also a movement away from institutions in general, with the story of an individual independently finding divine knowledge being a prime source of interest for Keith and the dissenting movement of which he was part. I. Tufayl would exert a strong influence on Keith's future work and, through him, English Protestant belief. As she does with Locke, Russell connects the interest in I. Tufayl's text with Keith's later works: "For Keith, the *Philosophus autodidactus* represented precisely what he summarized as the Quaker 'common notion' [described in the formal Quaker manifesto *Theses Theologiae*, which he co-wrote with Barclay in 1675]: 'the sufficiency of inner light.'"[21] Indeed, I. Yaqzan's example of finding divine truth through "the sufficiency of inner light" is a path Keith advocates that his readers follow in their lives. His break with older Christian traditions signals how radically different Dissenter goals were from those of the State Church. For Keith, his translation forms part of an attempt to re-educate English Protestants to judge knowledge not by the cultural or historical context that produced them but by an intellectual and spiritual standard that transcends time, culture, and even religion.

Keith's work differs from other translations in its insistence on readers viewing *Hayy* as directly applicable to their own religious lives. For example, George Ashwell's 1686 version, *The History of Hai Eb'n Yockdan, an Indian Prince: or, The Self-Taught Philosopher*, aligns itself with a more scholarly view of the text, and the introduction makes it clear that the translation is not meant to be an attack on the established political and social hierarchies.[22] The full title attempts to mediate the

---

[20] Ibid., iii.

[21] Russell, "The Impact of the *Philosophus autodidactus*," 248.

[22] The title's reference to I. Yaqzan as an 'Indian prince' comes from the opening lines of the narrative, which in Ashwell's translation reads: "We have received from our pious ancestors, that amongst the *Indian* islands lies an uninhabited one." Muhammad ibn Tufayl, *The History of Hai Eb'n Yockdan...*, trans. George Ashwell (London: Richard Chiswell, 1686), 1. According to Lawrence I. Conrad, this translation holds scholarly value for its innovations over the Pocockes: in his survey of translations of I. Tufayl's work, Conrad points out that this "translation by George Ashwell is

foreignness of the original author through the concept of universal reason. By noting that "Abi Jaafar Eb'n Tophail" is "a philosopher by profession, and a Mahometan by religion," Ashwell privileges the philosopher as part of a universal tradition, separating him from the cultural difference represented by his religion. Keith and the dissenting movement he represents saw I. Tufayl's text as a means of separating English Protestantism away from both the Roman Catholic Church and the close bonds between the Anglican Church and its state.

Ashwell, on the other hand, was an Anglican clergyman who, throughout his life, expressed support for monarchial and state power: "During the civil war Ashwell preached before the royal court assembled at Oxford.... Ashwell was a convinced royalist, who owned a manuscript copy of Sir Robert Filmer's *Patriarcha*, and at whose suggestion Peter Heylin wrote Parliament's Power in Laws for Religion".[23] His introduction presents the text as part of a scholarly endeavor toward rational Enlightenment by categorizing his translation and I. Tufayl's work as concerned with moral philosophy rather than culture or theology: whereas some men live by "giddily following their own Phancies, or other Mens Opinions," Ashwell offers a text "for the Guides of their Faith and Manners." I. Tufayl's philosophical tale, Ashwell contends, transcends time and culture.

True, Ashwell's universalized view of the text did require the reduction of the Islamic theology found in the text. This could be interpreted as a decision to deemphasize cultural and theological differences between the text and his audience in order to present Christian and Muslim thought as sharing a common ground through reason. As Nabil Matar points out, "In order to show the common grounds among all three traditions—Aristotelianism, Islam and Christianity—Ashwell deleted passages and Qur'anic citations which he feared would 'disturb the sense.'" But, the lack of emphasis on the Islamic passages could

---

noteworthy for his decision to drop Ibn Tufayl's extremely important introduction (a grave error followed by several later translators), and to prune out material unlikely to appeal to seventeenth-century English audiences, e.g., the account of Hayy's spontaneous generation and details on meteorology. He also provides section numbers through the text, a feature copied by several later English translators and the Cairo editor of 1322/1904." Lawrence I. Conrad, "Resources on Ibn Tufayl and Hayy Ibn Yaqzan," in *The World of Ibn Tufayl: Interdisciplinary Perspectives on Hayy Ibn Yaqzan*, ed. Lawrence I. Conrad (Leiden: E.J. Brill, 1996), 277.

[23] Philip Dixon, "Ashwell, George (1612–1694)," in *Oxford Dictionary of National Biography*, online ed., ed. Lawrence Goldman, Oxford: OUP, http://0-www.oxforddnb.com.library.colby.edu/view/article/788 (accessed January 22, 2011).

also be due in part to the reliance of translators such as Keith and Ash-well on the Pococke version, which "had been edited with the aim of reducing its Islamic content particularly in its allusions to the Prophet Mohammad" in the Latin translation.[24]

Regardless of these issues surrounding changes to the actual text, Ashwell presents the text as compatible with English beliefs. For him,

> the Philosopher, whose life is here described, will instruct them in such principles of Morality and Reason…as the light of Nature discovers, and which must needs be acknowledged for True by all those, who will judge and act as Men, according to the Dictates of Reason, and the Conclu-sions of resulting from Experience.[25]

Ashwell defines universal truth as resulting from human rationality and empirical knowledge. All, he argues, may arrive at universal truth "agreed in such principles as humane Reason teacheth out of the Book of Nature, which sets forth to our view of Gods works of Creation and Providence."[26] He may give credit to God but he emphasizes Nature more than theology.

Although both the Keith and the Ashwell help illustrate the impor-tance that I. Tufayl's text gained in both religious and scholarly circles, Keith's stands out as representing an alternative view of Arabic stud-ies not directly acknowledged by Pococke and Ashwell. This connec-tion between English Protestant identity and Islam was not wholly accepted in mainstream English belief. In 1708, Simon Ockley, a mem-ber of the Anglican clergy and later a professor of Arabic at Cam-bridge, published his translation that holds the distinctions of being the first English translation to use an Arabic source and of offering a direct rebuttal to Keith's claims. Reprinted again in London in 1711 and Dublin in 1731, this version would emerge as the English version used and respected by translators to the present day.[27]

---

[24] Matar, *Islam in Britain*, 100.
[25] George Ashwell, introduction to *The History of Hai Eb'n Yockdan* by Muhammad ibn 'Abd al-Malik ibn Tufayl (London: Richard Chiswell and William Thorp, 1686), iii.
[26] Ibid., iii–iv.
[27] Later translations, such as A.S. Fulton's, still rely heavily on Ockley's work. Ful-ton justifies his use of the Ockley version, arguing that Ockley's "keen relish of the spirit of the original and his aversion from pedantry reveal themselves repeatedly in the renderings of singular neatness." Fulton admits there are flaws in the Ockley: "he often takes liberties with his original which are quite unwarranted." However, the occasional correction of 'such lapses' are done out of the desire to maintain the

In the Ockley translation, the preface and appendix frame the text in dual sets of anxieties over English and Christian identity. The opening deals with Ockley's concerns that previous English translations have missed much of the original sense of the Arabic by relying on the Pocockes Latin translation rather than the source material. However, this seemingly scholastic argument also signifies an assertion of English identity. First, it invites the question of why an English translation is necessary at all, about which Ockley's anxieties emerge in the appendix. Second, by circumventing the Latin and using a straight translation from Arabic to English, he is pushing forward the scholarliness of the language in relation to Latin. These moves are a direct attack on Keith's use of the text to forward his Dissenter agenda. Viewing such attempts as a danger to English social order, Ockley lumps Keith and I. Tufayl into what he derogatorily refers to as Enthusiasts. This category of people, in his view, misapplies what knowledge they have, which is shown in their lack of scholarly and spiritual integrity. As the editorial material progresses, it becomes increasingly apparent that while I. Tufayl may be given this label, the true targets of Ockley's disdain are Dissenters such as Keith.

Ockley opens his preface by positioning the text within the bounds of solid English scholarship. Describing the success (academic, not necessarily financial) of the 1671 Latin translation by Pocockes, he positions his predecessor in the context of an ongoing scholarly project to translate other works by I. Tufayl. When he comes to the text itself—which he rechristens *The Improvement of Human Reason*—the preface's tone becomes more reserved and Ockley's views more obscured:

> The Design of the Author is to shew, how Human Capacity, unassisted by any External Help may, by due Application, attain to the Knowledge of Natural Things, and so by Degrees find out its Dependence upon a Superior Being, the Immortality of the Soul and all things necessary to

---

original integrity not of the Arabic original but of Ockley's: Fulton attempts to accomplish this "without offering any unnecessary violence to Ockley's work." Fulton also implies that these corrections are probably only necessary because he has access to better materials than Ockley, such as "the dictation of Gauthier's Arabic text, which is our best authority and much superior to the text upon which Ockley depended." A.S. Fulton, introduction to *The History of Hayy ibn Yaqzan*, by Muhammad ibn 'Abd al-Malik ibn Tufayl. (London: Chapman and Hall, 1929), 36–37.

For a comprehensive annotated bibliography of translations of *Hayy*, see Lawrence I. Conrad, "Resources on Ibn Tufayl and Hayy Ibn Yaqzan," in *The World of Ibn Tufayl: Interdisciplinary Perspectives on Hayy Ibn Yaqzan*, ed. Lawrence I. Conrad (Leiden: E.J. Brill, 1996), 267–93. English translations are listed on 276–79.

Salvation. How well he has succeeded in this Attempt, I leave to the Reader to judge.[28]

While the preface easily accepts or rejects the scholarship and religious views of the translators' preceeding Ockley, the place of I. Tufayl and his text in English culture is presented more ambiguously. Ockley distances himself from the argument by labeling it the "Design of the Author," placing even its success in question and refusing to offer judgment on it. Nor will he comment here on the text's view of revelation as unnecessary for individuals to know God, the quality that prompted Keith's translation. Both argument and interpretation are responsibilities Ockley rejects.

The claims of the source material reinforce rationalist arguments for understanding the cosmos through abstraction, but its claims of salvation through the individual's mind run counter to the nation's mainstream religious views. Given that oriental texts were used both for and against deism, it is difficult to determine where Ockley falls and why—aside from his scholarly scruples with earlier translations— he feels the need for an accurate English translation of *Hayy Ibn Yaqzan* to be available for the English reading public. His views of the earlier translations and his gestures toward an intended audience shed some light on his motivations. On Dr. Ashwell's translation, Ockley offers no commentary. But concerning Keith's, his criticism has a target, beginning a theme that will continue in the Appendix: "the *Quakers* who imagin'd that there was something in it that favoured their Enthusistick [*sic*] Notions." (ix). The non-scholarly use of the text seems to raise Ockley's hackles. His deriding tone toward the religious translator's "imagin'd" belief that I. Tufayl offered him support for "Enthusistick Notions" sets up the critique of the quality of these translations. By leaving Ashwell's position unembellished, he makes the Quakers the focus of his comments that earlier translations failed to live up to his scholarly standards. Both "were not made out of the Original *Arabick*, but out of the *Latin*" (ix), but since the Quakers have been singled out as less scholarly than Ashwell, his critique seems to fall more to them than to a potential colleague like Ashwell. Ockley goes on to argue that these earlier translations "had mistaken the Sense of the Author in many places"; since we do not know what 'sense'

---

[28] Simon Ockley, "Preface" and "Appendix," in *The Improvement of Human Reason, exhibited in the life of Hai ebn Yokdhan* (London, 1708), ix.

Ashwell aimed for, this critique seems once again aimed at those who would incorporate oriental sources into religion. Ockley seems to be trying to carve a space for oriental studies separate from the actual beliefs of his English readers.

Indeed, his increasing interest in oriental, specifically Arabic, scholarship is one of his stated purposes: "observing that a great many of my Friends whom I had a desire to oblige, and other Persons whom I would willingly incline to a more favourable Opinion of *Arabick* Learning, had not seen the book" (ix–x). Under this purpose, the Quaker's motivation may run counter to Ockley's scholarly mission. Fostering a "more favourable Opinion of *Arabick* Learning" includes outlining the correct uses of oriental texts. The danger of misreading becomes more apparent in the Preface's closing lines: "And lest any Person should, through mistake, make any ill use of it [his new translation], I have subjoin'd an *Appendix*, the Design of which the Reader may see in its proper place" (x). While he may have left the success of I. Tufayl's argument "to the Reader to judge," the Reader's own use of the text, it emerges, is restricted to the uses Ockley deems fit. The marginal anxieties over "ill use" and the "proper place" of the text come to fruition in Ockley's instructional Appendix.

While the preface leaves the success of I. Tufayl's attempt to the reader's discretion, in the Appendix this Anglican Vicar from Cambridgeshire carefully instructs the reader on how to judge the foundation behind that attempt. The title lays out his preliminary goal: it is a space "In which the Author's Notion concerning the Possibility of Man's attaining to the true Knowledge of God, and the Things necessary to the Salvation, without the Use of external Means, is briefly consider'd" (164). For Ockley, the meat of the texts is in the authority an individual can have in making pronouncements on the divine without any outside, institutional instruction. In a time and space where the religious and political were deeply intertwined, it is not too far a stretch to argue that Ockley is concerned about independence from the Church of England leading to independence from the Crown. His citing of the Quakers supports this: his motivation for writing comes from his desire to reclaim the text and its potential readers from dissenters.

That Ockley wants to save I. Tufayl's text in addition to Christian English readers is the claim with which the Appendix opens. The first line ends with a succinct admonishment of dissenting Christians: "So, as it [the text] contains several things co-incident with the errors of

some Enthusiasts of these present Times, it deserves to be consider'd"
(167). To a degree, this seems contradictory to the scholarly pursuit in
which he placed the text by dedicating it to Pocockes, but given that
missionary interests were deeply intertwined with Oriental Studies, the
slippage between academic and spiritual pursuits is not unconventional.
What I find interesting is his emphasis on the dangers of his 'present
time.' Opposed to a twelfth-century past where crusades were fought
and Spain was Islamic, Ockley locates the danger of a Muslim author's
philosophical-religious treatise in the manner that eighteenth-century
English Christians will use it. At the time, the Quaker beliefs that Keith
had seen as compatible with I. Tufayl's work represented a potential
threat to state power. During England's colonial expansion into the
Americas in the seventeenth century, dissenting churches were sites
of local power disconnected from the hierarchies in England. These,
according to Carla Gardina Pestana, "had the advantage of being local-
ized, with powers that would be vested in a church hierarchy in many
other Protestant churches instead of residing in the congregation.
The same could be said of the Quaker faith: the Society of Friends
flourished in the New World."[29] This, along with the history of political upheaval by radical Protestants (the Civil War, for instance) and
their resistance of existing social hierarchies, made Quakers and other
Dissenters a threat to civil order. This view permeates Ockley's presentation of Tufayl's work and explains his disdain for 'Enthusiasts'
attempting to change the existing social hierarchies through *Hayy*.

As the supplementary material unfolds, it becomes apparent that
Ockley is concerned with the potential power certain interpretations
of the text would offer: that of Old Testament prophecy. Given that
the biblical prophets were consistently at odds with the rulers of their
communities and acted outside of human hierarchies of power, the
role of prophet offers a real threat to the authority of the state and its
church. Ockley is critical of I. Tufayl's own beliefs, but forgives them
due to their cultural and historical distance from his own time: "There
are a Great many Errors both in the *Philosophy* and *Divinity*: And
it was impossible it should be otherwise, the one being a thorough

---

[29] Carla Gardina Pestana, "Religion," in *The British Atlantic World, 1500–1800*, eds.
David Armitage and Michael J. Braddick (New York: Palgrave Macmillian, 2002), 75.
Pestana adds that this trend also extended to "Muslims among the enslaved population... [who] had to manage with a highly simplified, even attenuated version of their
faiths, living without Qur'anic schools" (Ibid., 75).

Aristotelian and the other *Mahometen*" (168). However, while he will excuse a Muslim author, he uses Islam itself as a means to attack his true target—the Quaker 'Enthusiasts.' Closing his list of I. Tufayl's "errors," Ockley declares,

> I need not insist upon this any longer; I shall only remark, that as a true Piety is same in all Ages and Climates, and good solid Sense too, so also is Enthusiasm. And I have sometimes wondered when I have read the Whimsies and Conceits of the Arab Enthusiast [...] to find such a Harmony between them and ours at present. [...] Let the *Enthusiast* have never such great Abilities, there is always something or other which proves his Pretensions to Revelation to be false; as they tell us, that, let the Devil change himself into what shape he will he can never conceal his Cloven Foot; so neither can the *Enthusiast* make himself pass for Inspired, with any Person of tolerable discerning. (192–93)

Ockley uses Tufayl's Otherness as a Muslim to distance Quakers from 'true' Christianity. By performing the simple task of disproving I. Tufayl's beliefs as non-Christian, he then conflates Quaker belief with Islam, drawing upon the belief in Muhammad as a religious fraud.[30] The emphasis on dishonesty portrays the Quakers as intentionally using texts such as *Hayy Ibn Yaqzan* to deceive the English reading public, making it possible for Ockley to mark the progression from Quakers to Islam to Satan.

However, after making the connection between dissenters and the devil, Ockley attempts to reclaim I. Tufayl, severing the connection between his work and Quakers such as Keith. He closes his Appendix by integrating I. Tufayl into mainstream English Christianity by reading *Hayy Ibn Yaqzan* as a cautionary tale for the laity overstepping their intellectual boundaries, rather than a treatise in favor of increased religious independence for individuals: "It remains that

---

[30] An example of this belief can be seen Ockley's own work. In *The History of the Saracens*, Ockley begins his section "The Life of Mahomet" thusly:
> Though our author had good reason to take but little notice of the actions of *Mahomet*, because the life of that *impostor* [emphasis mine] had, but few years before, been published by the learned Dr. *Prideaux*; yet, as the present impression of the *Saracenic* history will probably fall into the hands of many persons who have not an opportunity of reading that excellent work, it is thought proper to premise a short account of the *Arabians*, the principal agents in the transactions hereafter related, of *Mahomet* and the progress of his arms which paved the way for the achievements [sic] of his successors, and of the *false religion* [emphasis mine] founded by him, which has since overspread so great a part of the earth. Simon Ockley, *The History of the Saracens. [...]*, volume 1, 3rd ed. (Cambridge, 1757), 1.

we [...] heartily apply our selves to the diligent Use of those Means which he has appointed for our Instruction, in his Church. That we seek for the knowledge of him in his holy Word, and *approach* to him in his Ordinances, and by a holy pious conversation" (194). The focus on adherence to the Bible, church ritual, and "holy pious conversation" mirrors the instructions a defeated Hayy Ibn Yaqzan gives to the civilized island he visits. Asâl convinces I. Yaqzan to accompany him to civilization by arguing that the "Sect [living on Asâl's island] was supreme to all other sorts of Men in Knowledge and Sagacity; and that if he [I. Yaqzan] could not work upon them, there was much lesser Hopes of doing any Good upon the Vulgar" (154). This island is set up as the true test of whether Yaqzan's utopia can transfer itself to the rest of humanity. It cannot.

Disheartened by the island inhabitants' inability to comprehend or even openly listen to new ideas based on rational thought and empiricism, I. Yaqzan gives them instructions similar to those Ockley gives to the reader:

> he understood the Condition of Mankind, and that the greatest part of them were like Brute Beast, [...] he begg'd their Pardon for what he had said to them, and desir'd to be excus'd and told them he was of the same opinion with them, and [...] persuaded them to stick strictly to their Resolution of keeping in the Bounds of the Law, and the Performance of External Rites [...] they should abstain from novel Opinions, and from their Appetites, and follow the Examples of their pious Ancestors. (158–59)

For Ockley to offer his readers in the British Isles the same advice conflates them with the "Brute Beast[s]" of the civilized island. What he omits in the Appendix is that in the story some people, such as Asâl, are capable of pursuing the religious independence outlined in the text. What separates him from his fellow islanders is his natural inclination toward contemplation and isolation (140). Placing this in the context of Ockley's praise of Pocockes and neutrality on Ashwell, it is plausible to see an implicit argument concerning who are proper readers for Arabic texts: Ockley and his fellow scholars.

Ockley's reinterpretation of I. Tufayl's text makes his closing lines ambiguous:

> These are the Ways [adhering to the scripture and tradition] which he has chalk'd out no fitter Bearer than Hai Ebn Yokdan, with whose Character and Language you are so well acquainted, and to whom you have

so long ago shown so great a Respect, that I have no reason to fear but he will be welcome.[31]

Is the story useful because it reminds the reader to follow I. Yaqzan's advice to stick with traditional beliefs or is the natural man—and by extension his author—an example of someone who has gone beyond the prescribed boundaries of religious thought? The openness of this ending draws attention to the way the tensions of the supplementary material parallel the tensions in the narrative. Just as I. Yaqzan and Asâl endeavor to find a means to connect the knowledge of one island with the inhabitants of the other, Ockley wants to reconcile his interest and promotion of Islamic texts with his professed beliefs in Christianity.

Ockley's dual desires to keep I. Tufayl's works in his own life as an academic while preventing others from 'misreading' or 'misusing' it to the detriment of Protestant England can be seen as representing the larger debate over Islamic influence on English culture. Coming out of the Civil Wars, the Restoration, and the 1688 coup, England was in the midst of a moment of self-definition: what kind of government, social hierarchies, and religious beliefs were 'English'? How was Protestant England in the seventeenth and eighteenth centuries different from its Catholic counterparts on the continent or, for that matter, its past as a nation loyal to Rome? To properly understand these issues, we must keep in mind that for this period, England was not simply trying to position itself in regards to Catholic-Protestant continental conflicts or the exploration of potential colonial holdings in the Americas. Islam, too, existed as a palpable force that extended into the political, scholarly, cultural, and spiritual lives of English subjects.

---

[31] Simon Ockley, "Appendix," *The Improvement of Human Reason, Exhibited in the Life of Hai Ebn Yokdhan*, (London: E. Powell, 1708), 194–95. Don Cameron Allen Renaissance Collection, Mandeville Special Collections Library, University of California, San Diego.

Whether due to a discrepancy between editions or a transcription mistake on my part, the last part of this passage which I took from a copy from the Don Cameron Allen collection at Geisel differs from the last page found on *Eighteenth Century Collections Online*. The latter reads:

These are the Ways which he has chalk'd out for us; and if any Persons will not be content with these Menns, but will walk in By Paths, and follow every *Ignis fatuus* [will-o-the-wisp] that present is self [*sic*]; if they beare the last convinc'd of their fatal Mistake when it is too late, they must blame themselves. God of his infinite Mercy lead them out of their Errors, and guide both them and us through this imperfect State, till at last we attain to the perfect Vision, and full Enjoyment of himself; though *Jesus Christ* our Lord. *Amen* (194–5).

Within the dueling discourses of the I. Tufayl translations lies an anxiety over the lack of a stable, monolithic English identity. Ockley's drive to incorporate the Arabic text into English scholarship without allowing it to be ingested by the broader body politic reflects both a fear of and an aspiration to join the outside world. For much of the English public in the long century, the Ottomans represented an exotic contrast to their forming domestic identity. Contradictorily, the Ottomans offered a model of cultural and political empire for England to model itself on as it steered a burgeoning British Empire, while also offering a threat to an already unstable internal identity. A fear of 'turning Turk' may have been found throughout popular and scholarly English thought, but the Ottomans as the most prominent representation of Islamic culture in Europe also held an allure as an alternate model of English identity.

CHAPTER THREE

THE OTTOMAN INFLUENCE IN *ROBINSON CRUSOE*: FAILURES OF ENGLISH IMPERIAL IDENTITY

In his work promoting government interests, such as the 1707 Act of Union between England and Scotland or the War of Spanish Succession, Daniel Defoe presents a fairly stable vision of English identity and overseas expansion. His novels do not follow this pattern. Identity in these texts is fluid. In *Captain Singleton* (1720), the titular hero moves between identifying categories from his childhood with an adoptive gypsy mother to his career of his pirate to his eventual financial rise as a merchant. Throughout *Moll Flanders* (1722), his heroine lacks a fixed identity: she enters life in mainstream Protestant England after an infancy with transient gypsies, takes on multiple identities as a maid, pickpocket, cross-dressed housebreaker, prisoner, and respected colonist. *Colonel Jack* (1722) charts the path of a slave turned plantation owner turned French soldier fighting against his native England until he learns his true heritage and repents. Although the narratives tend to return the protagonists to a financially and socially stable position in English society, each points to English colonial expansion as leading to failure and decay: Singleton turns to piracy, Jack is enslaved, and Flanders enters into an incestuous marriage when she leaves England for North America.

The seemingly happy endings of Defoe's novels are also ambiguous. For example, his last novel, *Roxana* (1724), ends with the heroine wealthy, outwardly religious, and entering a marriage based on mutual affection. Yet, the closing line undercuts this positive ending with the reminder that Roxana's success may be based on her daughter's murder:

> Here after some few Years of Flourishing, and outwardly happy Circumstances, I fell into a dreadful Course of Calamities,…the very Reverse of our former Good Days; the Blast of Heaven seem'd to follow the Injury done the poor Girl [Roxana's estranged and presumably dead daughter], by us both; and I was brought so low again, that my Repentance seem'd to be only the Consequence of my Misery, as my Misery was of my Crime.[1]

---

[1] Daniel Defoe. *Roxana* (1724), ed. Melissa Mowry (Peterborough, Ontario, Canada: Broadview, 2009), 326. Interestingly, Roxana's undoing originates from an

The portrayal of English identity as unstable and the recurring theme
of overseas disaster run throughout the major novels and has its origins in Defoe's first novel, *Robinson Crusoe*.

Published in 1719 and set in the mid-seventeenth century, Defoe's
Robinson Crusoe resonates with the anxieties over English imperial
insecurity of his later works while contrasting it with the threat of
Ottoman might and influence. The first half of the novel focuses on
the economic uncertainty created by English captivity in Ottoman
North Africa. Crusoe's predicament extends seventeenth-century fears
of apostasy into the eighteenth century. Since converts to Islam were
known to return to England without disclosing their conversions, this
opens up the possibility that English readers would have seen Crusoe's
Christian identity at least tested during his captivity and then seen the
tension between his outward non-English appearance and his inner
spiritual conformity as connected to that captivity. One of the novel's
first reviewers, Charles Gildon, attacked its "faulty view of Church
and State, the impiety of Crusoe's reflections, and, most significantly,
'making the Truths of the Bible of a piece with the fictitious Story of
Robinson Crusoe.'"[2] Gildon's concerns focus on Defoe himself and the
tension between truth and fiction. These issues quickly fell by the wayside as the narrative took on a mythic quality independent of author
or physical text. Gildon also commented—with no small amount
of disdain and trepidation—on the popularity of Defoe's novel and
its acceptance as a solidly Protestant text: in an imaginary dialogue
between Crusoe, Defoe, and Friday, the author attempts to pacify his
characters, flattering Crusoe that "there is not an old Woman that can
go the Price of it, but buys the Life and Adventures [of Robinson Cru-
soe], and leaves it as a Legacy, with *The Pilgrims Progress*, the *Practice
of Piety*, and *God's Revenge against Murther*."[3] The association between
Robinson Crusoe and English Protestant values, though satirical here,
became second nature as the popularity of the text grew.

Ottoman source. She attempts to leave her nationally and sexually ambiguous past
behind her and present herself as a conventional English Protestant. She is unable to
let go of the Turkish outfit that marked her rise as an exotic, desired mistress outside
of England. Her inability to shed her Ottoman dress leads her estranged daughter to
recognize and pursue her. Finally, Roxana send her servant to silence the daughter,
which, the text implies, may have resulted in murder.

[2] Joseph Bartolomeo, *A New Species of Criticism: Eighteenth-Century Discourse on
the Novel* (Cranbury, NJ: Associated University Presses, 1994), 38.

[3] Charles Gildon, *The Life and Strange Surprizing Adventures of Mr. D---- de F--,
of London* (London, 1719), ix–x.

By the end of the eighteenth century, the novel was consistently viewed as not only solidly English Protestant but also as an expression of British colonial might. Yet Gildon's critique points to an alternative view of the text in the early eighteenth century. I hold that this points to a change in the cultural context of this narrative over the century, which began in an atmosphere of colonial and religious insecurity. When read within the original context of English colonial efforts and debates over national religious identity, a narrative of anxiety emerges in Defoe's work. Centered on fears of a decaying identity, *Robinson Crusoe* locates the image of colonial power not within an emerging British Empire, but in the older, more established world of the Ottoman Empire. Defoe implicitly raises the specter of the apostate who sheds his Englishness in favor of an Ottoman identity, highlighting the anxieties of English overseas expansion. The interpretations that followed the novel's publication will reflect a different view of England's position in the world. But in its original setting, Defoe's novel is a backwards-looking text anxious about the possibility of an imperial future. Later, this vision shifts to one of English might and African slaves.

Gildon's critique is often dismissed as a sign of his inability to grasp the 'new' genre of the novel, but his censure of Defoe's representation of religion and transnational politics is often overlooked. Gildon was wary of the association of Defoe's book with Protestant values, viewing its popularity more as a source of discord than unity:

> If his works should happen to live to the next Age, there would in all probability be a greater Strife among the several Parties whose he really was, than among the seven *Græcian* Cities, to which of them *Homer* belong'd: The *Dissenters* first would claim him as theirs, the *Whigs* in general as theirs, the *Tories* as theirs, the *Non-jurors* as theirs, the *Papists* as theirs, the *Atheists* as theirs, and so on to what Sub-divisions there may be among us.[4]

Similar to my reading of the translations of I. Tufayl in the previous chapter, Gildon sees *Robinson Crusoe* as potentially being claimed by several sides in the feuds surrounding England's political and religious future.

Rather than looking forward to English imperial domination, this chapter looks back at the cultural environment that produced the

---

[4] Ibid., iv.

novel. In this context, the Ottomans—not the English—are the major imperial power, and Crusoe's efforts to rule his island expose national insecurities over the cultural and colonial influence of the Islamic Mediterranean. Reading Defoe's famous novel through the lens of an Ottoman influence helping to shape English Protestant identity, I argue that *Robinson Crusoe* is deeply embedded in the instability of English identity, especially in its relationship with Catholic Europe and the Ottoman Mediterranean. While the act of domination that most readers probably remember and that has generated the most controversy in *Robinson Crusoe* is the hero's subjection of Friday, this, like the novel's popularity, needs to be seen in a larger context that includes perceptions of the Ottoman Empire in eighteenth-century England. By doing so, an interpretation emerges that is an alternative to still-prevalent readings that focus on English colonial power. Instead, the text presents an Englishman's—and through him England's—failed attempts at colonization and loss of identity against a backdrop of perceived imperial success and superiority in the Ottoman Regencies in North Africa. Crusoe's—and through him England's—attempts at establishing an uniquely English religious identity and imperial power are repeatedly depicted in terms of failure and decay, especially when compared with the literary representations of a stable, powerful Ottoman identity.

Crusoe's Ottoman Captivity

Setting his first voyages in the 'Old World' of Sallee in Ottoman-held North Africa sets up a clear contrast to Crusoe's imperial endeavors. Why does Defoe begin Crusoe's adventures on the old side of the Atlantic rather than the new? I believe that he does so in order to set up the text's ideology of master-servant relations, placing his power over the island and Friday in an older and more complex context. Rather than 'civilized' man extending benevolent paternalism toward a 'natural' one, the African sequence leads the reader through a series of different power relations that later complicate Crusoe's relocation to the island and Friday.

The narrative begins with Crusoe's attempts to stabilize his identity as an English adventurer, after the loss of his former role as a dutiful son. This temporary identity soon decays, setting up the pattern of failed self-fashioning that remains until the end of the novel. His first voyage to West Africa, under the guidance of a captain he met in London, goes well. The captain plays a paternalistic role with the green adventurer, kindly guiding him in his new life. Their relationship is described in terms of mutual reciprocity: "For, as he took delight to introduce me, I took delight to learn."[5] That he is under the guidance of the captain and possibly still under the financial protection of his father signals that he remains in training to enter the realms of European mastery. It is further couched within the context of an familial endeavor, since despite his father's disapproval, he "had mustered it [the funds necessary to undertake the first voyage] by the assistance of some relations whom I corresponded with, and who, I believe, got my father, or at least my mother, to contribute so much as that to my first adventure" (16). The young Crusoe's relationship with his first captain reproduces the idea of an English family supporting its next generation. Both are free English Protestants, and Crusoe's relationship with the captain differs from those he will have with his servants. As an apprentice, he is being trained to one day become the captain's peer, but in Crusoe's future relationships as a master, the future independence of his charges remain ambiguous at best.

Following a pattern of the Englishman's identity becoming increasingly destabilized, the good English father-figure dies and is replaced on the second voyage by his mate, who proves an ineffectual father-figure. There is no mention of any bond, and the new captain fails to protect Crusoe from the dangers of the Ottoman Mediterranean. Near Morocco, Turkish pirates take their ship and Crusoe exits the world of fathers training sons and enters a world of masters and slaves. The former is defined by domestic, familial relationships; the latter by transnational, colonial hierarchies. Crusoe's enslavement initially places him under the command of the pirates' captain, placing him in circumstances "not so dreadful as at first I apprehended." What differentiates this from his first voyage is the shift from son/apprentice to slave. There, the English captain had focused on training him; here, the Muslim captain only values his ability to perform labor: "as his proper prize.... being young and nimble, and fit for his business." Crusoe moves from learning to create capital to being a means of producing that capital for someone else. His shift "from a merchant to a

---

[5] Daniel Defoe, *Robinson Crusoe* (1719), ed. John Richetti (London: Penguin Books, 2001) 16.

miserable slave" immediately puts him in mind of the loss of his father: "now I look'd back upon my father's prophetick discourse to me" (17). Crusoe's attempt to shape an identity as an English seaman potentially promoting English interests through trade declines into service to the more established and powerful Ottoman Empire.

The description of the pirates as Turkish and the taking of their prisoners to Sallee, "a port belonging to the *Moors*" (17), also places the adventure immediately into a discourse of power involved in eighteenth-century representations of English interactions with the Ottomans. Crusoe's first "taste of misery" as a slave to a Muslim master would have been familiar to English readers during the early eighteenth century. During the sixteenth through eighteenth centuries, audiences of English print and stage were exposed repeatedly to representations of Christian slaves, Muslim masters, and the ever-present possibility of apostasy. The concept of English captives in the Barbary would have been familiar to Crusoe's readers. Moreover, it would represent a challenge to the idea of an essentialist national Protestant identity, as captivity narratives were often fraught with the reality of English nationals converting to Islam out of a sense of cultural, financial, and military inferiority to Islamic culture, often represented by the Ottoman Empire.

Though the possibility of Crusoe's conversion to Islam is not explicitly stated in the novel, the historical context that produced it surrounds his actions during his enslavement with the sense that his identity as an English Protestant is in danger and makes his escape more urgent. As mentioned in the previous chapter, English sermons of the seventeenth and early eighteenth century frequently expressed domestic anxiety over apostasy abroad in areas such as Sallee. Nabil Matar points out that converts to Islam were known to return to England without disclosing their conversions:

> There is no information in English writings about the reasons why renegades gave up Islam and returned to their native homes. But it is evident from the sermons that of the 'thousands' of Christians who converted to Islam, some had returned to England without confessing their past. Evidently, there was easy mobility between Barbary and England, Islam and Christianity.[6]

---

[6] Nabil Matar, *Islam in Britain, 1558–1685* (Cambridge: Cambridge University Press, 1998), 65.

Similar to the fears surrounding coffeehouses that the outward activity of coffee dinking would change the inward religious and national allegiances of the drinker, the fears expressed in English sermons on apostasy while in the Ottoman Empire reject the idea that outward actions conforming to Islam do not correspond to an inward conversion. In a 1636 sermon, Charles FitzGeffry condemns the many Englishmen who claimed to "received the abominable circumcision in their flesh [i.e., converted to Islam while abroad], but not in their hearts. Some of them have professed so much in their private letters to their friends that outwardly they are Mahumetans, but in minde they remaine Christians."[7] Ironically, fears of apostasy also included the belief that outward conformity to Christianity in England might mask inner apostasy amongst those returning from abroad.

This tension between outward appearance and inward identity emerges explicitly in Defoe's novel when Crusoe is a castaway on the island, and I argue that it is also implicitly there during this episode in Sallee. There is a strong possibility that English readers would have seen Crusoe's identity as a Christian at least tested during his captivity. This threat of Crusoe losing his Protestant English identity becomes a reality when he becomes a castaway. The lack of others to identify with, nationally and religiously, leads to a destabilization of his own sense of self and causes him to reach back to a similar moment of cultural isolation: his enslavement. As a result, his stay in captivity shapes his view of himself and his actions on the island. Later, while still a castaway on the island, Crusoe will fear turning into a savage. To avoid this decline, he attempts to emulate the Turkish captors he observed in his Ottoman captivity.

During his time in Sallee, Crusoe, a gardener in his master's home (foreshadowing his experience as gardener of his own island), looks for a kind of solidarity with other slaves that would maintain his difference from the non-European Muslim majority surrounding him. However, he finds "no-fellow slave, no *English, Irishman,* or *Scottsman*" (18). Instead, he compromises on his choice of ally: a fellow slave who, while Muslim, is European—the Morisco Xury. Crusoe's actions after his escape are intended to change his position in relation to the Islamic system without actually changing the system. Desiring to be a master, he must obtain a slave. Xury's background as a Morisco

---

[7] Qtd. in Matar, *Islam in Britain*, 65.

is one that reinforces the narrative anxieties over apostasy through its challenge to the binary opposition of Christian and Muslim identity. His connection to Spain implies danger of apostasy during Crusoe's confinement. Beginning in early sixteenth century and continuing into the nineteenth, 'renegade' came to mean "a person who renounces his or her faith; an apostate; (in early use) spec. a Christian who converts to Islam."[8] Matar argues that the origin of the term, descended linguistically from the Spanish *renegado*, "suggests that the first converts were associated in English imagination with Spain."[9] Having been under Islamic rule during the medieval era, Spain became associated with conversion from Christianity to Islam as well as the reverse.

Between the fall of Toledo in 1085 and the taking of Granada in 1492, Christian forces began the conquest of Islamic Spain. A Muslim living under Christian rule was referred to as a *Mudejar*, or "the one allowed to remain." According to Middle Eastern and Hispano-Arabic scholar Anwar G. Chejne, while living in separate communities and allowed a degree of self-governance, "Mudejars served as intermediaries between Islamic and Christian societies, contributing to the integration of many Arabic elements."[10] However in 1501, a revolt in Granada led to a change in policy: all Muslims in Granada faced either conversion or expulsion. It is at this point that the term *Morisco* emerged:

> After the forced conversion of 1501, the neophytes—whether baptized by force or free will—came to be called Moriscos (little Moors), placing them in a special category within the Christian faith. They were differentiated from Old Christians not only by the recency of their conversions, but also by race. The label "Moriscos," or sometimes "Christian Mudejars," placed them at a greater disadvantage vis-à-vis their Christian fellows in that they were considered Arabs or Berbers and, thus, inferior to "Old Christians," who enjoyed "purity of blood" (*limpieza de sangre*).[11]

---

[8] Oxford English Dictionary (2009).

[9] Matar, *Islam in Britain*, 22. The OED supports this etymology, connecting its own definition of renegade to renegado, for which the earliest example it provides is a 1573 translation of *Supplication to Kinges Maiestie of Spayne:*
> And to that intent, haue they sought, to plant in this countrie the inquisition, deuised and inuented in Spaine by certaine Iewes, and Renegados, by that meanes to breake all priuileges, rightes, and auncient customes.

[10] Anwar G. Chejne, *Islam and the West: The Moriscos, a Cultural and Social History* (Albany: State University of New York Press, 1983), 4.

[11] Chejne adds that despite these claim of racial purity,
> it was almost impossible to distinguish one from the other at this juncture of history...The Arab conquest of Spain had been achieved by a small band of

In addition to the racial separation, Moriscos were viewed by their Christian rulers as a threat to Spanish security: during the fifteenth and sixteenth centuries, they "were considered a fifth column, not only an obstacle to the unity of Spain but also potentially a force colluding with North Africans, Egyptians, French, Turks, pirates, Lutherans, and other Christian heretics."[12] This continued suspicion illustrates that despite Moriscos' public conversions to Catholicism, neither Church nor State accepted them as 'true' Christians. This inability to lose the Muslim label explains why Defoe's text appears to present Xury as Muslim.

Robinson Crusoe aligns Xury with these destabilizing signs of apostasy found in captivity narratives and the struggle to define English religious identity separately from Catholic and Protestant Europe: he shares the same geographic space as Turks and pirates, but as their slave; he shares the same enslaved status as the Protestant hero. At the same time, Xury briefly stabilizes of English identity when his bond with Crusoe is trumped by their religious differences. Historically, Moriscos were also conflated with Protestants in the minds of the Church and Crown in Spain, which viewed the growing Protestant population as potential allies to the Morisco community, reasoning that the two groups shared "certain elements that conformed with some of their religious thinking—such as the denial of the supremacy of the pope, the frowning on images, and the freedom of the individual to scrutinize the Scriptures."[13] In response to fears of religious and therefore political unrest, by 1614 the expulsion of the Moriscos from Spain neared completion and those exiled "were scattered throughout the Mediterranean basin: the Balearic Islands, France, Sicily, Italy, Constantinople and other Eastern cities, but with the greatest concentration in Morocco, Algeria, and Tunis."[14] *Robinson Crusoe* is set in the mid-seventeenth century, just subsequent to the expulsion. Xury could have been taken from any of the above places or could have been the

---

Berbers and Arabs who intermingled with the overwhelmingly larger native population steeped in Christianity and Latin culture. Subsequent to the conquest, this native population underwent linguistic, religious, and cultural changes and hardly an ethnic or racial transformation. The neo-Muslims, mostly of Spanish stock and know as Muladíes (Ar. Muwalladūn), constituted the bulk of the Muslim population of the Peninsula preserving Islamic values and culture (7).

[12] Ibid., 8.
[13] Ibid., 9.
[14] Ibid., 14.

grandchild of exiled Moriscos who settled in Morocco. In either case, by creating this background for the character as well as ending the episode with a Catholic captain, Defoe evokes a history of displacement and religious conflict that sets up the themes and power dynamics of Crusoe's adventures on the island.

When Crusoe escapes from captivity, he has a choice between a Moor and a Morisco as his traveling companion. On a fishing boat with these two potential allies, Crusoe pushes the Moor, who has served as an easily manipulated companion for the protagonist for the majority of the captivity episode, overboard. The Moor, his master's brother Ismael, demonstrates his physical strength while verbally expresses his willingness to serve Crusoe: "he rose immediately, for he swam like a cork, and call'd to me begg'd to be taken in, told me he would go all over the world with me; he swam so strong after the boat that he would have reach'd me very quickly, there being but little wind" (20). In response, Crusoe threatens to shoot Ismael if he continues to follow the boat. Despite their past congeniality, Ismael's physical prowess, and his professed submission, Crusoe instead chooses Xury, of whom the narrative has made little mention up to this point.

One of Gildon's complaints against Defoe is the broken English spoken by Friday and Xury. His response to Xury's use of the language critiques the idea that those in the Barbary would assimilate to English practices: "it had been more natural to have made Robinson speak broken Arabick, which Language he must be forc'd in some measure to learn; whereas Xury had no Motive in the World to study so much English as he makes him speak; but this is a Peccadillo and not worth dwelling upon."[15] While he does not invest much meaning in this criticism and is using it mainly to point to the lack of logic in the narrative, Gildon's comment points to a world view of the time which assumed that an English subject would conform to Ottoman culture; Xury, who belongs fully to neither Europe nor the Barbary would have chosen the more dominant, powerful culture, as there was no incentive for assimilating into the weaker position of English culture.

In his one brief mention preceding this scene, little evidence is given of how Xury might surpass his Muslim masters as companion. First, Crusoe mentions that Ismael "always took me and a young *Maresco* with him to row the boat, we made him very merry, and I prov'd

---

15 Charles Gildon, *The Life and Strange Surprizing Adventures*, 13.

very dexterous in catching fish" (18). Here, the narrative emphasizes Crusoe's own abilities. "Me" precedes "young *Maresco*," making Xury almost an afterthought. Xury only rows the boat, while Crusoe shows extreme skill in making the fishing expeditions a success. Crusoe's justification of his choice lies in an unexplained belief that Xury is trustworthy while Ismael is not. He even goes so far as to imply that he could have been "content" in Ismael's companionship: "I could," Crusoe explains after threatening violence against the Moor, "have been content to ha' taken this *Moor* with me, and ha' drown'd the boy, but there was no venturing to trust him" (20). In this alternative, Xury would have met with a much more violent fate than what actually befalls Ismael. Given the choice of death or retreat, Ismael retreats to the shore. The ease with which his strength as a swimmer allows him to return to land is repeated four times in the paragraph describing Crusoe's betrayal of him. It even closes with Crusoe's reassurance—to himself or to the reader—that he "make[s] no doubt but he [Ismael] reach'd it [the shore] with ease, for he was an excellent swimmer" (20). The alternative scenario, in contrast, involves Crusoe and Ismael inaugurating their voyage by drowning Xury, with the description emphasizing his youth and vulnerability as "the boy" surrounded by two physically strong men.

While perhaps implicitly based upon their companionship in captivity, Crusoe explicitly bases his trust of Xury on an outward display of submission when he makes Xury "*swear by* Mahomet *and his father's beard*" to serve him (20). The difference between Ismael and Xury may lie partially in their age difference, with a boy being presumably easier to control and submissive to the older Crusoe as a father-figure. However, although youth plays a factor, I believe that by Crusoe specifying that Xury is of Spanish descent, he is making claims, though limited, about a European identity that supersedes other non-religious bonds. Roxann Wheeler points out that, in

> the context of Moroccan slavery, Xury and Crusoe resemble each other more than they differ.... [T]heir common difference from the Moors; their shared European origin counts most in this respect. Once out of the context of slavery, a different configuration is formed—first in relation to black Africans and then in relation to Europeans.[16]

---

[16] Roxann Wheeler, *The Complexion of Race: Categories of Difference in Eighteenth-Century British Culture* (Philadelphia: University of Pennsylvania Press, 2000), 59.

When compared to the black Africans, Xury is seen to be "neither as powerful as Crusoe nor as abject as the Africans on the west coast." The bond between them comes out of the "potential danger of the 'wild mans' and the resulting fear of being eaten lead Crusoe to notice that which most clearly separates Xury and himself from the West Africans: their light skin and clothed bodies."[17]

While no mention is made of physical description or skin color in the description of the "Negroes" and Xury, what is emphasized about the West Africans is their lack of civilization, signified by their lack of clothes and their darker skin. Their cannibalism at first frightens Crusoe, but later, when he encounters another group of natives and realizes that they lack weapons as effective as his gun, he is willing to accept help and food from them (25–27). His bond with Xury is due largely to a shared, generalized civilization defined by Wheeler, but Crusoe's assumption that he and Xury share values is also due in part to cultural assumptions in England of a past connection between Moriscos and Protestants in Spain and the early-eighteenth-century Quaker interest in an Andalusian Muslim scholar. With a lack of physical or personality description for Xury, his distinguishing feature lies in what Defoe and his readers assumed they had in common with Moriscos.

Robinson Crusoe is a narrative that often resolves potential instabilities of English Protestant identity. In a pattern that will be repeated with Friday, Xury's mixed background puts Crusoe's own position of colonial and individual power into question. Xury is often the more capable of the two, with frequent references to Xury's good advice as his master's "better councellor [*sic*]" (25). Relying on a non-Christian makes Crusoe's—and by extension English—identity unclear. Crusoe's own national and ethnic heritage was already called into question in the narrative's opening. As the son of a German immigrant, Kreutznaer, Crusoe and his family have endeavored to make themselves appear more English: "we are now call'd, nay we call our selves, and write our name *Crusoe*, and so my companions always call'd me"(5). Wheeler argues that the

> importance of Christianity as a significant bond between Europeans overrides even historical differences between the Church of England and Catholics by representing the greater difference as that between Christian

---

[17] Wheeler, *The Complexion of Race*, 60.

and Islam. It is clearly not Xury's Spanish national origin that casts him as a slave but his Islamic religion.[18]

I add to this that the text is not only resolving the blurring of religious categories under a general European banner, but also rearticulating Protestantism as closer to Catholicism than to the Islamic sects with which the Inquisition once associated it.

While at times England associated itself with Islam against Catholicism, a sense of shared identity through Christianity and an emerging biological view of race made it possible for English society to construct a hierarchy of worth based on religious and national affiliations.[19] Crusoe's eventual choice of a Catholic captain over Xury reinforces this hierarchy and reasserts his identity as an Englishman, superior to those around him and therefore fulfills his desire to have more power than them.

By selling Xury to a Catholic Portuguese captain, the novel comes closes to allegorically rewriting history. Spain, a traditional enemy of England, is not transformed into a Protestant ally, but instead the Catholic presence is displaced to another Iberian space. Rather than Moriscos and Protestants jointly persecuted by a Catholic power in Spain, the Protestant Englishman aligns himself with a Catholic Portuguese against a Spanish and Muslim Other.[20] However, even this resolution does not erase all the ambiguities Xury brings to the text. He is sold in a manner similar to the African slaves Crusoe traffics, but with a crucial difference. Seeing that Crusoe is conflicted on whether selling the boy is a betrayal of their previous companionship, the Portuguese captain offers an alternative: "he [the captain] would give the boy an obligation to set him free in ten years, if he turn'd Christian; upon this, and *Xury* saying he was willing to go to him, I let the

---

[18] Wheeler, *The Complexion of Race*, 60.
[19] As Matar points out,
   Although some Britons adopted customs, texts and ideas from the Muslims, others reacted with a pride that inspired poets and theologians to think of God as English and to see the nation as an 'English Zion,' [a pride which]...sometimes extend[ed] to notions of religious-racial superiority as can be seen in the popular saying that one Protestant Englishman was worth three Catholic Portuguese, and one Portuguese was worth three Muslim Moors (Matar, *Islam in Britain*, 120).
[20] In other places, Crusoe aligns himself against Catholicism. For example, he decides against settling in Brazil since living there would require either conversion or persecution: to be
   resolv'd to be a sacrifice to my principles, [or] be a martyr for religion, and die in the Inquisition; so I resolv'd to stay at home (Defoe, *Robinson Crusoe*, 238).

Captain have him" (29). Unlike other slaves, Xury enters consensually into indentured servitude, placing him in a position of privilege compared to the African slaves.

This situation also mirrors the historical situation of the Moriscos, with the Portuguese captain standing in for the Catholic Church and Spanish Crown who also demanded conversion in exchange for the Moriscos receiving acceptance into the Reconquista's new political order. But this promise of freedom through social citizenship did not materialize. What then are readers to make of Xury's chances of future freedom? The ambiguous status of Xury throughout the episode and the uncertainty of his future are based upon the complicated history of Muslim, Catholic, and Protestant relations and sets up the complex relationship at the heart of the novel: the paternal and imperial interactions between Crusoe and Friday.

Empty Signs of Sovereignty: Crusoe Turns Turk

Although he physically leaves the Ottoman Mediterranean of his captivity, Crusoe continues to operate under the same systems of values and hierarchies of power when he arrives on his island in the New World. After being shipwrecked while on a slave-trading expedition and having established himself and secured his survival on the island, the narrator's description evokes an edenic state with Crusoe reborn as natural, pre-lapsarian man. This description, however, is consistently undermined throughout the narrative, acting as a counter to the philosophies of property, man, and contentment that characterized the post-1688 ideology, ardently supported by Defoe in much of his political writings. In this light, what emerges is a study on the instability of English Protestant identity, in which the Ottoman Empire becomes the symbol for civilization against the threat of barbarism offered by the island.

Though he seems to control the island, Crusoe finds his reign constricted by the way his isolation alters his sense of need and use. An excess of property without the social context to make its ownership meaningful oppresses him. Images of thwarted imperial potential emerge as Crusoe emphasizes the inability to trade or build a fleet. Following his declaration of himself as the island's sovereign, his power is quickly undercut:

> There were no rivals. I had no competitor, none to dispute sovereignty
> or command with me. I might have rais'd a ship loadings of corn; but
> I had no use for it;…I had timber enough to have built a fleet of ships.
> I had grapes enough to have made wine, or to have cur'd into raisins, to
> have loaded that fleet when they have been built. But all I could make
> use of, was, all that was valuable. (103)

The seemingly positive connotation of the lack of rivals to his dominance is undercut by the repeated declarations of his possessions,
power, and potential followed with a 'but' for the emptiness they produced. All these images require other people with whom to interact.[21]

Crusoe's sense of need is redefined by the lack of use to which he can
put his goods. With his physical needs met, he considers his surplus
goods a burden and not a blessing. He has access to goods frequently
traded between the Old and New Worlds, the profit from which partly
motivated him to travel to this area. In this context, the earlier lines
about competition also foreshadow the conflicts he will fantasize over
and seek with the other islanders as well as some of the European sailors he meets at the end. Just as possessions are worthless if they carry
no value, power loses its allure without subjects to rule and rivals to
subdue. Being forced into a life of subsistence instead of one of profit
devalues what he does rule, and for Defoe's protagonist, sovereignty is
valuable only when it includes dominion over another.

In fact, he is fettered by the abundance he possesses and the lack of
population (or consumers) to share, trade or sell it to:

> If I kill'd more flesh than I could eat, the dog must eat it, or the vermin.
> If I sow'd more corn than I could eat, it must be spoil'd. The trees that I
> cut down, were lying to rot on the ground. I could make no more use of
> them than for fewel [sic]; and that I had no occasion for, but to dress my
> food. In a word, the nature and experience of things dictated to me upon
> just reflections, that all good things of this world, are no further good to
> us, than they are for our use, and that whatever we may heap up indeed
> to give others, we enjoy as much as we can use, and no more. (103)

---

[21] In addition, his desires for trade involve a wish to exchange his American goods
for English ones:
> I would have given it [the money he found in the shipwreck] all for a six-penny-
> worth of turnip and carrot seed out of England, or for a handful of pease and
> beans, and a bottle of ink (103).

This wish reflects both the existing triangular trade thriving in the British empire—
without trade, his labor on his little colony carries little meaning in the greater economics of the Atlantic—as well as his desire to stay attached to his native identity,
which is destabilized by his time on the island.

While Crusoe may rule the island, Nature, especially the nature of his own physical body (with its limited capacity to consume), oppresses him. He lacks the ability to use much of what he possesses, because without others to recognize his wealth and potentially share in it, property has no real value to its owner. The plentiful island turns utopian conventions on their heads: removing strife and want from a man's life leads to a virtually sinless life in Defoe's text but also leads to an oppressive and sterile existence. Crusoe needs companionship for his property or his authority to have any meaning. It is not enough to gain mastery over himself; he must have other humans to rule for his 'kingdom' to satisfy him.

As with property, religion fails to offer a stable identity or stay the growing sense of decay on the island. Though he reads his Bible regularly, it only helps to stem his discontent and teaches him a gratitude that he would otherwise lack, as his religious identity is always associated with others: his identity as an Englishman, as a Protestant, as civilized, as European. Crusoe describes his contemplations of God as exercises in gratitude: "I learned to look more upon the bright side of my condition, and less upon the dark side; and to consider what I enjoy'd, rather than what I wanted; and this gave me sometimes such secret comforts, that I cannot express them" (104). Despite his difficulty in expressing the "comforts" he "sometimes" experiences, he has little problem spending long passages expressing his discontent despite the abundance surrounding him. In other words, his relationship to God is shaped by his relationship to others. As a result, Crusoe tries to develop human-like relationships with his animals with limited success. With his parrot, he is able to simulate human companionship while remaining aware of the superficiality of the parrot's 'concern' for him. After returning from scouting the island's coast, the parrot 'greets' Crusoe with the phrases he taught it to mimic:

> *Poll*, the sociable creature came to me, and sat upon my thumb as he used to do, and continued talking to me; *Poor* Robin Crusoe, and *how did I come here?* and *where had I been?* Just as if he had been overjoy'd to see me again; and so I carry'd him home along with me. (114)

Poll's noises simulate concern, which give Crusoe the sense that his presence does matter to his subjects by producing this illusion that he was missed. That Crusoe chose to teach this "bemoaning language" (113) to the bird demonstrates his desire to feel needed and wanted by someone else.

Through his animals, Crusoe tries to bring meaning to his sovereignty of the island by making them further mimic not simply human companionship in general, but specifically a life at court. In terms of power, he sees himself as clearly superior to the animals, having "the lives of my subjects at my absolute command." While he makes his daily routines into a performance of his sovereignty, the power of his position rings as hollow as Poll's empty words: "like a King I dined too all alone, attended by my servants, *Poll*, as if he had been my favourite, was the only person permitted to talk to me" (118). Poll's ability to mimic human emotions grants him a favored position in Crusoe's 'court' and the parrot's centrality in Crusoe's kingdom points out the emptiness of the castaway's own life. Just like Poll, Crusoe is parroting sovereignty.

The dialogue between Poll and Crusoe mirrors passages of Defoe's earlier political writing and points to a potential critique of the monarchy and Dissenter movements. Paula R. Backscheider points out parallels with the emotional state Defoe himself presents in *A New Test of the Church of England's Honesty* (1704). Backscheider notes that Poll's empty consolation to Crusoe mirrors Defoe's earlier prison writing: "'Alas, *Poor De Foe*! What hast thou been doing, and for what hast thou suffer'd?'...At this point both Defoe [writing from Newgate Prison] and Robinson Crusoe feel sorry for themselves and puzzle endlessly over why they have been 'singl'd out' for suffering."[22] And while he produced numerous defenses of Dissenter rights and post-1688 monarchs William, Anne, and George I, these efforts often had negative effects on his personal life. Although he supported William's ascension, the new king's military policies helped bankrupt Defoe;[23] and though he went to prison for writing Dissenter propaganda, his experience at Newgate left him less enthusiastic for them:

> Prison and its aftermath left Defoe with an uneasy peace with the Dissenters. He never trusted them again, never felt himself truly one of them, and they returned the feeling. Although he continued to write in their interest, he often slipped into making wry, slightly bitter comment and consistently recognized that he could expect no gratitude.[24]

---

[22] Paula Backscheider, *Daniel Defoe: His Life* (Baltimore: John Hopkins Press, 1992), 131.

[23] Ibid., 51.

[24] Ibid., 134.

Given the bitterness that his prison experience lent to Dissenter positions, I think it can be argued that the financial, legal, and employment difficulties he found in politics could color his view of the monarchy as well. The emotional desolation Crusoe finds in his paradise could be an example of his "wry, slightly bitter" commentary on Protestant beliefs in self-reliance and the individual's relationship with God.

Not only is Crusoe always aware that the bird is not truly expressing joy at seeing him, the companionship he does manage to find with Poll and the other animals degenerates along with the goods he forces himself to see as divine blessings. His sovereignty is a hollow parody of colonial power. Crusoe's perfect kingdom where he can "hang, draw, give liberty, and take it away, and [have] no rebels" is undercut through the narrative's ironic descriptions (118). He has the power to favor some subjects over others. But Poll's words have already been established as empty of real meaning, and while that might on its own fulfill a satiric view of a courtier, the descriptions use this pretense of companionship to point to the intimacy Crusoe lacks. Poll is described as "the only person permitted to talk," which carries the depressing limits of his power: "permitted" implies Crusoe's power but is undercut by the knowledge that the parrot is the only one of his subjects with this ability. Similarly, that Poll is "the only person" points to the thing Crusoe desires most at this point—another *person*. Poll, despite his verbal tricks, will never be a true companion because he can only mimic the language of devotion, not feel that devotion himself. Similarly, Crusoe is sovereign of the island, but the lack of real subjects makes his performance of kingship empty.

The passage continues to undercut Crusoe's courtly display of power. His dog may sit "always at my right hand" like a privileged companion, but he has degenerated and "grown very old and crazy" (118). The insufficiency of the comfort the dog offers is further emphasized by finiteness of the resource, as the dog "had found no species to multiply his kind upon" and will be the last of his kind on the island (118). This theme of degeneration continues in the passages leading up to his encounter with Friday. These courtier animals die and are replaced with new, less companionable ones. The cats—that in the early passage sat "one on one side the table, and one on the other, expecting now and then a bit from my hand, as a mark of special favor" (118)—"multiply'd...to that degree, that I was oblig'd to shoot several of them at first to keep them from devouring me and all I had" (143). Earlier, he described a kingdom without rebellion against his authority, but the cats alter this already compromised utopia through attacks on his power and property. He may consider a few of the cats' descendants as "part of my family" but he must exert a considerable amount of control over them to prevent further threats to his rule: the "two or three favorites [of the cats], which I kept tame and whose young, when they had any, I always drown'd." The pitiable albeit humorous need to squash potential rebellion among his subjects' points to the impotency of his rule. Even Poll's successors are found lacking: "I had two more parrots which talk'd pretty well, and would all call *Robin Crusoe*; but none like my first; nor did I take the pains with any of them that I had done with him" (143). This final image of Crusoe ruling over the animals is one of a tired monarch barely holding on to his authority over his subjects.

The devolution of his relationship with the animals does not lead him to a deeper contemplation of God as it does for the titular hero of I. Tufayl's *Hayy Ibn Yaqzan*, discussed in the previous chapter. Instead, the decline of his material kingdom leads to the symbolic deterioration of his faith. Initially, he thanks Providence for the material blessings he receives:

> [a] reflection [that] was of great use to me [in keeping faith in God and positive view of his isolation]...[was] to compare my present condition with what I at first expected it should be; nay, with what it would certainly have been, if the good Providence of God had not wonderfully ordered the ship to be cast up nearer to the shore,

supplying him with tools, weapons, and ammunition to ease his life there and preventing him from living as a "meer savage" (14).

Like the animal court, these supplies too are represented with images of increasing decay. Within a few paragraphs, his ink "had been gone for some time, all but a very little"; this item played an important role in his spiritual meditation as he used it to record "the various Providences which befell me." Along with the ink, his bread—reminiscent of both the manna God gives the Israelites in the wilderness as well as the communion host—runs out before he can grow corn to make it on his own. His clothes "decay too mightily." He cannot go naked because he "could not bear the heat of the sun" and must make new—and, he admits, badly made—clothes out of animal skins (106–7). For Robinson Crusoe, true contentment is not found purely in property or in divine revelation. It is firmly placed in interaction with a companion similar enough for him to relate to but different enough so he may still subjugate him as an Other.

The decay of these remainders of civilization further blurs the line between civilized and savage. Specifically, he views it as the loss of his identity as an Englishman: "had any one in *England* met such a man as I was, it must either have frighted them, or rais'd a great deal of laughter" (118). While he feels he has not devolved into a "savage," he recognizes that his outer appearance no longer reads as 'English,' and interestingly, he connects his Otherness to his captivity in Sallee. In order to stem the decay and impotency surrounding his English identity, he literally 'turns Turk.'

The only example of stable power found in the novel is Crusoe's captivity with the Ottomans. In fashioning a new identity powerful enough to subdue his island colony, he models himself on the imperial representatives he observed in North Africa. After improvising an outfit of mostly goatskin and remnants from the shipwreck, he chooses to style his facial hair after the Turks he saw while in captivity. This is seen as a step toward civilization from the "beard I had once suffer'd to grow till it was about a quarter of a yard long," especially since he stresses the need for tools, "both scissars and razors." Yet, the turn away from natural disarray does not make him more recognizably English:

> I had cut it [the beard] pretty short, except what grew on my upper lip, which I had trimm'd into a large pair of *Mahometan* whiskers, such as I had seen worn by some *Turks*, who I saw at *Sallee*; for the *Moors* did not wear such, tho' the *Turks* did…they [the whiskers] were of a length and shape monstrous enough, and such as in *England* would have pass'd for frightful. (119)

While he makes a point that he is not imitating his former captors, he needs a means to explain his status as neither savage nor Englishman and accomplishes this by using Islam as an alternative mode. The reference back to his servitude in Sallee at this point when he feels a loss of identity may connect to the tradition of captivity narratives the North Africa episode draws upon.

Placing this scene within the seventeenth-century context of English anxieties about reintegrating apostates into society after their experience in the Barbary, Crusoe's anxieties take on a new dimension. The loss of the outward appearance of Englishness would carry a deeper reference to apostasy for Defoe's readers. Reflecting anxieties similar to those surrounding coffeehouses turning their patrons into Turks or Englishmen in Ottoman spaces such as Sallee converting to Islam, there is a strong connection between outward appearances revealing an inner truth about a person's identity. The novels explicit connection between Crusoe's Ottoman captivity, his fears of no longer looking English, and his decision to 'turn Turk' in appearance opens up the possibility that English readers would have linked the Sallee episode and this later scene with domestic discussions of apostasy. The narrative's movement from Crusoe's loss of English resemblance to his adoption of "*Mahometan* whiskers" thus illuminates the connection between Crusoe's adventures on both sides of the Atlantic. While there may not be the possibility of conversion, there is both the fear of losing signs of his cultural identity and the insistence—similar to those Englishmen who claimed to have only outwardly converted to Islam—that his physical appearance does not signify a lasting inward change. His adventures in the Mediterranean world draw on existing narratives of captivity and apostasy, where English identity is threatened by the specter of conversion, and provide a prism for reading his experiences in the New World.

Friday and Crusoe's Colonial Failures

Beneath the breakdown of identity shown when Crusoe reimagines himself as a Turk, Crusoe has failed to fulfill his other desires for companionship in his dealings with animals or even God. When he puts his plan to capture 'a savage' into effect, he is immediately drawn to Friday as a human being. Upon first examining his new find, Crusoe describes Friday in tender terms of admiration:

> He was a comely handsome fellow, perfectly well made, with straight strong limbs, not too large; tall and well shap'd...[he] seem'd to have something very manly in his face, and yet he had all the sweetness and softness of an *European* in his countenance too, especially when he smiled. (161)

Crusoe's association of femininity with European identity seems to strengthen the ties between his time on the island and the captivity episode. The association of power and therefore masculinity with a non-European culture (the Ottoman Empire) influences his overall view of Europe in the world. Crusoe transfers the feminized position that Christian Europe holds in the Old World into his encounters in the New. This may explain his overwhelming fear of the natives, even when they seem to pose no real threat to him. That European features are associated with 'sweetness and softness' and not a 'manly' appearance demonstrates that Crusoe does not align himself as a European with a sense of imperial potency. By seeing Friday as similar to a European, he does not associate his companion with a threat to his identity as he does the Ottomans and other natives.

Little description is provided of what Xury looked like or the traits Crusoe admired in him, but this is not the case with Friday. Crusoe now possesses a subject to make his rule over the island meaningful. Friday's presence allows Crusoe to expand his farms and increase his cultivation with the added labor, whose added needs prevent the waste that earlier oppressed him. Yet the pleasure he gains from Friday's presence is not aligned with Friday's role as a servant, but with one of companionship. When he describes his first year with Friday as "the pleasantest year of all" his time on the island, the narrative breaks from a description of labor to one of education: "Friday began to talk pretty well…I began now to have some use for my tongue again." By teaching English to Friday, Crusoe enjoys the mutual benefit of regaining speech himself. This elevates their bond, with Crusoe declaring that he "began really to love the creature" and "believe he lov'd me more than it was possible for him to ever love any thing before" (168). The intensity of Crusoe's pleasure in Friday's company elevates the Carib from the role of a servant or slave to an apprentice or son to be educated.

Despite this elevation, though, Crusoe still maintains the hierarchy where he is sovereign over his companion. Friday, for his part, perfectly performs his role of subject: "for never man had a more faithful, loving, sincere servant…without passions, sullenness, or designs, perfectly oblig'd and engag'd; his very affections were ty'd to me, like those of a child to a father, and I dare say, he would have sacrific'd his life for saving mine" (165). This conception of Friday makes him the perfect subject to finally give meaning to Crusoe's sovereignty over the island. Poll only mimics the language of faithfulness, obedience, and love. Friday embodies these traits.

Crusoe's ability to rule the island remains flawed, as seen when he tries to impress his new subject with an English identity. As Friday's education progresses, Crusoe is frequently shown to be either lacking or soon to be surpassed by his companion, making their relationship less one of Friday's permanent servitude but more one of apprenticeship from which Friday may one day become independent. This is bolstered by Crusoe's identification with Friday as being more similar than Other to him. Crusoe's description of Friday differentiates him from the other natives. Besides his European countenance, his description is dominated by how he is not like non-Europeans: his

> hair was long and black, not curl'd like wool... The colour of his skin was not quite black, but very tawny; and yet not of an ugly yellow nauseous tawny, as the *Brasilians* and *Virginians*, and other natives of *America* are... his nose small, not flat like the Negroes, a very good mouth, thin lips, and his fine teeth well set, and white as ivory. (162)[25]

Crusoe's to racially identify with Friday, and to educate him both culturally and religiously, forges a strong bond of identification between master and servant. This bond undoes the Christian European alliances that allowed Crusoe to sell his previous companion, Xury. Instead, when Crusoe gains other subjects, Friday becomes elevated not just over the Caribs in the group, but over the Europeans as well.

Reassured of his position of power, Crusoe begins to regard the other natives as less of a threat to his power and more as unknowing subjects to be subdued or destroyed. The desire for power over the natives is seen in his desire to play God over them—to judge and execute them. His belief in Friday's goodness makes him ponder God's own choices in ruling Earth:

> however it had pleas'd God... in the government of the works of his hands, to take from so great a part of the world of his creatures, the best uses to which their faculties, and the powers of their souls... And this made me very melancholy sometimes, in reflecting as the several occasions presented, how mean a use we make of all these [as Christian Europeans]... and why it has pleas'd God to hide the life saving knowledge from so many millions of souls, who if I might judge by this poor savage [Friday], Would make a much better use of it than we did. (165)

While Crusoe shifts his critique mainly to the misuse of divine gifts by Christian Europe, the critique is strangely framed in a critique of God's governance of his creation—His own mismanagement of

---

[25] As Wheeler points out, Friday's racial difference from natives and Africans becomes obscured as centuries pass. Much like the effect of the abolitionist movement on the racialization of Oroonoko that I discuss later, Friday begins to be seen as an African slave:

> Changes in the laboring population [of the West Indies] were not the only factor resulting in confusion between Carib and African. Friday's Negroization in eighteenth-century illustrations is also connected to the makeup of the colonial population... [which] gave rise to many blended identities (*The Complexion of Race*, 83).

properties of virtue and scriptural knowledge. The concept of use also relates back to Crusoe's negative views of his property when he first arrives on the island. Knowledge, like goods, only carries value if it can be put to use. Despite already possessing the "saving knowledge" of God, Crusoe cannot put it to use when he arrives on the island because he is preconditioned to see the world through the material lens of human interaction.

From this Crusoe comes very close in his own estimation to challenging God as supreme ruler of the islands. He admits, "I sometimes was led too far, to invade the sovereignty of *Providence*, and as it were arraign the justice of so arbitrary a disposition of things, that should hide that light from some, and reveal it to others" (165–6).[26] Yet this mismanagement with which he charges God is also close to his own. He makes no attempts to convert the other natives, and the religious teaching he provides to Friday points to both his own inadequacies and an implicit critique of God. Crusoe finds it difficult to explain the existence of evil in the world because he himself does not understand it: "I found it was not so easy to imprint right notions in his [Friday's] mind about the Devil, as it was about the being of a God" (172). When Friday asks, *"if God much strong, much might as the Devil, why God no kill the Devil, so make him no more do wicked?"* (173), Crusoe is at a loss to answer. He tries to place his inability to answer as one of his own flaws, not God's—much as he does in the scene discussed above: "tho' I was now an old man, yet I was but a young doctor, and ill enough qualify'd for a casuist, or solver of difficulties" (172). However, this argument is undermined by the frequent references to his daily Bible devotions and almost constant reflections on God, especially the reasoning behind Crusoe's exile on the island, which is explicitly discussed in terms of why God would allow a seemingly evil act to occur. His initial response to Friday's question is avoidance: "at first I could not tell what to say, so I pretended not to hear him" (173). After a brief failed attempt to answer the question, Crusoe successfully distracts his companion from the issue. While containing a critique of God, the

---

[26] Crusoe catches himself challenging God's sovereignty when he debates whether or not he had the right to 'condemn' the Caribs' beliefs and lifestyle:

> What authority or call I had to pretend to be judge and executioner upon these men as criminals, whom Heaven had thought fit for so many ages to suffer unpunish'd[?] (135).

castaway's inability to answer Friday's biblical queries also shows Crusoe's own lack of authority.[27]

Crusoe's earlier dealings with Xury act as a foil to his more profound relationship with Friday. By foreshadowing the events on the island through the illustration of a similar relationship with a young, culturally different man, the text raises the question of why Crusoe parts with one with callous ease while he clings jealously to the other. Xury can be gifted to the Portuguese captain because Crusoe views the boy as a tool and slave in contrast to the bond he shares with the fellow Christian. The only acknowledgement of a sense of kinship on Crusoe's part as he leaves his Morisco companion is the stipulation that if Xury converts to Christianity his time in bondage will be limited. In other words, Christianity holds significance beyond a supernatural belief system for Crusoe—it is the sign of equality and, when we define it as the ability to be free and self-governing, full humanity for him.

Within a framework that equates Christianity with free man, Friday's conversion to Christianity explains his rise in Crusoe's estimation, but it also complicates the existing system of racial, cultural, and religious alliances. Crusoe's similarities with the Catholic Europeans trumped any similarities with Xury, but Friday's conversion changes the situation.

Gaining other subjects after he and Friday rescue a Spaniard and Friday's father from the cannibals, Crusoe revels in his increased sovereignty: "My island was now peopled, and I thought my self very rich in subjects; and it was a merry reflection which I frequently made, how like a king I look'd. First of all, the whole country was my own meer property; so that I had an undoubted right of dominion" (190). This joy in his undisputed authority over the island is increased because of its growing population. Throughout the text, there has been little or no threat to his control of the island itself, so the change in his attitude toward it comes from others recognizing his dominion. Like Friday, these new subjects "were perfectly subjected: I was absolute lord and lawgiver; they all ow'd their lives to me, and were ready to lay down their lives, *if there had been occasion of it*, for me" (190). This echoes his earlier description of Friday's ideal submission. When Crusoe asks

---

[27] This weakness in the spiritual education of Friday forms part of a larger critique of religion in the text—in particular, the vision of a just and well-ordered universe.

if his companion will defend and obey him, Friday goes even further by pledging, "*me die, when you bid die*" (182).

Nevertheless, although these new subjects are similar to Friday, Crusoe does not trust or identify as much with them. His two new subjects represent the binary of European and Other set up in the Xury episode, but unlike his predecessor, Friday is able to supersede the European Christian in Crusoe's eyes. In describing the diversity of his subjects, Crusoe defines them by religion: "My man *Friday* was a Protestant, his father was a pagan and a *cannibal*, and the *Spaniard* was a Papist" (190). This triangulation echoes Crusoe's reintroduction to Europeans with Xury: then, he needed to choose how to align himself amongst Xury the Morisco, a load of pagan African slaves, and a Portuguese captain. The crucial difference this time is that Friday's religious conversion has shifted Crusoe's allegiances so that he values this inward quality more than the outward markers of race and culture. Earlier, he welcomed the Portuguese captain, but at the end of the novel he is filled with suspicion for these Catholic Others:

> I fear'd mostly their treachery and ill usage of me...I told him, it would be very hard, that I should be the instrument of their deliverance, and that they should after wards make me their prisoner in *New Spain*, where an *English* man was certain to be made a sacrifice...I had rather be deliver'd up to the *savages* and be devour'd alive, than fall into the merciless claws of the priests, and be carry'd into the *Inquisition*. (192)

After Friday's conversion, older models of alliance and similarity fall to the wayside. Friday is aligned with Englishness through his Protestant education, while the Catholic Europeans are seen as worse than savages.

Because of this deeper bond, Friday is able to transcend the servant role. Like an apprentice or son, he becomes increasingly self-reliant and enters into forms of self-hood recognized by Crusoe (and readers). This is demonstrated by his ability to enter European society. Leaving the island together changes their bond. In Europe, Friday is no longer really a servant, since someone else is hired to take care of their needs (227). The ease with which Friday is able to adapt to Europe reinforces the power of his conversion. While occasionally comical, Friday shows no fear or lack of adeptness in his new surroundings. Crusoe, by contrast, expresses fear at his new surroundings: "the howling of the wolves run much in my head; and indeed, except the noise I once heard on the shore of *Africa*,...I never heard any thing that filled me with so much horror" (233). The novel's last account of Friday's actions demonstrates his desire to confront the wolves but obeying Crusoe's fearful hesitancy (234).

Crusoe does not manage to reintegrate himself into Europe or England, and the novel ends with his return to the New World to re-subdue his island. At least in this novel, the last image of Friday shows a Protestant youth, seemingly at home in the civilized European world. Friday successfully crosses the boundary between Old and New Worlds with which Crusoe has such difficulty coping.[28] Like Friday, Defoe's novel also acts as a bridge between old and new as it incorporates the older order of a world dominated by Mediterranean empires alongside a new one, still intimidated by the legacies of the Old World and unsure of what the future holds.

---

[28] I am not including Defoe's sequel in this analysis. In *The Farther Adventures of Robinson Crusoe*, Friday accompanies Crusoe on his return to the island, where Friday is killed but Poll the parrot is set free.

PART TWO

CHAPTER FOUR

RACE AND ROMANCE:
OTHELLO, OROONOKO, AND THE DECLINE
OF THE OTTOMAN INFLUENCE

From 19 February 1704 to 6 June 1713, Daniel Defoe produced the propagandistic periodical *A Review of the Affairs of France* as part of the campaign to garner support for the English government's role in the War of the Spanish Succession. But this publication frequently went beyond its intended parameters to touch on the unstable constructions of Protestant and Catholic European identities fueling the conflict. These identities, he argues, were evoked in order to mask the non-religious political mechanisms actually at the heart of the conflict: "Religion, we see, made the Stalking Horse of the World, and serves for a Varnish to all these State Intrigues; but all Centers in this mighty Circle; Men are all Working themselves in, and their Neighbours out."[1] The French king may claim that he "Fights for the Church of which he passes for the most Christian Head;...yet nourishes Hereticks, and gives Arms into their Hands, to Fight against that shame Catholick Religion he pretends to." Similarly, the Swedish king, "a Protestant Prince, Fights against...the whole Body of the Protestant Church in Europe." This, Defoe contends, is no Holy War, but

> a War of *State*; Europe is Embroil'd by the Ambitious Designs of one Man aiming at *Universal Power*; We are fighting to bring him to *Reason* and *Rule* to maintain *Right*, preserve *peace*, open and Encourage *Trade*, and bring the World to a Temper, fit for Honest Men to Live in.[2]

Notably, by shifting the conflict away from religion, the article recasts it as a—rather violent—attempt at persuasive reasoning: the English fight France, not to destroy all Catholics, but to "bring" its king to "*Reason*" in order to "preserve peace" and trade between European nations regardless of religion. Although Defoe ends this article with a

---

[1] Daniel Defoe, *A Review of the Affairs of France*, No. 77 (28 November 1704), Facsimile Book 2 of Volume 1 (New York: Columbia University Press, 1938), 322.
[2] Ibid., 322.

Pro-Protestant/Anti-Catholic stance, he remains insistent that this is not a war of religion.

The distinction matters, in part, because of the long history of religious causes as a justification for European states going to war both within the continent and beyond its borders. Contextualizing these Catholic-Protestant conflicts are the sixteenth- and seventeenth-century Ottoman incursions into Central and Eastern Europe and the eighteenth-century Ottoman-Russian conflicts, but perhaps the deepest cultural memory for Europeans would be the memory of the medieval Crusades. In the article discussed above, Defoe proclaims,

> Commend me to the *Turks*, [for] they are the Truest Fighters for Religion, that I know of in the World; they scorn the Assistance of Christians to Erect *Mahometanism*; we never Read since the Battle between Tanerlain [*sic*] and Bajzette, that ever the *Turks* accepted the Aid of the Christians in any of the Wars.[3]

Nor was this an isolated moment of Defoe defining 'true' Holy War through his example of Ottomans. Early that year, he referenced the 1683 Battle of Vienna, before "which all *Europe* ran the hazard of being over-run by the Banners of *Mahomet*."[4] Defoe critiques the stance of some English Protestants, who privileged sectarian divides within European Christianity over what he perceives as a larger danger posed by the Ottoman Empire: "in those days we had abundance of People, that had so little Sence [*sic*] of Publick Safety, and so much Zeal for the Protestant Religion in *Hungaria*, that they wish'd every day the *Turks* should take *Vienna*."[5] Perhaps foreshadowing the privileging of Robinson Crusoe's connections with the Catholic Portuguese Captain over those with his Morisco companion Xury, or the anxieties that the novel would express over Ottoman might, Defoe argues that England must fear Ottoman incursions more than those of any Catholic power:

> I am not for having the *Whore of Babylon* pull'd down by the *Red Dragon*, and Popery run down by the Power of Mahometanism.... I had rather

---

[3] Ibid., 322.

I.e., Tamberlaine, the fourteenth-century Central Asian Emperor perhaps best known for his depiction in Christopher Marlowe's sixteenth-century *Tamburlaine the Great*.

[4] Defoe, *Affairs of France*, No. 55 (12 September 1704), 234.

[5] Ibid., 234.

be Prosecuted by *Rome*, than by *Constantinople*; nay, if you will come to the extream, I had rather be Persecuted by the *Roman* Catholick Power, than Tollerated by the *Turks*.[6]

He continues this argument into the following issues, highlighting Protestant-Catholic similarities over Ottoman difference:

> if I am to be Murthered, Rob'd, Plundered and Destroyed, I had rather a *Roman* Catholick was the Butcher than a *Turk*; had rather he had the Power over me, that acknowledge Christ, than he that despises him, and defies him; rather he that kills me, because I don't Worship Jesus his way, than he that does it, because I own him [i.e., acknowledge Christ] at all.[7]

Defoe's objections to a English Protestant preference for Ottoman might damaging Catholic influence in Europe points to the contradictory perspectives shaping England's relationship to the rest of the world. Did the Ottomans represent a military and cultural threat greater than that posed by the geographically closer Catholic powers? In an era when religion could mask political motives for conflict and alliances, were the Ottomans that different from other European powers? Informing these questions, the narrative tradition of romance had preserved histories of Crusader conflict as well as sympathetic portrayals of Muslims within English culture. Although by the eighteenth century the genre would have been associated more with continental—specifically French—tradition, its roots are embedded in the Mediterranean world later dominated by the Ottomans. Romance scholars such as John J. Winkler and Elizabeth Archibald locate the genre's origins in accounts of Alexander the Great. Winkler sees the narrative tropes of romances as "a resident alien in Greek culture" and being "born in and (presumably) appropriate to the social forms of a Near Eastern culture...Hellenized in the wake of Alexander's conquests."[8] Adding to this viewpoint, Archibald points out that

> within a few years of [Alexander the Great's] death his history was being turned into a romance which proved so popular that versions of it survive not only in Greek and Latin and in all the European vernacular

---

[6] Ibid., 234–35.
[7] Ibid., 237.
[8] John J. Winkler, "The Invention of Romance," in *The Search for the Ancient Novel*, ed. J. Tatum (Baltimore: John Hopkins University Press, 1994), 35.

languages, but also in Arabic, Persian, Turkish, Malay, Ethiopian, and even Mongolian.[9]

In this light, romance is founded in the merging of 'Eastern' and 'Western' traditions, making it difficult to distinguish what cultural elements in each are free of the other's influence.

Over the course of several centuries, these narratives offered a model of race that differed from empiricist-driven scientific models of the mid and late eighteenth-century Enlightenment. The romance model of race is based in the genre's consistent portrayal of nobles being innately fit to rule commoners. Winkler describes Greek romance as "an elaboration of the period between initial desire and final consummation" (28), allowing the potentially dangerous sexual passion (*eros*) to find containment within marriage (*gamos*). The common plot line for many romances follows the outline Ronald McCail provides in his introduction to Longus's *Daphnis and Chloe*:

> [The] main characters are a newly married couple or a betrothed couple or a pair of lovers. Some mishap causes them to be separated and conveyed far apart from one another...Both travel far over land and sea...They are sold into slavery, and their chastity is assailed by a lustful master or mistress. Their lives are repeatedly endangered, by warfare or cruel punishments. There are trial scenes.... At last the lovers are reunited, by the agency of chance, or with the help of well-wishers or faithful slaves.[10]

The status of the romance's two lovers as belonging to the noble race innately separates them intellectually, morally, and physically from the commoners who raise them. Each of their trials throughout the text rearticulates their fitness to rule over their companions. From this point of view the romance racial model seems to reinforce existing views of social hierarchy by dividing people into two major groups: nobles and commoners. Even as a nationalist perspective emerges in English romances in the Middle Ages, it is complicated by this racial division between subjects from their rulers. This division between castes also lends itself to making unusual connections between peoples: the medieval form of romance focuses, for the most part, on the interactions

---

[9] Elizabeth Archibald, "Ancient Romance," in *A Companion to Romance from Classical to Contemporary*, ed. Corinne Saunders (Malden, MA: Blackwell Publishing, 2004), 17.

[10] Ronald McCail, introduction to *Daphnis and Chloe*, by Longus (Oxford: Oxford University Press, 2002), x.

of nobles across cultural and religious boundaries. Unlike the almost universally negative portrayal of Jews, these stories were just as likely to depict Muslim nobles as positive counterparts to Christian aristocrats as they were to portray them as demonic monsters.

Over the course of the seventeenth and eighteenth centuries, parallel shifts occurred in the portrayal of race and in England's relationship to other world powers. When England is less secure in terms of transnational relations, most English portrayals of Europe and North Africa focus on the Ottomans as an established power that held an influence over this region. A powerful international player, the Ottoman Empire is presented in texts as both an example for imperial imitation and a potential threat to English sovereignty and national-religious identity. Later in the eighteenth century, when England emerges as the center of its own empire, these depictions change. The Ottoman holdings become a site of past glory, now an older, declining, courtly, and possible corrupt world reminiscent of that portrayed in medieval romances.

At times, these representations obscure and erase their original inclusion of references to the Ottoman Empire. Chapters Five and Six will focus on the transformation of two narratives, William Shakespeare's *Othello; or, the Moor of Venice* (1603) and Aphra Behn's *Oroonoko; or, the Royal Slave* (1688). Both inject the Ottoman Empire into English debates over Protestant and Catholic alliances. The theatrical afterlife of both narratives also chart the rise of English Empire as its cultural representations of a powerful Ottoman Empire give way to images of a non-unified West and North Africa under English control. The transformation of the English audiences' supposed power relations with the characters is striking: depictions of Othello and Oroonoko range over the seventeenth and eighteenth centuries from powerful foreign figures to be feared, to images of a universalized (which for English audience at the time meant Europeanized) Everyman, to the figure of an African slave popularized throughout the nineteenth and twentieth centuries. This history of representation points to an implicit transition in the popular representation of England itself. The increase in its own transnational power led to an alteration of how it perceived other races: the image of a powerful, potentially threatening Ottoman-like figure evolving into one of an African slave that questions how English imperial power should be used demonstrates a shift in discussion of what comprised English identity and what role England was perceived to be occupying on the world stage.

The Ottoman Empire in European Romance: Orient(ing) Africa and the Mediterranean

Surrounding the ambiguity of English racial categorizations of the Ottomans are European portrayals of Africa as a racially Other space. Africa, when not occupied by Macedonian, Ottoman, or other forces, was presented, as Natalie Zemon Davis points out, as undifferentiated by the many cultures it contained: "The land mass that for centuries in Europe was called Africa, in expansion of the ancient Roman province by that name, was rarely identified by a single place-name in the Arabic tradition."[11] Except for a few places such as Egypt, this presentation of Africa required the blurring and often the omission of its diversity. Despite this ambiguity, these depictions of Africa often present a clear divide between Northern Africa and the rest of the continent. The former is commonly presented in European texts as more 'civilized'—the Africa that is associated with the succession of Mediterranean empires of Alexander the Great, the Romans, and the Ottomans. The latter mixed with images of other groups, but was represented as dark, exotic, and wild. Debra Higgs Strickland points out that during the Medieval Era "the terms 'Black' and 'Ethiopian' were synonymous" and both were portrayed with "a very consistent set of physiognomical features: dark skin, woolly or tightly coiled hair, large eyes, flat nose, and thick, everted lips."[12] Within this model, "at best, stereotypical Ethiopian features were interpreted as aesthetically repellent and as signs of wildness," and at its worst, "Blackness [was read] as a sign of sin" with Ethiopians being "not just [affiliated] with the demons themselves but with things Demonic writ large."[13] Even as new information was gained during the sixteenth and seventeenth centuries, older ideologies dating back to these narratives continued to flourish; these racial theories reflected little knowledge of the continent of Africa, and were largely limited to North Africa and some of West Africa. In her analysis of the influences on and of Leo Africanus's *De totius Africae descriptione*, Oumelbanine Zhiri argues that, rather than falling away as new information surfaced, the old view of the majority

---

[11] Natalie Zemon Davis, *Trickster Travels: A Sixteenth-Century Muslim Between Worlds* (New York: Hill and Wang, 2006), 126.

[12] Debra Higgs Strickland, *Saracens, Demons and Jews: Making Monsters in Medieval Art* (Princeton, NJ: Princeton University Press, 2003), 83, 79.

[13] Ibid., 85, 84, 82.

of Africa as unknown and uncivilized persisted and emerged in new ways: "The recent knowledge [gained in the sixteenth and seventeenth centuries] did not eliminate the old image, which survived in these texts with all their elements."[14] Africa, for the most part, was associated with demons, black skin, and other markers that signaled its Otherness to Europe.

It would make sense, then, for Muslims in Crusade romances to follow suit: as the enemy of Christians in a Holy War, as opposed to the Ethiopians (who ironically were historically one of the oldest Christian groups in the world, dating back to the fourth century CE), the derogatorily labeled 'Saracens' would logically be seen as equally, if not more, monstrous, demonic, and Other. In some Crusade depictions, Muslims seem to adhere association of skin color with barbarity, monstrosity seen in the representations of the Ethiopians. In the thirteenth-century *King of Tars*, conversion to Christianity turns the sinful black skin of the titular character virtuously white. Yet, Strickland points out, this was not a uniform representation: they were "sometimes described as extraordinarily *handsome*, and some are blond rather than dark."[15] Negative depictions occur, such as the anachronistic placement of Muslim figures at the Crucifixion that clearly represents them as enemies of Christianity, but literary representations "were just as likely to describe the Saracen opponents as admirable foes embodying many noble and chivalric qualities."[16] Strickland contends that the frequently positive portrayal of Muslims within chivalric romance is informed by a desire to increase the sense of chivalric honor associated with Crusader victories: "the idea here seems to be that Christian victory would be all the more glorious if the vanquished were both dangerous and worthy. From an artistic perspective, worthiness had to be translated into some conventionally recognizable form."[17] Out of the desire to make a foreign character's worthiness legible to a European audience, romances employed domestic conceptions of nobility.

When placed in a favorable light, Muslim nobles were beautiful, brave, honorable, and possessors of highly refined feelings. In the

---

[14] Oumelbanine Zhiri, *L'Afrique au Miroir de l'Europe* (Geneva: Droz, 1991), 209. My translation. The French reads: «Les connaissances récentes n'avaient pas éliminé la vieille image, qui avait survécu dans les textes avec tous ses éléments» (209).

[15] Strickland, *Saracens, Demons and Jews*, 173.

[16] Ibid., 177, 188.

[17] Ibid., 188.

early thirteenth-century German romance *Parzival*, the nobility of its two principal Muslim characters, Belacane and her son Feirefiz, are described in terms of European standards of nobility. Despite her dark skin, Belacane possesses "a woman's manner... and was on other counts worthy of a knight"; despite her non-Christian beliefs, "[h]er innocence was a pure baptism."[18] Similarly, her son Feirefiz is admired by the Arthurian knights and desired by the European women, eventually marrying the Grail Maiden. In romance, the noble races have exclusive ownership of emotional and aesthetic sensitivity. Romance privileges the ideas of emotions, and people are driven not by reason but by their honorable feelings. Swooning, crying, and blushing all serve as more examples of how their outer appearances mark inner superiority. This romance model of rank set up a tradition of a peculiar variation of universalism: while peasants and the nobles who ruled them were presented as innately different, this separation was seen as crossing cultural and religious boundaries, binding nobles together as part of one race destined to rule.[19] Even in romances such as *Song of Roland*, in which animalistic and demonic characteristics are placed on Muslim forces, there is still a sense of similarity between Christians and Muslim knights: in a mirror image of their Christian counterparts, the Muslim soldiers carry a demonic trinity of Tervagant, Muhammad, and Apollo; and just as treacherous knights exist among the good Christians, the Muslim forces contain some valiant, good knights, such as Grandonie and Margariz, simply serving the wrong side. When the Ottoman Empire emerged at the beginning of the fourteenth century, it entered into this complicated religious-racial representation of Islam. As the empire spread into North Africa, European views of that continent also changed. A dark face associated with an Ottoman Orient would be presented as more of a cultural equal—and perhaps even a superior—to a European than one of a pagan African.

---

[18] Wolfram V. Eschenbach, *Parzival: A Romance of the Middle Ages*, trans. Helen M. Mustard and Charles E. Passage (New York: Vintage Books, 1961), 14, 17.

[19] This vision of universal nobility is similar to the historical reality of the educated elite of the ancient Roman Empire: men of a certain status received a nearly identical education to those of the same station as them throughout the empire. In this way, a citizen from Spain could socialize with another from Byzantium with little cultural conflict: their manners, reading habits, and other social niceties would be nearly identical.

Restoration Romance

Romance depictions of Islam originate from a historical reality of
cultural, political, and economic exchanges in which foreign powers
such as the Ottoman often represented the more powerful player. This
romance view of race maintained its popularity into the eighteenth
century. Shakespeare's narrative of a Moor's incorporation into Venice
in the 1623 play *Othello* mirrors the ending of many romances where
a Muslim noble integrates and marries into a Christian culture. Behn's
narrative provides Oroonoko's kingdom with an Ottoman gloss of
veiled harems and citrus alcoves, thus making a pagan African culture
feasible to her audiences by associating it with the Ottomans. Both
Oroonoko and Othello receive the respectively contradictory titles of
"Royal Slave" and "Moor of Venice," signifying their dual position as
outsider and insider. Oroonoko's rank raises him above the other African slaves, allowing him to circulate in and at times defend an English
colony's ruling society; ultimately, though, his title of slave leads to his
own destruction. Othello defends Venice from a foreign threat, yet at
the same time is seen as a foreign element, disrupting the domestic
lives of those he serves. Both Behn's and Shakespeare's narratives fall
in line with romance racial models in that their protagonists' flaws and
virtues transcend national differences to fit within a universal chivalric
code. Othello's eloquent wooing of Desdemona—as well as the coun-
cils listening to the description of the courtship—emphasizes his martial prowess, and she reacts like a romance heroine, responding to him
with "a world of sighs" (1.3.158). Similar, Oroonoko's innate nobility
wins over his African wife, Imoinda, as well as the English narrator
who attempts to shelter him from Surinam's slave system.

Othello and Oroonoko serve as bookends to a century during which
the romance racial model flourished and evolved. During seventeenth
century, romances referenced the chivalric tradition that produced
them while juxtaposing it with a new cultural order. Marie-Madeleine
de La Fayette's 1670–1671 romance *Zaîde: Histoire Espagnole*, for
example, mixes military and amorous battles between Muslim and
Christian characters; however, while the text favorably presents the
occasional conversion of a Muslim character to Christianity, the two
cultures are seen as equally admirable and share a common, noble
race. In the case of La Fayette, the new order is less political and more
stylistic. La Fayette uses romance conventions but subverts them: she
has characters misread their situations by judging others by romance

standards. For example, both Consalve and Zaïde disbelieve each other's love because they assume an imaginary rival: first he believes she
mourns a dead lover and then ignores the plentiful evidence that she
does not love Alamir; meanwhile, she remains skeptical of his shows
of affection and eventually imagines he still loves his ex-lover, Nugna
Bella. Nicholas D. Paige notes that "[e]verything in Zayde indicate that
twists like these are the result of astonishingly canny reflection on the
devices of romance, whose tropes the novel systematically subverts."
He argues that the text should be viewed as "a pastiche of romance"
straddling the transition from this old genre to the new one found in
the novel: "all the elements of the old genre are there, and they are
recognizable as such, but they no longer function as they once did."[20]

In *Zaîde*, rank becomes a universal point of connection for nobles,
even in the middle of a military conflict. When the hero Consalve res-
cues Zuléma, one of the Moorish commanders, from the excessive violence of his own soldiers, he happily finds his expectations of a shared
noble culture are met: Zuléma, "this valiant man, perceiving that he
could no longer defend himself, relinquished his sword with an air so
noble and bold that Consalve could not doubt at all his worthiness of
the great reputation he had acquired."[21] Where his soldiers saw only
an enemy who had killed many of their own men, Consalve recognizes
him as a fellow noble through his actions and bearing. Zuléma also
seems to relate to Consalve in a way he cannot with the lower order of
Christian soldiers he encounters: with them, he seems willing to fight
to the death, but with Consalve he graciously surrenders his sword
and, at the end of the text, his daughter.

In the text's many examples of lovers, religion seems to matter
less than the lovers' shared rank. Zaïde is the product of a Christian/
Muslim marriage, and while she spurns the advances of Alamir based
on his religion, her objections are less on the grounds of theology and
more on those of fidelity—she cannot bear the thought of being one of
many wives.[22] Further undermining the potential differences between

---

[20] Nicholas D. Paige, introduction to *Zayde: A Spanish Romance*, by Marie-Madeleine de La Fayette (Chicago: University of Chicago Press, 2006), 19, 21.

[21] Marie-Madeleine de La Fayette, *Zaïde: Histoire Espagnole* (1670–1671), (Paris:
Garnier Frères, 1970), 143.

My translation. The French reads: « ce vaillant homme, voyant bien qu'il ne pouvait
plus se défendre, rendit son épée avec un air si noble et si hardi que Consalve ne douta
point qu'il ne fût digne de la grande réputation qu'il avait acquise. »

[22] Ibid., 173.

Muslim and Christian nobles in the text, her companion Felime would gladly marry the Muslim prince and dies out of longing for him. The narrative ending presents the two religious groups as symbolically part of the same noble family. It is discovered that not only does the Spanish Christian Consalve share a close physical resemblance with the Prince of Fez, they are also first cousins. The last lines of the text emphasize the compatibility of the two sets of nobles as Consalve and Zaïde's wedding is celebrated with "all the gallantry of the Moors and all the civility of Spain."[23]

Shakespeare and Behn similarly tie their protagonists' downfall to a move away from old romance deference to nobility: *Othello* portrays a dangerous lower order in Iago's resentment of Othello and Cassio's bond as fellow nobles, and *Oroonoko* depicts a colonial government overrun with the lower ranks persecuting their 'natural' superior by making a prince into a slave. Yet, by the end of the eighteenth century, a different image would emerge for both *Othello* and *Oroonoko*. Their narratives would transform on stage for their audiences' evolving perception of England's role in the world. As the reality of a stable English Empire became more apparent, depictions of overseas failures in Cyprus and Surinam became less emphasized. The titular heroes evolved, as well. Both Othello and Oroonoko grew increasingly disconnected from the romance tradition that produced them. Rather than representing the complex racial depictions of Islam and the Ottomans, their darkness signified the oppression of a European-controlled Africa that raised questions of English moral responsibility to those countries less powerful than it rather than anxieties over Ottoman might.

---

[23] Ibid., 235. My translation. The French reads: «toute la galanterie des Maures et tout la politesse d'Espagne.»

CHAPTER FIVE

"I AM NOT WHAT I AM":
REIMAGINING SHAKESPEARE'S MOOR OF VENICE,
1603–1787

Over the course of the seventeenth century the *Othello* narrative used
an Ottoman threat to explore anxieties over ambiguities of English
identity as well as England's place in international politics; while its
representations during the long eighteenth century represent a significant change in English and Ottoman power, as the focus becomes
increasingly on the positives and negatives of English imperial power.
During this period, *Othello*'s titular Moor loses his gloss of oriental
power, emerging as a nearly English figure of *universal* humanity and
eventually as a meditational object on racial difference and the treatment of Africans in a burgeoning British Empire.

I do not aim to present a definitive production history of Shakespeare's play; instead, I am seeking to give a sense of how cultural
and political shifts during the era shaped ideas about the play in a
larger popular context. As Virginia Mason points out, it is difficult to
pin down what racial and religious identities Othello represented to
seventeenth- and eighteenth-century English audiences: "Outside the
magazines and other standard theatrical sources, there is admittedly
slender but nonetheless suggestive evidence as to how Othello was
constructed within the larger culture."[1] Nevertheless, an examination
of references to the play in terms of political events and cultural definitions as well as the noted rejections of certain interpretations point to
common assumptions that critics, scholars, and audiences held about
the meaning of the play.

Before Shakespeare: Othello's Origins in Gli Hecatommithi *and* Lepanto

The basic *Othello* narrative remains a common cultural touchstone
in many cultures today. A celebrated military leader of ambiguous

---

[1] Virginia Mason, "Race Mattered: Othello in Late Eighteenth-Century England,"
Shakespeare in the Eighteenth Century: Shakespeare Survey 51 (1998), 61.

background, foreign Othello weds Venetian-born Desdemona against his father's wishes. Immediately after, they go on a military campaign in Cyprus, where their marriage erodes. Othello's duplicitous ensign plots to undermine his superiors by convincing the Moor that his wife is having an affair with his lieutenant, Cassio. Tormented by his jealousy, Othello kills his wife, learns of the plot, and kills Iago and then himself.

As with many of Shakespeare's plays, the plot draws on existing sources. It is widely accepted that the majority of the narrative is drawn from Giraldi Cinthio's *Gli Hecatommithi* (1563). In the tradition of Giovanni Boccaccio's fourteenth-century *Decameron*, this Italian text builds its narrative around storytellers sharing tales that fit around a series of themes. The story of Otello contrasts to the surrounding stories, which focus on deceptive spouses. In his study of the alterations *Othello* makes to the *Gli Hecatommithi* narrative, Ned B. Allen presents the Otello tale as "a kind of exemplum": "the preceding tale, mentioned in the head-link, concerns a dissolute, adulterous wife justly killed by her husband. Of the many narrators within *Gli Hecatommithi*, the teller of this specific story, Curtio, prefers not to be so erotic as the others, whose pretence of preaching morality is usually little more than an excuse for dwelling on salacious adventures, and he therefore, here and in his later tales, describes chaste rather than adulterous characters. Here his purpose is to show that not all women are unchaste and not all jealous husbands are justified in their suspicions."[2]

The basic plot of the Otello tale clearly prefigures Shakespeare's *Othello*. Yet there are significant changes made in the play. Written roughly half a century later, Shakespeare's narrative reflects a different political and religious situation than Cinthio's. Allen outlines a major change between sources: *Othello* alters the action of the first act in a way that opens up the original's domestic focus and places it into a transnational context through the introduction of an Ottoman threat in Cyprus.[3] Such changes, I argue, blur boundaries between foreign and domestic. It places the allure of the exotic and its complicated reception into a Christian European society. The *Gli Hecatommithi*

---

[2] Ned B. Allen, "The Two Parts of *Othello*," *Aspects of Othello: Shakespeare Survey* 21 (1977): 75.

[3] Ibid., 75.

narrative offers scant details of Otello and Disdemona's courtship, but *Othello* directly connects it to the allure of exotic power. Defending his marriage to the Venetian Duke, the Shakespearean Moor relives his courtship. Upon hearing of his encounters with "the cannibals that each other eat/The Anthropophagi, and men whose heads/ Do grow beneath their shoulders. This to hear /Would Desdemona seriously incline" (I.iii.142–44, 145). Yet it is not just that Othello has witnessed strange sights that wins Desdemona: it is the power behind his extensive travel and what he has encountered that inspires both a terror of him as well as a desire to associate herself with him: "She wish'd she had not heard it, yet she wish'd/That heaven had made her such a man" (I.iii.161–62). This mix of fear and awe parallels the Venetian attitude towards Othello. On one hand, they consider him a source of protection from foreign threat; on the other, they fear the decay of a Venetian identity through his incorporation into their domestic space. Further emphasizing this conflicting view of Othello is the contrast between Brabantio's view of Othello and Desdemona's marriage and that of the Duke and Senators. Mirroring the anxieties over an Ottoman influence outlined in the first half of this book, Desdemona's father, Brabantio, declares that "if such actions" as his daughter's marriage to the foreign Othello are allowed "passage free,/ Bondslaves and pagans shall our Statesmen be" (I.ii.98, 99). He rejects the incorporation of the Moor into Venetian society, but the rulers are more concerned with threats from the outside, namely from a powerful Ottoman Empire.

With the addition of an Ottoman threat to the narrative, Shakespeare's *Othello* seems to amplify this connection between Othello and attempts to articulate an English identity in an Ottoman context. In *Gli Hecatommithi*'s Othello tale, the newlyweds' voyage is merely part of "a change in the troops whom they used to maintain Cyprus."[4] The seventeenth-century, English *Othello* adds military crises due to an Ottoman attack. The focus of the first two acts on the exotic and international, Allen points out, signals the strongest break with the source material in the entire play. When the play shifts more towards the domestic tragedy, it returns to its source material:

---

[4] J.E. Taylor, Trans., "Selection from Giraldi Cinthio's *Hecatommithi*," in *The Tragedy of Othello: Moor of Venice*, ed. Alvin B. Kernan (New York: Penguin, 1998), 135.

Instead of enlarging on the bare outlines of Cinthio, instead of improvising and digressing as he has in the first two acts, Shakespeare here shows such respect for the details of the sources that he leaves out scarcely any of them.... Nearly all of Shakespeare's most striking verbal reminiscences of Cinthio are in this part of the play.[5]

Yet the context of these events was altered considerably by the earlier Turkish context of Act One.

I connect this entanglement of the domestic and foreign to the way another sixteenth-century text dealing with the Ottomans and Cyprus received a resurgence of attention which coincides with the 1603 Shakespearean *Othello: The Lepanto,* a poetic account of an European-Ottoman military conflict by James Stuart, King of England and Scotland. Written in 1585 and first published in 1591, the heroic poem by then James VI of Scotland commemorates the 1571 naval victory of an alliance of Catholic powers over the Ottomans in the Gulf of Lepanto. As in the play, the Ottoman navy threatened a Venetian-held portion of Cyprus, but the play takes a more ambiguous view of the conflict through its emphasis on the Venetian turmoil over the extent to which its Moorish general should be accepted into their society. This more complicated landscape reflects several changes that had occurred both in terms of the Ottoman presence in Cyprus and the political shifts taking place in the British Isles.

James VI of Scotland became James I of England and Ireland in 1603. That year also saw renewed interest in *The Lepanto* as a means of better understanding the nation's new monarch. In "*Othello, Lepanto* and the Cyprus Wars,*" Emrys Jones argues that just as *A Midsummer Night's Dream* and *Macbeth* are frequently seen as pleasing the king in the early years of his rule, *Othello* must be viewed in this light as well. Certainly, references to the king as poet and his most ambitious poem, *The Lepanto,* were plentiful at the time of *Othello*'s production:

A sonnet by Drayton addressed to James opens, 'Of Kings a Poet, and the Poets King,' and an epigram of Jonson's class him 'best of poets.'... Among the poems and translations[,] which he had published, the best known was his original heroic poem *Lepanto*. It is this poem, I suggest, which provides the link between *Othello* and the king.[6]

---

[5] Allen, "The Two Parts," 76–77.
[6] Emrys Jones, "*Othello, Lepanto* and the Cyprus Wars," *Aspects of Othello: Shakespeare Survey* 21 (1977): 61.

Although political opportunism (and necessity) on the part of Drayton and Jonson may have sparked their flattering notice of the poem, Jones argues that the poem was perceived as an important means of assessing the political and religious views of the new king. Supporting this view is the renewal of interest in the Ottomans, which was, in turn, linked to James. In 1603, the same year *The Lepanto* was republished, Richard Knolles dedicated his *Generall Historie of the Turks* to James, describing the new English king as a "prince of so great learning and judgment" whose own work had "induced" Knolles to give a history of the "strange successe of the great and mightie *Othoman* Empire." He praises *The Lepanto* for unifying Christian nations in Europe for "the state and good of the Christian commonwealth in generall," who have "never by any so much impugned or endangered, as by these naturall & capitall enemies [the Ottoman Empire]."[7] Even without Knolles making the connections explicit, Jones holds that the events of *Othello*

> could hardly have failed to arouse the memory of anyone in Shake-speare's audience who was at all aware of recent European history. For if we were to seek to give an approximate date to the action of *Othello*, we should be driven to the crucial years round about 1570, the year of the Turkish attack on Cyprus.[8]

I add to this that any anxieties that an Ottoman threat may have conjured for these early seventeenth-century playgoers would likely have been mixed with anxiety over the new Stuart dynasty.

In many quarters, these anxieties over a Scottish king with Catholic affiliations represented a threat to English national and religious sovereignty, an anxiety that would remain throughout the Stuarts' rule. As a result, the reception of *The Lepanto* was not entirely favorable. Sandra Bell's "King James VI and Lepanto: Basilikon Doron, Castalian Band, Helgerson" views the poetry of James I as an attempt to shape national and religious identity, which is rejected by a more complicated reality among the public, but his control over its reception was undermined by public fears that he would return the nation to the Catholic Church.

---

[7] Richard Knolles, *The Generall Historie of the Turkes* (London: Adam Islip, 1603), iii, iv.

[8] Jones, "*Othello*, Lepanto, and the Cyprus Wars," 63.

James presents the Battle of Lepanto as a heroic example for all Christian nations to follow when dealing with the predominantly Islamic Ottomans. Bell posits that *The Lepanto* acts as a Pan-Christian battle cry that largely ignores debates between and within Christian sects: "James appears to have envisaged the victory as a Christian rather than specifically Catholic one, and therefore as safe subject matter. James chose the subject of Lepanto in order to rouse confidence in a newly created league of European Protestant princes." Yet even at this imaginary stage, his plan of Christian unity is clearly complicated by intra-religious differences: it was, after all, Catholic and not Muslim incursions that "prompted James to arrange a league of European Protestant princes for the mutual defense against the Catholic forces."[9] In 1603, it was unclear which posed a greater threat to England: the Ottomans or the many Catholic European powers.

The success of *The Lepanto* as a means of garnering support from James's new subjects rests on the perception of the Battle of Lepanto to be seen as a positive event for England. Instead, it reveals a great deal of cultural naivety on the part of the new Stuart dynasty. It underestimates the insecurity the majority of English men felt towards a pan-Christian identity and James' own mixed-religious heritage. Not all readers would naturally see themselves so opposed to the Ottomans that they would align themselves even ideologically with Catholics.

As mentioned in earlier chapters, Elizabeth I had made overtures towards the Ottomans in order to distinguish England from Catholic nations—and to a certain extent from other Protestant powers. Bell's work supports this view that James's new English subjects feared (as they did with almost all Stuart monarchs) that he could be a crypto-Catholic, so this poem's celebration of Catholic military triumph—by divine will no less—did little to set them at ease. Generously, Bell posits:

> James over-estimated his readers' ability to remain dispassionate about religious differences, an ability he took for granted because of his extraordinarily mixed upbringing. Offering assurances to both his Protestant and Catholic subjects was one means—however unstable—James used to

---

[9] Sandra Bell, "Writing the Monarch: King James VI and *Lepanto*," in *Other Voices, Other Views: Expanding the Canon in English Renaissance Studies*, eds. Helen Ostovich, et al., (Cranbury, NJ: Associated University Presses, 1999), 194.

retain control in both Scotland and England; recognizing Catholic heroism in a Protestant poem is analogous to this method of ruling.[10]

Bell reads James's religious policy as founded on a hierarchy of groups.
Protestants are considered more religiously correct than Catholics,
but God still prefers the latter to 'infidels' like the Turks. Although
Bell does not credit the seventeenth-century charges that James was
secretly Catholic, she is clear that this view is not to be found in the
Protestant reactions of the time: "Despite James's protestations that he
intends *Lepanto* as an expression of Protestant superiority, the choice
of a Roman Catholic victory as its subject is an excellent example of
how James tries to play both sides of the religio-political division."[11]
Indeed, the king poses a threat as the head of England and its Church,
a distinction that was crucial to the reception of both the poem and
its author.

The attempt to use *The Lepanto* as a unifying force within England
was further complicated by the aftermath of the actual battle. As Jones
points out, "the victory of Lepanto did not in fact restore Cyprus to
Venice.... At the time of *Othello's* composition therefore (c. 1602–4),
Cyprus had been in Turkish hands for over thirty years."[12] Bell believes
that at the time of the Stuart ascension,

> Cyprus could be seen as an outpost of Christendom, rich, vulnerable,
> and perilously situated: a highly suitable setting for a play showing
> Christian behaviors under stress. After Cassio's drunken brawl has been
> put down, Othello is to say:
>
>> Are we turn'd Turks, and to ourselves do that
>> Which Heaven hath forbid the Ottomites?
>> For Christian shame, put by this barbarous brawl.
>
> His words, skillfully placed in the scene, are emphatic and ironic. For if
> Shakespeare's fictitious action can be said to belong to the years 1570–1,
> those were historically the very years when Cyprus underwent a violent
> conversion from Christian to Turkish rule—the years when it literally
> 'turned Turk.'[13]

If we see *Othello* as, at least in part, responding to existing tensions
over the ascension of James I, the reimagining of *Gli Hecatommithi's*

---

[10] Ibid., 196.
[11] Ibid., 197.
[12] Jones, "*Othello*, Lepanto, and the Cyprus Wars," 63.
[13] Bell, "Writing the Monarch," 65–66.

Otello tale into the context of the Battle of Lepanto points to a complicated English religious identity being formed. A century later, Daniel Defoe's *A Review of the Affairs of France*, discussed in Chapter Four of this book, would advise readers not to allow their anti-Catholic bias to lead them to underestimate the non-Christian threat of the Ottoman Empire. His fear of the public's mistaken prioritizing of foreign threats comes out of a long standing distrust of the geographically nearer Catholic empires such as Spain and France frequently, which were perceived as posing a potentially greater threat to England than the Ottomans. Compounding this mixed attitude towards the Ottomans, James I raised anxieties over whether he would protect English identity from foreign influence or betray it.

Among English subjects fearful of the loss of the Church of England and a return to Catholicism, a suspicion lingered during much of the Stuart dynasty that these kings were secretly Catholic and conspiring with the rulers of Catholic empires. To varying degrees, this was true: in the late seventeenth century, Charles II would enter into secret agreements with the king of France while his brother and successor, James II, openly converted to Catholicism. James I alienated members of his English court by surrounding himself with Scottish favorites and shows signs of leniency towards English Catholics early in his reign. Highlighting the manner in which James's wife, Anne, worked to allay fears that her religious beliefs would unduly influence the king, court, or nation, Albert J. Loomie concedes:

> Suspicions about a Catholic household within the royal establishment could create frictions at court. For the alert Puritan there would be the threat of a papal influence secretly on the king's counsels, and there would be the inference that the mother of the royal children might seek to influence them to her own view.[14]

Yet despite her efforts to downplay her religion, others saw her as a possible proponent of Catholic emancipation. In his 1610 *A Briefe Admonition to All English Catholikes*, Michael Walpole compares Anne to the Biblical Queen Esther, who saved her fellow Jews from destruction by interceding on their behalf with her husband, the king:

---

[14] Albert J. Loomie, "King James I's Catholic Consort," *The Huntington Library Quarterly*, 34. 4. (1971): 304.

why should not Queene Anne prevaile as farre with King James for Ancient and Christian Catholikes? Can any doubt, but that he would extend the Golden Rod of Clemency, toward his dearest spouse? Yea rather devide his Kingdome then deny her request? His Majesty is already informed of former services, performed by Catholikes, both to his Mother of Happy Memory, and Himselfe; for which they crave no other recompence nor reward, but the recalling, and repeating of such Proclamations, & Lawes, as their Adversaries upon false suggestions have procured against them.[15]

Walpole urges English Catholics to obey their king and, to a certain extent, conform with religious restrictions placed upon them. Yet his language points to the more widespread belief that James was tied to Catholicism through his past and present relationships. Although Walpole places it in a positive context, the threat that the king's actions could "divide his Kingdome" needs to be kept in mind when considering public reactions to *The Lepanto*.

In his Preface to the 1603 reprint of *The Lepanto*, James I reacts to criticisms that the poem is too favorable towards foreign, Catholic powers. He presents himself as correcting the "special thing misliked in it": "that I should seem far contrary to my degree and Religion, like a mercenarie Poet, to pen a worke, ex professo, in praise of a forraine [sic] Papist bastard."[16] James I points to a Catholic victory over the Ottomans as an event to align the Protestantism of England and the rest of the British Isles with European Christianity in general. He presents the Ottomans as a common enemy, dividing the world into "the baptiz'd race/ And circumcised Turbanded Turkes" (l. 10–11). The Shakespearean *Othello* is first produced before James I placed further restrictions on dissident religious groups, such as non-Anglican Protestants and Catholics; it is before a Catholic conspiracy attacks the king and Parliament in the 1605 Gunpowder plot.

It is, however, playing at a time when the king is seen as a potential Catholic ally and after the publication of his 1599 *Basilikon Doron*, which instructs his son, Prince Henry, on how to rule the kingdoms of the British Isles. In her examination of Catholicism under the Tudors and Stuarts, Stefanie Tutino reminds us that the text expresses views

---

[15] Michael Walpole, *A Briefe Admonition to All English Catholikes* (Saint-Omer, 1610), ii–iii.
[16] James Stuart, *His Maiesties Lepanto, or Heroicall Song Being Part of His Poeticall Exercises at Vacant Houres* (London, 1603), i.

on religion not entirely unfavorable to Catholics: presenting Catholics
and dissenting Protestants as the main threats to the Church of England, *Basilikon* argues that

> English Catholics and Protestants shared the foundations of true reli-
> gion, and consequently it was necessary that the latter did not bitterly
> rail against manifestations of Catholic worship in order to avoid the
> spread of Catholicism itself, and to promote the 'peace of the Church.'[17]

This emphasis on a shared religious ground seems to shape the message of *The Lepanto* as well as the implied message of the peace James
would enter into with Spain in 1604—that unity is necessary within
Christianity, especially when faced with foreign, non-Christian threats,
such as the Ottoman Empire.

Similar to attempts by James I to unify all of his Christian subjects,
the Duke in Act 1 of the Shakespearean *Othello* seeks to smooth over
the domestic conflict between Othello and Brabantio concerning the
former's marriage to the latter's daughter. After validating the marriage but not resolving the conflict, the Duke moves his attention to
what he presents as the more pressing threat: the Ottoman attack on
Cyprus and the need to defend a Christian outpost against a non-
Christian enemy. This opening act seems in line with the overt goal
of *The Lepanto*, but the following acts undermine this goal. The Ottomans do not play an explicit role in the rest of the plot. Instead, the
play focuses on internal dangers: fears of adulterous wives (both Iago
and Othello suspect their wives of unfaithfulness) and of false friends
(Othello suspects Cassio has betrayed him whilst Iago actually is betray-
ing him; Iago also manipulates one of Desdemona's rejected suitors,
Rodrigo, into believing that Iago's plotting will benefit Rodrigo); all
point to threats within Venice as more deadly than those posed by the
Ottomans in Cyprus.

The anxieties surrounding the internal dangers to society are highlighted by those in power marking them as a lower priority than
the external threat of the Ottomans. In his study of cross-cultural
exchanges within and through Shakespeare's plays, Lemuel A. Johnson points out that initially the anxieties expressed by characters
such as Brabantio over Othello's incorporation into Venetian soci-

---

[17] Stefania Tutino, *Law and Conscience: Catholicism in Early Modern England,
1570–1625* (Burlington, VT: Ashgate, 2007), 83.

ety are largely ignored. Brabantio objects strongly to his daughter's marriage and the social ills he argues it represents, but "[o]f course, he does fails to get a hearing" from the Duke and Senators. Instead "the urgency of the *state's* foreign relations quickly makes his son-in-law 'more fair than black.'"[18] Similarly Brabantio and his position are marginalized again:

> Consider in Act 2, Scene 3 the degrees of visibility that the Ottomite threat confers on the Venetian magnifico [Brabantio] and the foreign general [Othello], even when the Turkish fleet appears to be steering away, 'with due course toward the isle of Rhodes':
>
> *Enter Brabantio, Othello, Cassio, Iago, Roderigo, and Officers*
> Duke: Valiant Othello, we must straight employ you
> Against the general enemy Ottoman
> (*To Brabantio*) *I did not see you* [Johnson's emphasis]. Welcome, gentle signior.[19]

I find it ironic that Brabantio's decreasing visibility seems to coincide with the audience increasing awareness of the domestic strife within Othello's marriage and the growing danger his jealousy poses for his Venetian bride.

Yet these competing anxieties between external and internal threats overlap in the figure of Othello. His identity as a foreigner and a Moor connects him to the Ottoman threat he is meant to combat. In his examination of images of the Ottomans on the Early Modern English stage, Daniel Vitkus sees Othello's fear of martial betrayal as "linked in the play to racial and cultural anxieties about 'turning Turk'—the fear of a 'black' planet that gripped the Europeans in the early modern era as they faced the expansion of Ottoman power." This connection between sexual, racial, and cultural anxieties complicates the binary set up in *The Lepanto* of Christian Europe united against an Ottoman threat. Vitkus emphasizes audience fears of 'turning Turk' when *Othello* was first performed: "there had been extensive, direct contact with Muslim pirates—both in the British Isles and in the Mediterranean, where English merchant ships sailed with greater frequency after trade pacts with both the Barbary principalities and the Ottoman

---

[18] Lemuel A. Johnson, *Shakespeare in Africa (and Other Venues): Import and Appropriation of Culture* (Trenton, NJ: Africa World Press, Inc., 1998), 97.
[19] Ibid., 97.

sultanate were signed."[20] His excellent analysis of the play places it in the context of other theatrical representations of Ottomans and Moorish villains; yet, for my argument, the evocation and then suppression of the Ottoman threat seem to turn the issue of 'turning Turk' to a more general sense of threatened English identity.

Othello, then, echoes not only to the Ottoman threat posed in *The Lepanto*, but also to the poem's skeptical reception that questioned whether a greater threat of foreign domination was posed by Catholic forces. After the 1605 treaty with Spain, James I still needed to issues warnings against his subjects who continued "their unlawful and ungodly course of living by spoil" as they pirated Spanish ships.[21] In *The Lepanto*, Catholics are included in a larger concept of Christian identity, against which the Ottomans stand as a threatening outside force. Many English subjects, however, rejected this shared Christian identity, seeing Catholic powers such as Spain as the Other that threatened the nation.

Within *Othello*, this tension over who is the true outside threat plays out in a complex way. There is a fear of foreign attack, but it contrasts the outright danger represented by the Ottoman navy with a fear of internal contamination from miscegenation. Othello's Otherness is emphasized continually. Iago baits Brabantio into acting against Othello by negatively depicting Othello's racial difference: "an old black ram/ Is tupping your white ewe. Arise, arise;/ ... /Or else the devil will make a grandsire of you" (I.i.89–90, 91). Even when discussed in a positive light, he is exotic and foreign. Desdemona falls in love with his tales of foreign places, and he is best fit to defend Venice against the Ottomans because the "fortitude" of Cyprus "is best known" to him (I.iii.200). The difference in his physical appearance from his Venetian companions is frequently brought up.

Othello's marriage to and murder of Desdemona echo the Ottoman threat introduced in the opening act. Demanding legal intervention to remedy the damage he feels his daughter's marriage inflicts upon him, Brabantio links the Ottoman threat to Othello, Venice's chief

---

[20] Daniel Vitkus, *Turning Turk: English Theater and the Multicultural Mediterranean, 1570–1630* (New York: Palgrave Macmillan, 2003), 78, 82.

[21] Qtd. in ibid., 215.

protector against the Ottomans. In response to Brabantio's claim his daughter has been "stol'n…and corrupted/By spells and medicines" (I.iii.60–61), the Duke declares:

> Whoe'er he be that in this foul proceeding
> Hath thus *beguiled* your daughter of herself
> And you of her, the bloody book of law
> You shall yourself read in bitter letter
> After your own sense, yea, though *our proper son*
> Stood in your action. (66–70, emphasis mine)

After learning that Othello stands accused and listening to his defense, the Duke reverses his position, instructing Brabantio to "smile" at events that cannot be changed. An embittered Brabantio responds, "So let the Turk of Cyprus us *beguile*,/ We lose it not so long as we can *smile*" (I.iii.208–9, emphasis mine). Othello and the Ottomans "beguile" Christians out of their possessions. Brabantio loses his daughter; Venice stands to lose Cyprus. The connection of the two emphasizes Othello's Otherness, but it also questions whether the main threat to domestic stability comes from an outside military threat or from an internal conflict.

Othello, too, blurs the lines between domestic and foreign, Self and Other when he punishes himself for Desdemona's murder. His last words begin as a catalog of exotic but unfixed cultural signifier, as he describes himself as "one whose hand/ Like the base Indian, threw a pearl away/ Richer than all his tribe" (V.ii.342–44).[22] But his metaphorical links between himself and the exotic takes a strange turn as he evokes the Ottomans.

The threat of an external Ottoman attack drives much of the action of the first act, only to drop to the side once the characters arrive in Cyprus. In the majority of the play, domestic betrayals result in more damage to the Venetians than military attacks. This focus on the internal makes the case that the true danger to a society comes from within,

---

[22] There is some debate whether Othello compares himself to "the base Indian" (as he does in the 1622 First Quarto) or "the base Judean" (1623 First Folio). For succinct yet thorough accounts of both the Indian and Judean positions, respectively, see Richard Levin, "The Indian/Iudean Crux In Othello," *Shakespeare Quarterly* 33, no. 1 (Spring, 1982): 60–67 and Naseeb Shaheen, "Like the Base Judean," *Shakespeare Quarterly* 31, no. 1 (Spring, 1980): 93–95.

but in his closing speech, Othello links that threat back to the foreign in general and the Ottomans in particular:

> [...]Set you down this;
> And say besides, that in Aleppo once
> Where a malignant and a turban'd Turk
> Beat a Venetian and traduced the state,
> I took by th'throat the circumcised dog
> And smote him thus. (V.ii.348–51)

In the lines prior to these, Othello represents himself in exotic images: the Indian, the Arabian trees (V.ii.343, 346). The last image changes it. He evokes the idea of avenging a Venetian beaten by a Turk, before killing himself, his lines echoing the opening of *The Lepanto* that called for unity against "circumcised Turbanded Turkes" (l. 11). Yet, the question of who is of the "baptized race" (l.10) and who is a Turk remains unclear in the play.

After connecting the circular language of this final threat that "turns" Othello from a Christian warrior into a murderous apostate then into an avenging figure that destroys the apostate, Vitkus reminds us of another reference to cutting and turning: circumcision. To a seventeenth-century English audience, circumcision was believed to be a requirement for male converts to Islam: "For Othello to cut himself [when he commits suicide at the speech's end] reiterates the ritual cutting of his foreskin, which was the sign of his belonging to the community of stubborn misbelievers, the Muslims."[23] In Vitkus's analogy, Othello is both the Turk and the one who destroys the Turk. He is both the Christian's avenger against an Ottoman threat, which remains in line with the role the Venetian Duke casts him in at the beginning of the play, and, conversely, he is the Ottoman threat from which Christian Europe must be protected. His speech may "beguile" the Duke and his cohorts, denying Brabantio the chance to avenge himself, but as Desdemona's violated body represents Othello's motive for suicide, the Moor acts in place of his Christian father-in-law—reading for himself "the bloody book of law" by acting as his own judge and executioner. Connecting back to the first act, he is both the one who defends Venice against foreign threats as well as the foreign element that threatens to change it from within by marrying Desdemona.

---

[23] Vitkus, *Turning Turk*, 104.

It is not, I believe, too far-fetched to connect this ending to the ambiguous reception in England of James I. Othello is *of Venice*; James, king *of England*. Yet neither is completely accepted as a member of either of those nations. The reception of *The Lepanto* anticipates the ambiguities exploited in *Othello*. Shakespeare's play has often been presented as one of stark binaries—foreign vs. native, black vs. white, non-Christian vs. Christian—but the play also explores the inability to make such clear distinction. Similarly, *The Lepanto* seems to be a clear-cut endorsement of a Christian victory over an Ottoman enemy, but for many English readers at the time of the Stuart ascension, it was complicated by the newly formed, and still largely undefined, Protestant identity introduced by the Tudor dynasty and solidified by its last monarch, Elizabeth I, Only to be followed with the more religious ambiguous Stuart dynasty.

If we think about the linking of the Ottoman Mediterranean to fears of an internal threat, Shakespeare's *Othello* resonates with a fear of losing a sense of English national-religious identity. Whether it was the personification of a fear of turning Catholic or Turk, the figure of Othello resembles the figures discussed earlier in this book, whose outward markers of religion and nationality do not necessary match their internal affiliations. In this way, Othello can be linked back to fears of James Stuart's potential non-Englishness, of the upwardly mobile Englishmen in the Levant who gain higher status through foreign means and are perhaps apostates, of the English coffee-drinkers losing their identities cup by cup.

Othello consistently questions who is an ally and who an enemy. When *The Lepanto* put forth what James I seemed to see as a relatively straightforward definition of friend and foe, the public reacted with skepticism. Indeed, at this stage, England's state Church was still in its infancy, as were its imperial ambitions. The widespread insecurity felt by English subjects was rooted in part to its complex and contradictory relationships with other countries. For James I, the Ottomans could represent a clear choice for a symbolic enemy, but for some of his subjects this empire posed less of a threat than the geographically closer Catholic empires, and, as discussed in earlier chapters, a stay in the Levant could materially improve the status of a poor, low-rank Englishman. The never-seen Ottomans contrast the unstable alliances and identities of *Othello*'s Venetians.

Seeing English actors speaking in English colloquialisms, the play's first English audiences could reasonably relate the scenes before them to their own situation. Their rulers might tell them that the Ottomans posed a threat to them, but the most prominent threat in the play is an internal one. In the opening scenes, the Venetian Duke presents the military threat of the Ottoman army as being of more concern than the marriage of Desdemona and Othello. Yet Othello does not present himself as a clear ally or enemy, as he simultaneously plays the role of Christian defender and Moorish threat. Instead, the only clear-cut villain is an internal one: Othello's trusted ensign, the Venetian-born Iago manipulates the tragedy with unrelenting malice and unclear motives. He declares in the play's opening scene, "I am not what I am" (I.i.66), and, indeed, this seems to be the greatest threat within the play: an unknowable, unstable identity that cannot be properly categorized into *The Lepanto*'s neat divisions between a "baptized race" and "Turbanded Turkes."

Noble Turks and Tortured Slaves: Re-Imagining Othello *in the Long Eighteenth Century*

The ambiguities of *Othello* would play out differently in the various productions that followed. Of particular interest here are the productions of the long eighteenth century. Following the period of the mid-seventeenth-century Commonwealth and Protectorate which closed the theaters, this era witnesses not only a change in England's position as an imperial power, but also the canonization of William Shakespeare and his plays as representative of a type of English national identity. Shakespeare is now commonly viewed in many traditions as quintessentially English—a signifier of English cultural worth—and at times English imperial superiority. But just as the journey to a self-image of England as successful empire takes place over the course of the long century, so Shakespeare's rise as national symbol is one steeped in political change during the era.

There is a widespread effort to promote and defend Shakespeare as he transitioned from simply a noted author who is respected but contextualized by his peers to a national icon during the eighteenth century. During the twentieth and twenty-first centuries, scholars frequently looked back at this transformative moment with disdain—criticizing the editing (and at times, outright bowdlerization) of the plays being performed as well as the lack of attention to Shakespeare as a poet, both in terms of his actual poems and a lack of attention to his use of language in general. Sometimes this disdain is bemused, sometimes it is accusatory, but the majority of scholars are critical when they note the changes the plays underwent during this era.

Marvin Rosenberg, who is perhaps the seminal scholar of the past fifty years on production history and the author of the foundational performance history *The Masks of Othello: The Search for the Identity of Othello, Iago, and Desdemona by Three Centuries of Actors and Critics*, characterizes the eighteenth century as a time of prudery that strips the plays of their sexual content and moral ambiguity:

> *Othello* inevitably suffered. Depending so much upon spoken thoughts and physical action involving the sexual act, the play troubled a culture self-conscious of 'indelicacy.' As the theaters worked to eliminate verbal and visual imagery that was erotic or in 'bad taste,' many references to physical love came to be deleted and the erotic implications of Othello's jealousy and of Iago's evil were diminished.[24]

What is most telling about his attitude towards the eighteenth century's treatment of Shakespeare in general and *Othello* in particular is his blurring of the lines between the nineteenth and eighteenth centuries: "The changing content of formal drama and specifically the changes in *Othello* indicate an unmistakable tide moving strongly toward the rigid pattern of outward behavior and language that would be called 'Victorianism.'"[25] While certainly some chronological compression occurs when one does such an expansive survey, this misrepresents the debates over theatrical morality in the eighteenth century, which characterizes the changes in Shakespeare's plays, and obscures the change in racial representation between the two eras, which is reflected in the production history of *Othello*. The long century's production and scholarly history of this play shows a definitive shift in English attitudes towards themselves, the Ottomans, and race. Othello begins as an ambiguous but universal figure only to shift eventually into an emotionally out-of-control racial Other. The ambiguity during the seventeenth and early eighteenth centuries mirrors England ambivalence both to its place in the world and to its Stuart monarchs, but during the long century the universalism of a 'noble' Othello

---

[24] Marvin Rosenberg, *The Masks of Othello: The Search for the Identity of Othello, Iago, and Desdemona by Three Centuries of Actors and Critics* (Cranbury, NJ: Associated University Press, 1992), 31.

[25] Ibid., 30.

mirrors a growing sense of confidence, until finally the Moor is cast away as lesser, as Other. He is no longer a defender against Turks, but a sign of that threat becoming internalized within White Christian nations. The religious part is important. As mentioned in the previous section, religious divides within Christianity were arguably as prominent and bloody as those between Christianity and Islam. A shift does not show an increasing tolerance of Catholics in England, but a sense of confidence as a uniquely religious nation following the Church of England.

The abridgement of *Othello* begins to make sense when some of the early criticism is examined. In the 1693 *A Short View of Tragedy*, Thomas Rymer makes one of the first true critical analyses of *Othello*. Rymer offers faint praise for the play's poetry, focusing instead on its inattention to classical models and perceived implausibility of its plot and characters. Chief among his complaints is its flouting of what he presents as the natural social, racial, and sexual orders. Due to her marriage to Othello, Rymer declares, "there is nothing noble in *Desdemona*, that is not below any Country Chamber-Maid with us."[26] His complaint about the heroine extends to the portrayal of all the Venetians in the play:

> shall a Poet thence fancy that they will set a *Negro* to be their General; or a *Moor* to defend them against the *Turk*. With us a Black-a-moor might rise to be a Trumpeter; but *Shakespear* [sic] will not have him less than a Lieutenant-General. With us a *Moor* might marry some drab, or Small-coal wench; *Shakespear* would provide him with the daughter and heir of some great Lord, or Privy-Councellor.[27]

Rymer's complaints over the acceptance and promotion of Othello point to a sense of 'natural' order, one he insists is adhered to in English society. But his analysis does not merely focus on perceived racial and social hierarchies. Instead, the complaints about Othello's place in a fictive Venice create a larger issue with the emotional excess in the characters that he hopes English audiences will reject. He finds Othello's "Love and his Jealousie are no part of a Souldiers [sic] Character, unless for Comedy" (93) just as Iago "shews nothing of a Souldier,

---

[26] Thomas Rymer, *A Short View of Tragedy It's Original, Excellency and Corruption* (London: Richard Baldwin, 1693), 91. For more on the context of Rymer's criticism, see Andrew Hadfield, ed., *A Routledge Literary Sourcebook on William Shakespeare's Othello* (New York: Routledge, 2003), 37–38.

[27] Rymer, *A Short View of Tragedy*, 91–92.

nothing of a Man, nothing of Nature in it" (127). He finds an appall-
ing lightness in the characters; for example, Iago and Desdemona's
dialogue "runs on with little plays, jingle, and trash below the patience
of any Country Kitchen-Maid with her Sweet-heart" (110–11). As for
Othello's jealous confrontations with his wife, Rymer decries it as
ridiculously overwrought: "So much ado, so much stress, so much
passion and repetition about a Handkerchief! Why was this not call'd
the *Tragedy of the Handkerchief*?" (139). That the characters act with
too much sensibility and too little sense is presented as something in
which an English audience should not pleasure. That the characters
possess nothing that is "either true, or fine, or noble" (95) is seen as
part and parcel with the lack of a coherent plot that asks audiences
to "deny their senses, to reconcile it to common sense: or make it in
any way consistent, and hang together" (123). The Venetians' lack of
application to Rymer's sense of propriety is presented as one of the
flaws of a play that does not hold to established classical models. Every
fault he finds relates back to his assertion of the play's failed formal
elements that make it so that "the tragical part is, plainly none other,
than a Bloody Farce" (146).

In the eighteenth century, however, a different perspective of the
play and its author emerged. In his 1709 essay "Some Account of the
Life &c. of Mr. William Shakespear," Nicholas Rowe counters that
although Rymer "certainly pointed out some Faults very judiciously,"
he wishes that "he would likewise have observ'd some of the Beauties
too; as I think it became an Exact and Equal Critique to do. It seem
strange that he should allow nothing Good in the whole." Rowe goes
on to list the qualities of *Othello* and its author, declaring that Shakespeare's "Sentiments and Images of Things are Great and Natural; and
his Expression (tho' perhaps in some Instances a little Irregular)."[28]
That *Othello* is both "Great" artistically and "Natural" in its sentiments
would prove to be qualities set up as uniquely English as the century
wore on.

Rowe's positive view of the play, more than Rymer's, continued
to gain followers over the course of the eighteenth century. In 1753,
Charlotte Lennox's *Shakespear* [sic] *Illustrated* directly challenged
Rymer's objections to *Othello*. Whereas "Mr. *Rymer*, in his Criticisms

---

[28] Nicholas Rowe, *Some Account of the Life* (1709), in *Eighteenth Century Essays on Shakespeare*, ed. D. Nichol Smith (Oxford: Claredon Press, 1963), 19, 20.

of this Play, severly censures the Characters as well as the Fable, and the Conduct of the Incidents," Lennox finds them highly plausible. Rymer deems Iago's behavior unnatural for a solider; Lennox counters that "*Iago* was a Soldier, it is true, but he was also an *Italian*; he was born in a Country remarkable for the deep Art, Cruelty, and revengeful Temper of its Inhabitants," and argues that Shakespeare

> improved on the Novelist [Cinthio, who she also analyzes in the section on *Othello*] by making him jealous of the Moor with his own Wife; this Circumstance being sufficient, in an *Italian* especially, to account for the Revenge he takes on *Othello*, though his Barbarity to *Desdemona* is still unnatural.[29]

Her argument that Iago's behavior is credible based on his cultural background and race extends to the rest of the play, resulting in a positive portrayal of Othello and his marriage to Desdemona. Although in Cinthio's version "the Moor is mentioned without any Mark of Distinction," in the play Othello is "descended from a Race of Kings," and as a result, "the Dignity which the *Venetian* Senate bestows upon him is less to be wondered at."[30] Rymer presents Desdemona's "Love for the Moor" as "out of Nature," but Lennox posits that

> [s]uch Affections are not very common indeed; but a very few Instances of them prove that they are not impossible; and even in *England* we see some very handsome Women married to Blacks, where their Colour is less familiar than at *Venice*; besides the *Italian* Ladies are remarkable for such Sallies of irregular Passions.[31]

As in her analysis of Iago, the portrayal of Italians as cruel, conniving and possessing "irregular Passions," plays a role in her view that Othello's incorporation into Venetian society is plausible.

But her reading of Othello also draws upon the romance racial model discussed in Chapter Four. His nobility of character is established by the rank to which he was born. Similarly, his marriage to Desdemona is seen as 'natural,' because of their shared status as nobles:

---

[29] Charlotte Lennox, *Shakespear Illustrated: or the Novels and Histories, on which the Plays of Shakespear are Founded, Collected and Translated from the Original Authors. With Critical Remarks. In Two Volumes. By the Author of* The Female Quixote, vol. 1. (London, 1753), 129, 130.
[30] Ibid., 127.
[31] Ibid., 131.

> Mr. *Rymer* alledges [*sic*], that *Shakespear* makes *Desdemona* a Senator's Daughter instead of a simple Citizen; and this he imputes to him as a Fault, which is perhaps a great Instance of his Judgment.

> There is less Improbability in supposing a noble Lady, educated in Sentiments superior to the Vulgar, should fall in love with a Man merely for the Qualities of his Mind, than that a mean Citizen should be possessed of such exalted Ideas, as to overlook the Disparity of Years and Complexion, and be enamoured of Virtue in the Person of a Moor.[32]

Rymer sees Desdemona's love for Othello as inconsistent with her rank in the play, but Lennox argues that it is instead a sign of it: because Desdemona is noble, she can recognize Othello as similar to and worthy of her, despite difference of skin color, age, or geographic origin. Lennox goes on to dismiss Rymer's inability to recognize the characters nobility with his flaws as an scholar, pointing out what she sees as Rymer's mistranslation: "*Cinthio* calls her [Desdemona] *Cittadina*, which Mr. *Rymer* translates a simple Citizen; but the *Italians* by that Phrase mean a Woman of Quality."[33] Rymer, according to Lennox's critique, cannot recognize the nobility of the characters—whether in their inner qualities or their rank—because he lacks the cosmopolitan view possessed by these noble characters and Lennox. Through her discussion of nobility, Lennox undermines Rymer's authority as a critic: in her assessment, he cannot recognize Othello's worthiness, Desdemona's rank, the "naturalness" of interracial unions, or the merits of Shakespeare's play, because he does not understand nobility. Arguing that she does understand nobility, Lennox ranks herself above Rymer in a different sort of hierarchy: as a writer, reader, and translator she supersedes him, implicitly aligning herself with the rising author she defends, William Shakespeare.[34]

---

[32] Ibid., 132.

[33] Ibid., 132.

[34] Charlotte Lennox's friend and colleague Samuel Johnson wrote some of the most famous of the eighteenth century commentary on Shakespeare. I have omitted him largely for the same reason that Alexander Pope's 'corrected' version of Shakespeare's plays is not included; I wish to use Rymer, Rowe, and Lennox's work to show shifting attitudes towards Shakespeare in general and *Othello*, in particular. Johnson's analysis of the play draws in part Rymer's arguments, but still, like Lennox, finds much of the plot and characters 'natural.' Another reason I chose not to focus on Johnson, because his treatment of Shakespeare's tragedies is less nuanced than his work on the other plays and I feel, less representative of his era's views. G.F. Parker argues despite some superficial similarities, "the eighteenth-century criticism which recoils from certain aspects of Shakespearean tragedy" differs from Johnson's "protest, dismay, or shock"; "Johnson is unique among those eighteenth-century critics sensitive to what

The contrast between Rymer and these two later writers corresponds to the changing status of Shakespeare within English society
closely connected to concepts of English national identity. In *The
Making of the National Poet: Shakespeare, Adaptation and Authorship, 1660–1769*, Michael Dobson provides a persuasive argument for
why these changes occur. Similar to the way I purpose we must look
backwards to a pre-imperial England to understand its relations to the
Ottoman East, he purposes that we must remember that Shakespeare
was not always the cultural and, indeed, national icon he is today. He
argues that these changes helped introduce audiences to the Bard and
increased interest in him—making it possible to have the expansive
and global production history we have today. Between Shakespeare's
death and the reopening of the theaters during the Restoration, Shakespearean texts were not the dominating cultural objects they would
become after the long century:

> Shakespeare's plays had not been republished in a collected edition since
> the Second Folio appeared in 1632; very few living actors had any experi-
> ence of performing them, and that experience dated from twenty years
> earlier, before the Civil Wars, at which time the number of Shakespeare
> plays had already dwindled to perhaps five—*Hamlet, Othello, Julius Cae-
> sar, The Merry Wives of Windsor*, and *I Henry IV*.[35]

During the long century, the status of Shakespearean works and the
idea of William Shakespeare as a national symbol would come into
prominence over four phases. The first regards Shakespeare "at worst
as an artless rustic, at best as an archaic father-king" in need of revi-
sion in order "to finish and update his works"; the second "coincided
with the constitutional crises of the 1670s and 1680s, [during which]
Shakespeare's plays are rewritten sometimes to court such immediate
topicality but more often to avoid it." This era emphasized the image
of Shakespeare "as a king…but his dominion is now primarily over
the private realms of the passions."[36]

---

is shockingly unnatural in the tragedies, in the degree to which he simply registers his
sense of shock without translating it into a pejorative judgment" (173). For a good
overview of Johnson's work on Shakespeare, I recommend Parker's *Johnson's Shakespeare*, especially the final chapter, "Johnson and Tragedy." See G.F. Parker, *Johnson's
Shakespeare* (Oxford: Clarendon Press, 1989).

[35] Michael Dobson, *The Making of the National Poet: Shakespeare, Adaptation, and
Authorship, 1660–1769* (Oxford: Claredon Press, 1992), 2.

[36] Ibid., 13.

In the third of Dobson's phases, from the 1688 establishment of a constitutional monarchy through the 1730s, Shakespeare appears in the prologues of his rewritten plays "as a disembodied author," whose "plays are increasingly purged of their grosser, fleshlier comic details as he becomes a proper, and proprietary, Augustan author."[37] In other words, although he holds the status of a valued English author, his work is seen as outdated and in need of correction. Anticipating the changes that would dominate productions of this period, I argue that Rymer's critique over the excessive emotionality and deficient nobility of *Othello*'s characters reacts to the emphasis on emotions in Shakespearean plays at the time. His cries to remove vulgar emotionality reflect the changes made during this era, which Dobson describes as illustrating "a new insistence on the separation of 'popular' from 'literary' drama."[38] Shakespearean plays figure into both sides of this tension: on the 'popular' side, they legitimized "a variety of ephemeral entertainments; on the 'literary' side, often while being purged of just those 'low' elements which appealed to the popular entertainers, Shakespeare is constructed as a fully decorous Enlightenment author."[39] These alterations fit into a larger attempt to create a new, morally safe theatrical culture.

Dobson envisions this process culminating at the end of the century as the adaptations of David Garrick, along with other contemporary material, "despite virulent disagreements between themselves[,] assimilate Shakespeare to a common agenda of domestic virtue at home and colonial warfare abroad," which in turns results in the "rise of Bardolatry, with Shakespeare enshrined as the transcendent personification of a national ideal."[40] In this final phase, Dobson argues that the idea of Shakespeare as author and national symbol begins to overshadow the work of his adaptors:

> The promotion of Shakespeare as both symbol and exemplar of British national identity…had some profound and paradoxical consequences for contemporary treatments of his texts. The plays, now established as the productions and property of the national poet, acquired a new sanctity (which is one reason why so few successful adaptations were produced after the middle of the eighteenth century), but at the same

---

[37] Ibid., 13, 14.
[38] Ibid., 100.
[39] Ibid., 100–1.
[40] Ibid., 14.

time they came to seem almost beside the point, so extensively did Shakespeare's authority now exceed the texts from which it supposedly derived. Less than an author in the 1660s, Shakespeare was by the 1760s something more than an author: both he and his characters, invested with significances no longer containable within the framework of the Complete Plays, began to escape from the Folio and appear in poems, novels, anthologies of quotations, pageants.[41]

I wish to build off Dobson's assertion that the cuts to Shakespearean plays acted as a means of accustoming the audience to the plays and led to the establishment of Shakespeare as embodying an idea of Englishness that was culturally equal if not superior to other national identities. By focusing on the depictions of Othello, especially in terms of race, we can see a growing confidence in England's imperial status and a lessening fear of the Ottoman East.

Rosenberg's critique of eighteenth-century revisions to *Othello* presents the dialogue cuts as diminishing the titular hero: it "diminished the humanity and exoticism of the Moor, seems to indicate that a proper, neoclassic hero was aimed at.... [T]he deepest and cruelest cuts were made to reduce the atmosphere of sexuality into which Othello was betrayed."[42] Rather than simply viewing this as prudery, we can also see this as an articulation of a different sense of racial hierarchies. Clearly, for some late seventeenth-century critiques such as Rymer's, Othello's racial identity is presented as inferior to that of an English audience member. Yet, as seen in earlier chapters, the depiction of racial hierarchies in England was convoluted and contradictory at this time.

The tendency at this time to lessen the "exoticism of the Moor" would answer Rymer's objection to his high status. It would also fit into another racial model that focused more on rank than on their physical appearance or geographic origin. *Othello* draws on a model of race based on the romance tradition, discussed in the previous chapter. Though anxiety may be expressed about the Ottomans as a military force, the romance racial model allows for a universalism among those labeled 'noble,' which allowed the early eighteenth century to reinterpret Othello as a figure to which eighteenth-century English audience can both relate and aspire. If we survey the print culture surrounding *Othello*, it becomes clear that the titular hero was widely viewed as

---

[41] Ibid., 185.
[42] Rosenberg, *The Masks of Othello*, 34–35.

far more noble and less exotic. In its summaries and brief analysis of plays, *A Companion to the Theatre* (1736) emphasizes Othello's racial ambiguity and unambiguous nobility:

> Of what Country or Extraction *Othello* was, neither our Author, nor *Giraldi Cinthio*, from whom he took the Story, have thought fit to inform us: All that can be learned of him is, that he was a very valiant Commander; and having done many signal Services to the Republick of *Venice*, arrived at length to be General of the whole Army. The fame of his great Atchievments [sic], and that honest Openness of Soul which appeared in all his Words and Actions gained him the Affection of the beautiful *Desdemona*.[43]

In the text's summary of the play's plot, any physical or cultural difference that contrasts Othello to his audience or the Venetians is obscured. The violent result of his jealousy is downplayed, as are the negative commentaries by other characters on his skin color. In fact, he is only identified racially three times, and each time he is portrayed favorably. It is Iago who is villainous because he "bore the noble *Moor* most deadly hate." When Othello learns that he is being removed from Cyprus and unable to revenge himself, the text presents his anger as a reasonable reaction: "If any Thing could have added to the Rage of this deceived *Moor*, it would have been this Turn of Fortune." His "Rage" will turn deadly, but the text mitigates his culpability by reminding readers that he is also "deceived." Finally, Othello's confession made over his wife's strangled body is presented as the speech of a rational man: "the *Moor* relating the Motives which led him to commit this Murder, *Emilia* confesses that she stole the Handkercheif at her Husband's Request."[44] The Moor relates the logic that led him to murder; the attendant "confesses" her role in the crime. The syntax elevates Othello by stressing the blame held by others.

The erasure of both Othello's exoticism and his culpability is seen in other areas as well. Oration manuals frequently cite Othello's speeches as worthy of imitation, especially by young English schoolboys. Later in the century, we see a continued effacement of Othello's race and an implicit emphasis on his nobility. Othello's eloquence is held up as a model for imitation when John Walker's *The Academic Speaker* (1796) includes the Moor's defense to the Duke regarding his marriage to

---

[43] Anon., *A Companion to Theatre* (London, 1736), 232–33.
[44] Ibid., 233, 236, 237.

Desdemona. No Rymer-like asides or emendations are made questioning the propriety of the marriage. It is not Othello's scenes of murderous jealousy that *The Art of Speaking* qualifies with an asterisk.[45] It justifies including a scene of Cassio's drunkenness, conceding that although "it may, perhaps, seem strange to some" to include "such an example" of poor behavior, the inclusion of such as passion has a benefit: "the moral is good. For this very frolick costs Cassio his place." When two scenes follow depicting Othello's violent jealousy, no validation or excuse is given for their inclusion. The implicit message holds that there is nothing truly damaging to young children in imitating the Moor, but imitation of his light-skinned, European lieutenant needs an accompanying warning. This position is clarified by the handbook's introductory essay on oration, which details the components of different human passions.

Othello's fatal flaw of jealousy is accorded a surprisingly high position in Burgh's hierarchy of emotions. "Jealousy," he holds, "is a ferment of *love, hatred, hope, fear, shame, cruelty, vengeance, madness,* and if there be any other tormenting passion, which can agitate the human mind." To express it requires "that one know how to represent justly all these *passions* by turns...and often several of them *together.*"[46] By elevating the artistic difficulty of representing the emotion, Othello's embodiment of it places him above the petty drunkenness of Cassio.

Although Burgh does not touch on Othello's identity as a Moor, the introductory essay exhibits an anti-Catholicism that would make imitation of a Moor preferable in its eyes to that of a Catholic. To understand jealousy, Burgh asserts, is to understand torture—and the greatest tortures are that of the Inquisition and of Hell: "For next to being in the pope's, or Satan's prison, is the torture of him who is possessed by the spirit of *jealousy.*" Indeed, the entire essay framing the selection of speeches acts explicitly as an anti-Catholic track and implicitly as an anxious admiration of the Mediterranean. English is presented as a young language that must assert itself globally in order to be respected. In order to prove its worth, it must differentiate itself from the more established ancient and modern languages that have so far framed the measure of linguistic greatness: English "is not quite so tractable as the Italian, and consequently, not so easily applied to *amo-*

---

[45] James Burgh, *The Art of Speaking* (Dublin, 1763), 204, 267, 307.
[46] Ibid., 39.

rous, or to *plaintive* music," and the "Greek, among the antient [sic], and the Turkish and Spanish, among the modern languages, have a *loftier* sound," but English holds a capacity for "variety."[47]

In this context, the passion and violence of Othello fits in well with this vision of the English language. Jealousy, after all, is the culmination of a variety of passions, and English is the language best suited to express that variety. This book of oration is a polemic piece on religion that feels the need to justify its inclusion of Cassio's drunkenness but not Othello's jealousy. It presents oration as a way of preserving the Church of England against Catholic intrusions: "by keeping clear of every thing *disagreeable*, grating, and by consulting all that may *please, entertain*, and *strike*, that the sagacious Roman Catholic keep up, in their people, a *delight* in the public services of their religion." In order to combat this menace, children must be trained in the art of oration in order to become effective clergy and statesmen for the nation by learning how to speak as pleasingly but with more truth and variety.[48] Yet in this lengthy essay on the need to teach oration to prevent the loss of English religious identity to Catholicism, no mention of the threat of the Ottomans is mentioned. Instead, Turkish is a noble language that English cannot match in terms of classical standards, and Othello is a figure that young boys can imitate as they are molded into future religious and political leaders.

By the end of the century, Othello has been adopted as a model for the English because of the Ottoman gloss placed upon him. His difference from the Venetians is noted, but his racial difference from English actors and audiences is ignored. In Edward Capell's *Notes and Various Readings to Shakespeare* (1779–80), which details the inflections needed for key lines and words in the plays, no mention is made of playing Othello as culturally different. Desdemona may occasionally use "a Scottish twang" when pronouncing some words, but Othello is never given any direction that he is anything other than English.[49] Even his discussion of scenes explicitly dealing with light and darkness, such as the scene where the darker Othello considers smothering the lighter Desdemona, Capell emphasizes "putting out the light" in terms of an end of life, arguing here Othello "questions himself about of this

---

[47] Ibid., 39, 5.
[48] Ibid., 72.
[49] Edward Capell, *Notes and Various Readings* (London, 1779–80), 144.

metaphorical extinction."[50] Potential racial implications of the lines are ignored. Othello the philosopher matters more in this interpretation than Othello the Moor.

Notably, during the eighteenth century, Othello is depicted as vaguely Ottoman. Rymer objects to the logic of Othello defending against the Ottomans by conflating the two: Venetians are "bred up with that hatred and aversion to the *Moors*" because these are the Ottomans from whom they "suffer by a perpetual Hostility."[51] Ironically, the less jealous and irrational protagonist would be elevated by solidifying his ambiguous identity as a civilized and Ottoman-like. In her overview of *Othello*'s production history, Julie Hankey asserts that during the first productions of the play, Richard Burbage, one of the principal actors at the Globe Theatre, "would probably have painted himself as black as possible" so "he would have stood out against a background of faces, listening to his tale in the afternoon light" of a Jacobean out-door theater.[52] Following the reopening of the English theaters in 1660, Restoration audiences would have seen a very different production. Besides performing in indoor theaters, with scenery and women in the female roles, actors and critics of the eighteenth century seemed to downplay the idea of racial difference in the play, "neither pointing to Othello's Africa origins nor arguing them away.... The black face was, in effect, neither here nor there. There was no pressing reason to abandon it, nor to make it part of a thoroughgoing foreign costume."[53] When objections arose to the hero's blackness, the response seemed to be to adopt an Ottoman gloss. Hankey illustrates this connection:

> Boaden, it is true, said that above the general's uniform it [the black face] "begets a ludicrous association at first sight," and perhaps it was for that reason that Barry (according to the frontispiece of a 1777 edition of the play) adopted a vaguely oriental costume. But he surely had not always worn it, for when J.P. Kemble assumed "the Moorish habit" in 1787, he was praised for it as though it were not yet customary.[54]

The two modes of costuming for Othello seem to be clothing culturally associated either with the Ottomans or with Europeans. The frontis-

---

[50] Ibid., 155.

[51] Rymer, *A Short View of Tragedy*, 92.

[52] Julie Hankey, introduction to *Othello*, by William Shakespeare (Cambridge: Cambridge University Press, 1987), 11.

[53] Ibid., 40, 41.

[54] Ibid., 41.

piece of a 1709 edition of Shakespeare by Nicholas Rowe highlights the difference in color between Othello and Desdemona, but Othello's angry facial features are not distorted by racial stereotyping nor would his clothing be out of place in London. Othello exists here as a universal figure, much like some of the romance depictions of Moors in the preceding century.

More telling is the kind of interpretations of Othello that audiences rejected. Throughout much of the century, Othello is physically depicted in either European or oriental dress. His foreignness is downplayed in favor of a universalized idea of a tragic hero. Although he is not explicitly Ottoman, he resembles someone from the Ottoman Mediterranean more than the groups of Africans associated with the European slave trade. As noted earlier, the seventeenth-century Othello represented both an external Ottoman threat as well as an internal Catholic one; as the eighteenth century progressed, he retains the Ottoman gloss but becomes a more universalized and less threatening character. It is towards the end of the century that we see the beginnings of the 'African' Othello that would come to dominant nineteenth- and twentieth-century productions. Yet, as the negative reviews garnered by Shakespearean actors for their innovative interpretations of Othello show, critics and general audiences resisted the interpretation of Othello as exotic, passionate, and Other.

Despite being widely acknowledged at the time and today as a major reformist of eighteenth-century acting as well as the creator of Shakespearean adaptations that were one of the main means of popularizing the plays, David Garrick's three performances of Othello in 1745–6 were some of the least admired in both the play's production history as well as in Garrick's own career. Hankey rightly points out that Garrick experienced "a variety of successes in both comic and tragic roles, but when it came to Othello the magic failed."[55] The negative reaction was due largely to the belief that his small stature, black face, and turbaned costume diminished the noble hero. He restored the sexualized language that previous productions found unfit for a proper, tragic hero.[56] Oddly, the turbaned performance was ridiculed because it was not in line with the image of a noble Moor or Ottoman price: "James Quin [a major proponent of a rival school of acting] ridiculed this [the turban]

---

[55] Ibid., 24.
[56] For a good overview of the linguistic cuts, see Hankey, introduction, 18–19.

by remarking loudly enough for a large part of the audience to hear: 'Why does not he bring the tea-kettle and lamp?' (The reference is to a small black boy in a plumed turban and holding a kettle in William Hogarth's series *A Harlot's Progress* [1731])."[57] The oriental turban referenced by Quin points to a rejection of Othello as an African slave. Virginia Mason argues that Garrick's and others' Othello portrayals— and the negative reviews they received—reflect the visual culture of slavery in London. She insists that the play's production history be read with the awareness that it occurred at "a time when the justice of British enslavement of black Africans in England and the West Indies was hotly debated," making it therefore folly to insist that "Othello's race and his relation to a white woman seem, in the eyes of most theatre historians, not to have mattered."[58] Garrick was interpreting Othello as an African and inserting, however apolitically or unintentionally, a reference to England's enslavement of black, non-Arab Africans.[59]

Garrick's performance occurred in the 1740s, in the middle of a century when the image of Africa was still dominated by the Ottoman holdings, and English identity was still being shaped. Shakespeare was performed and studied with growing respect, yet there was still a tendency to correct him. In the later part of the century a different failed performance of Othello shows a shift in attitudes towards race. A revered eighteenth-century actor and brother of actress Sarah Siddons, John Philip Kemble also received negative reviews, inconsistent with those of his other roles, when he played Othello as too much like an African slave and not enough as a noble Moor. The 29 October 1787 *Public Advertiser* approves of what is noble in the performance, which it labels as the Ottoman-like costuming, but decries the lack of emotion: "The reviewer praises the actor's performance in the later scenes, but in a curious aside, comments: 'We much approve his dressing Othello in the Moorish habit... [but] is it necessary the Moor should be as *black* as a native of Guiney?'"[60]

---

[57] Ibid., 24.

[58] Mason, "Race Mattered," 57.

[59] The eighteenth century also saw the rise of Iago as a desirable role for actors. Garrick had "conceded [Spranger] Barry's superiority as Othello, he 'took care' wrote [Garrick biography Arthur] Murphy, 'not to let himself down' in the part of Iago" and as Hankey puts it, was not "content to play second fiddle" to Othello. Hankey, introduction, 27.

[60] Qtd in Mason, "Race Mattered," 59.

The reaction of critics and audiences points to a different understanding of racial and national identity in England than what would
come to pass in the following centuries. The Othello of the eighteenth
century was presented as a universal figure with whom the audience
could identify—this shows a shift in the view of the Ottomans from
a threat to an equal to a peripheral interest to Africa corresponding
with growing confidence in an English-centered empire. Mason rightly
points out the importance of race in these 'failed' performances:

> That Kemble's Moor was too like an African from Guinea (most likely a
> slave to be exported to the West Indian sugar plantations) suggests that,
> to some viewers at least, the distinction between a white actor playing
> a black man and the real thing had to be maintained. This may be one
> explanation for David Garrick's failure in the role of Othello—not that
> he was too black, but that in his turban and feather, he looked too much
> like the black servants fashionable Londoners encountered every day.[61]

Although I agree with her call to examine the racial context of the
play, I would like to place this in a larger context of the shift in England's attention from the Ottoman world that threatened them in the
Mediterranean world (including Africa) to an African world they were
exploiting for their own imperial gain.

What was the perceived failure of these performances? It is clear
that audiences did not want a small, dark, emotional Othello, signaling
their preference for a light-skinned, noble, physically attractive one.
But I believe that these two performances reflected other changes as
well. The first is the changes made to the play itself: Garrick notably
gave a much fuller version of the text, including the more sexual lines,
for which audiences and critics were not yet ready. While esteeming
the play more than Rymer, audiences and critics appear to still want
a traditionally tragic hero, a form to which Shakespearean characters
did not fully ascribe.

The second is the growing association of blackness with African
slaves. It is true that this association existed in England during earlier
centuries, but as we have seen, it was not in *Othello*, nor do I believe
it was firmly in the public's mind.[62] However, as England's imperial
might rose, so did its expectations of how it treated others. Rather

---

[61] Ibid., 59.
[62] For excellent accounts of racial discourse in Early Modern England, see Ania
Loomba, *Shakespeare, Race, and Colonialism* (Oxford: Oxford University Press, 2002)
and Kim F. Hall, *Things of Darkness: Economies of Race and Gender in Early modern
England* (Ithaca, NY: Cornell University Press, 1996).

than be threatened by Ottomans, debates shifted over its treatment of Africans. Fear of white slavery transformed into concerns over the empire's own African slave trade.

I believe Garrick and Kemble's audiences rejected a blackening of Othello from a more Arab version that the new reality of a multiracial London and an imperial England challenged with new views and visual associations. England's position had changed. Rather than the English being the ones going abroad to a more powerful empire in the Mediterranean, an increasing number of people were coming to the British Isles. Of course, there had been immigration in the seventeenth and eighteenth centuries, but what had changed in the late eighteenth century was England's self-image as a significant world player. There was an increasing black presence in the country, especially in London. These were not always the slaves that had been present since the sixteenth century. Some were free men and women: some prosperous, like ex-slave turned abolitionist and successful author Olaudah Equiano, some poor, like the black loyalists from the American War. Directly and indirectly, all of them raised the general public's awareness of the presences of African slavery within the empire, and helped a growing number of British subjects question the moral role of England as the center of a powerful empire.

The increasing association of blackness with slavery and growing abolitionist movement shaped the reaction of audiences and critics to the darker-skinned, more emotional Othellos offered by Garrick and Kemble. Charges that Garrick's Othello resembled the house slave in a Hogarth print or Kemble's "native of Guiney" points to the increased association within the public sphere of blackness with slavery. These images were not necessarily heroic. In the panel of the 1731 Hogarth engraving *A Harlot's Progress* Quin would reference a few years later as a critique of Garrick's Othello, the house slave's grand, exotic, oriental attire complete with turban juxtaposes his diminutive stature as a child, low status as the slave to a Jew's promiscuous mistress, and his objectification as a fashionable domestic adornment. He a marginal figure in the engraving's narrative, lacking the heroic authority or power eighteenth-century audience associated with Shakespeare's Moor.

When Kemble performed the role, the issue of slavery had gained a more prominent place in the public discourse. Here, too, the images of blackness differed from the popular image of Othello. Josiah Wedgewood's effective abolitionist seal depicting a kneeling male slave dressed in rags beseechingly asking the viewer, "Am I Not a Man and a Brother," appeared around the same time as Kemble's performance of Othello. In the famous broadside "Description of a Slave Ship," put out by the Society for Effecting the Abolition of the Slave Trade in 1788, tiny, faceless figures of slaves are packed nightmarishly close to each other in the vessels hold. Both the Wedgewood seal and slave ship diagram were effective in turning public opinion in England against its empire's role in the slave trade. Yet, though the motivations that produced these images and the political change they elicited are undeniably admirable, their image of a dark-skinned man contrasts the image of Othello observed in this chapter.

As the long century ended, Othello was increasingly associated with the enslavement of black Africans by white Europeans. England was solidifying its place as one of the most powerful empires while Ottoman influence faded. As Mason discusses *Othello* within the context of contemporaneous slavery images, she makes the apt point that by the end of the eighteenth century Othello was being consistently tied to ideas of an African blackness:

> His blackness, of course, was a given, so it is not surprising to find Othello as the name of a slave or a member of an all-black military musical regiment. That Othello married a white woman was also a given. Thus the white chambermaids who flirted with the Duchess of Queensberry's black servant, Julius Soubise (notorious for womanizing and other vices), called him 'the young Othello.' Othello was jealous. So, when Hester Piozzi reported the jealous quarrel between Francis Barber, Samuel Johnson's black servant, and his white wife, she called the wife 'his Desdemona.'[63]

I think, however, this trend points to two larger and more complicated issues. First, a shift towards African blackness does not mean that the Ottoman construction has been completely lost. We see this in the resistance to Kemble and Garrick's black, passionate, less-universalized (which for the audiences and critics meant 'civilized' Europeans and Ottomans) interpretations of the role.

Second, this shift invites the questions of what it meant for Africans to be associated with a previously Arab-Ottoman inflected role. Mason

---

[63] Mason, "Race Mattered," 61.

expresses surprise "that literate Africans also used Othello as a self-construction."[64] She implies that it is illogical for a slave turned abolitionist such as Olaudah Equiano to respond to critics with a quotation from Shakespeare's Moor. I believe Equiano and other ex-slaves used this association precisely because it dealt with a kind of non-European identity that fit into another vision of Africa—an Ottoman one. It was a step up from the racial position accorded to them as African slaves. It was also a way of ennobling Africans by attaching themselves to a part of Africa the English had long recognized as civilized—and, indeed, powerful.

Conclusion

In the seventeenth century, Othello's racial ambiguity coupled with his high rank allowed for a complicated exploration of English anxieties over external and internal threats. As discussed in previous chapters, the Ottomans represented both an outside military threat as well as the internal threat of apostasy. In this chapter, I argue that Othello's dual role mirrored anxieties James I. Othello acts as both an insider in Venice as well as a foreigner, who is occasionally linked to the Ottomans through speeches such as Brabantio as well as his own final proclamations. Similarly, a Scot as English king or a possible Catholic as head of the Church of England was viewed as contradictory and potentially dangerous by some of his subjects.

This interpretation begins to shift in the eighteenth century. The 1688 constitutional monarchy barred Catholics from the English throne, which, along with historical distance, lessened the play's links to James I in the minds of Shakespeare's new audience. Similarly, the rise of Shakespeare as national poet outlined by Dobson resulted in an emphasis on the nobility rather than the passion of the play's titular character. Reinforced by the romance racial model already surrounding the play, Othello's nobility was reinforced by his rank. Critically successfully portrayals of the Moor as well as the oratory books that highlighted his speeches placed less emphasis on his foreignness and more on his presumed heroism.

---

[64] Ibid., 61.

The negative reactions to Garrick and Kemble's performances superficially seem to fit the above interpretation, but the language of the criticism points to a cultural shift. Detractors invoke the image of slavery when describing these portrayals. That they saw an African slave and not a noble Moor illustrates the rising public awareness of the slave trade in the mid to late eighteenth century. Whereas the discussion of English captives in the Ottoman Empire earlier in the century focused on English vulnerability to a stronger imperial power, the debate over the slavery at the end of the pitted concerns over the strengthening of a British transatlantic empire against the moral and ethical responsibilities of that empire to less empowered nations.

CHAPTER SIX

ORIENTAL PRINCES AND NOBLE SLAVES:
ROMANCE MODELS OF RACE IN *OROONOKO*, 1688–1788

While the popularity of Aphra Behn as an author wavered over the past three centuries, her last work, *Oroonoko; or, the Royal Slave* (1688), has continually been seen as relevant to audiences and scholars. Recent attention has focused on Behn's position as the first professional woman writer as well as on the novel's examination of race and gender in the slave-holding plantation colony of Surinam. However, during the century following Behn's death in 1689, her narrative took on a new form: eighteenth-century audiences were often more familiar with the stage adaptations of *Oroonoko*. The popularity of the plays reached the point where it becomes difficult to determine if eighteenth-century commentators refer to the novel or its dramatic reincarnations. The change from one genre to another—along with the subsequent new variations of the play—resulted in alterations not just to accommodate staging concerns but also to shift the political stance taken by the novel. Reflecting changing conceptions of romance and Africa, each version is driven by a new need to make amends or apologize for the political indiscretions of its predecessors. The removal of an Ottoman gloss to Behn's African prince plays a crucial role in the narrative's later association both with abolitionism and with perceptions of England as a rising imperial power.

In the original prose narrative, Behn outfits her African kingdom and its characters with elements from romance depictions of Muslim cultures in order to make a political statement on late-Restoration politics. The use of romance evokes an association with an idealized past and seeks to validate the text's ideological stances by inserting itself into the romance tradition reaching back to the Classical and Medieval eras. As subsequent adaptations attempted to distance themselves from the ideological message of the novel, the depiction of Oroonoko loses its association with the Ottoman holdings of North Africa and Muslim nobles of romance; the hero of the plays emerges instead as a symbol of the pagan African slaves of the West Indies. The differences between the source material and its adaptations demonstrate the interconnectedness of romance and Ottoman power in the English cultural imagination: a vision of Africa associated with Islam evokes images from romance of military prowess and a long-established civilization; without this connection to a romance discourse of the Orient, Africa is presented as a continent victimized by the transatlantic slave trade and lacking a culturally sophisticated society. This chapter deals with the first half of this transformation by focusing on the way the romance tradition shapes the representations of politics, class, and race in the novel.

The *Oroonoko* narrative, from its initial prose narrative form through its stage adaptations, reflects a changing relationship between Britain, its subjects, and its colonies in the period 1688 to 1787. Behn's version presents a pro-Tory argument against representative governments and gives a fairly positive view of colonial plantations' reliance on slave labor. The original prose version is divided into four sections. The first is a description of the nearly pre-Lapsarian innocence of the Surinam natives that serves to critique London immorality; this theme is expanded in the subsequent play adaptations. In the second section Oroonoko—the seventeen-year-old heir to his centenarian grandfather's throne in the African kingdom of Coramantien—falls in love with an old general's beautiful daughter, Imoinda, but shortly after they pledge themselves to each other, his grandfather forces her into his harem. Too impotent to rape her, the king is further enraged to discover her relationship with Oroonoko. The king informs his heir that Imoinda is dead when in fact she has been sold into slavery. The third section recounts how Oroonoko's intellectual curiosity allows him, his French tutor, and about a hundred courtiers to be tricked onto an English slave ship headed to Surinam. There he meets the unnamed narrator often associated with Behn herself and is reunited with Imoinda. In the last section, Imoinda's pregnancy prompts him to rebel so that his children will not be slaves. The rebellion fails, in part owing to the other slaves' passivity. Oroonoko kills Imoinda to prevent her from falling into enemy hands, and he is brutally executed by the colony's provisional government. Later stage adaptations, chiefly those of Thomas Southerne (1696) and John Hawkesworth (1759), reflect a change in how British audiences viewed their domestic and colonial spaces, trending more toward Lockean ideas of universal suffrage.

This concept of universal suffrage replaced another definition of universality found in the romance idea of a noble race, in which rank presents a means of connecting the ruling class across cultural boundaries. Though the romance model is limited to a small group of individuals and serves to justify a system of power, Locke's concept of universality possesses its own limitations on who could claim to be a subject as opposed to a slave. Property ownership played a large role in determining who could and could not be enslaved. Those who possessed property were at liberty, while those without it became property themselves. Locke's symbolic use of the term 'slavery' to represent a lack of property and individual power allows Southerne to draw a connection between the poorer classes of England and the enslavement of Africans for colonial labor. Later in the eighteenth century, multiple transitions occurred in power relations in the Transatlantic and Mediterranean regions, altering the way audiences responded to the themes of monarchal rights, race, and slavery in the narrative. In the Transatlantic, the British power in the Caribbean declined while support in the British Isles for abolition rose. This also corresponded with the increasing decay of Ottoman power in the Mediterranean while England existed at the center of an increasingly powerful British Empire spreading eastward.

Throughout Britain in the long eighteenth century, the stage adaptations of Behn's novel portrayed slavery and the plantation as inherently corrupt. As a result, Behn's narrative of a royal slave experienced an ideological drift as stage adaptations and audience response reflected changes in cultural attitudes toward the West Indian colonies and the slavery that supported their economy. By the end of the eighteenth century, the narrative's roots in romance depictions of Islam and its preoccupation with the divine right of kings had been obscured in favor of a new era's political issues.

Recent criticism on the many manifestations of the *Oroonoko* narrative focuses mainly on the depiction of race and female authorship. For example, both Laura Brown's "The Romance of Empire: *Oroonoko* and the Trade in Slaves" and Margaret Ferguson's "Juggling Categories of Race, Class and Gender: Aphra Behn's *Oroonoko*" see the novel's depiction of Oroonoko's blackness as bound up in the gender of his author.[1] Brown interprets Behn's text as downplaying the racial difference between Oroonoko and the female characters, chiefly

---

[1] Laura Brown, "The Romance of Empire: *Oroonoko* and the Trade in Slaves," in *The New Eighteenth Century: Theory, Politics, English Literature*, eds. Laura Brown and Felicity Nussbaum (New York: Methuen, 1987).

Moira Ferguson, "Juggling Categories of Race, Class and Gender: Aphra Behn's *Oroonoko*," in *Aphra Behn*, ed. Janet Todd (New York: St. Martin's Press, 1999).

the narrator. In doing so, she argues that Oroonoko is Europeanized enough to symbolically represent Charles I, to whom the good Englishwomen of Surinam remain loyal. Women, slaves, and king become linked by a common political stance against mercantile imperialism. Ferguson uses the categories of race, class, and gender to analyze the intellectual history behind U.S. feminism. In her analysis, Oroonoko and Behn's narrator persona are embroiled in common struggles for power: he with his grandfather and she with Byam, the provisional Governor of Surinam. Together, they are a potentially subversive threat, but Ferguson ultimately sees the conflicting desires of Behn's narrator to critique yet profit from colonial slavery as leading to Oroonoko's demise.

Focusing on Behn's political stance as a Stuart supporter, Laura Doyle and Elliot Visconsi continue this discussion of race but place it in a different historical context.[2] They see Oroonoko's difference from the other slaves and alignment with Behn's narrator persona as signally a racial model that, instead of focusing on physiological or geographical divisions, categorizes people according to rank. This chapter relies largely on their readings to support my interpretation of the Coramantien court scenes as a deliberate evocation of an idealized past found in medieval romances. Reading the novel within the context of romance highlights the connection between the shifting views on race and sovereignty that this chapter traces from Behn's prose narrative to her dramatic descendants. Under the romance equation of race with rank, Oroonoko is not a common African slave but a royal member of a culture with heavy Islamic overtones. Positioning him within the romance context, Behn evokes medieval crusade narratives that—despite a frequent reliance on negative stereotypes—positions Islam as a cultural equal to Christian Europe. As the *Oroonoko* narrative experienced a series of stage revisions, this romance view of race gave way to a dual portrayal of African slaves as part of a universal humanity as well as a pagan, uncultured people in need of Christianization.

Critical treatments of the play versions of the novel focus primarily on the first adaptation by Thomas Southerne. Reflecting the concern with intersections of race and gender in the novel's scholarship, ana-

---

[2] Laura Doyle, "The Folk, the Nobles and the Novel: The Racial Subtext of Sentimentality," *Narrative* Vol. 3, No. 2 (May 1995): 161–187.
Elliot Visconsi, "A Degenerate Race: English Barbarism in Aphra Behn's *Oroonoko* and the *Widow Ranter*," *ELH* 69 (2002): 673–701.

lytical work done on this first stage adaptation frequently focuses on Southerne's choice to present Imoinda as a white European instead of African. Jennifer Elmore interprets the heroine's color change as a sign of her sentimentalization and domestication in order to prompt audience sympathy both with Imoinda herself and with what Elmore reads as an abolitionist agenda in this first play version.[3] This shift, she argues, represents the silencing of black women in the British public. Joseph Roach incorporates the first stage version into his reading of performativity across the Atlantic world, citing it as a "disclosure of how these distinctively circum-Atlantic relationships—reproduction and abundance, surrogation and memory, miscegenation and violence—emerge out of the performance of Behn's narrative through the staging of Southerne's dramatic adaptation."[4] For him, the staging of the play allows these issues to emerge out of Behn's original plot in a way unavailable to the novel. Felicity Nussbaum also focuses on the blanching of Imoinda, linking it to the disappearance of the nar-rator and the emergence of the comic plot's female characters.[5] When combined, she argues, these changes point to the play's desire to rein in women in general, and in particular the changes are interpreted as a mode of chastising Behn for the independence she displayed through-out her life.

While drawing on this scholarship, I take the position that the stage adaptations, such as Southerne's and Hawkesworth's, do not necessar-ily point to an anti-slavery stance until John Ferriar's 1788 production, which was directly connected to the local abolitionist movement in Manchester. This reading places the novel and plays within the his-torical context of England's domestic debates over sovereignty and the changing fortunes in the plantocracy of the Caribbean in order to highlight the way romance depictions of Islam are deeply embed-ded in the ideology of the original novel and how the removal of the Oriental romance elements results in a drastically different vision of English-African relations. This shift reflects my larger thesis that the

---

[3] Jenifer B. Elmore, "'The Fair Imoinda': Domestic Ideology and Anti-Slavery on the Eighteenth-Century Stage," in *Troping* Oroonoko *from Behn to Bandele,* ed. Susan B. Iwanisziw (Burlington: Ashgate, 2004).

[4] Joseph Roach, *Cities of the Dead: Circum-Atlantic Performance* (New York: Columbia University Press, 1996), 154.

[5] Felicity A. Nussbaum, *The Limits of the Human: Fictions of Anomaly, Race and Gender in the Long Eighteenth Century* (Cambridge: Cambridge University Press, 2003).

decentralization of the Ottomans from the cultural imaginings of English culture over the long eighteenth century connects to another shift in power relations as the older, established Ottoman Empire waned on the world stage while England ascended into its new role as the central player in the British Empire.

Properly contextualizing the romance tradition that Behn's *Oroonoko* evokes in the late seventeenth century requires an examination of the romance tradition in the preceding centuries. As discussed in the earlier chapters, during the eighteenth century England emerges as an imperial power while struggling for cultural and political recognition. This insecurity gave rise to fears of cultural instability—of the loss of identity to the more powerful nations surrounding it. In order to highlight this fear, I combine my discussion of romance and the novel with a focus on England's interactions with the Ottoman Mediterranean.

With this in mind, I want to recontextualize the discussion of the use of romance and depictions of the Orient within eighteenth-century English culture. Seeing the eighteenth century as a period before the imperialism of the nineteenth century solidified, I believe texts such as Behn's *Oroonoko* need to be read backwards into the past that produced them. Rather than examine the imperial success represented by England's eastward swing to Africa, India, and the Far East, I want to re-examine its insecurities in regards to the Ottoman Empire's holdings in the Near East.

The Problem of Abolition and Royal Slaves

It seems as if a tragedy of a prince kidnapped into slavery who goes on to lead a revolt against plantation owners in a Caribbean colony would in its bare plot lines carry some sort of abolitionist critique of British colonial practices. In fact, the Behn version's narrative of a slave revolt does lend itself to a superficially anti-slavery reading. Oroonoko's process of self-awakening to his condition as a slave leads directly to his rebellion. For most of his stay in Surinam, Oroonoko occupies himself with the white, mainly female, colonists while awaiting the royally appointed Lord Governor's arrival. Aphra Behn inserts herself into the text as the narrator at the center of Oroonoko's group of female colonial supporters. Throughout much of the novel, the prince spends his time freely in the company of these sympathetic women, while occasionally helping the colonists by mediating treaties with the native Caribs. His compliance is due largely in part to the narrator and her compatriots' insistence that his freedom will be restored once the royally appointed Governor arrives to take power from the provisional government. Oroonoko's freedom—and not that of the common slaves—is the concern of Behn's narrator persona.

The Governor's drowning in a hurricane, along with the introduction of Oroonoko's unborn child, shifts the dynamics of the situation. Until this time the narrator and her companions had "diverted" Oroonoko from any thoughts of rebellion, but the European women's power over him wanes when his wife Imoinda begins to use her pregnancy to assert her authority. Doing "nothing but Sigh and Weep," she urges her husband to consider the fate of their future children, who will belong to the plantation owners and not to them. Presenting the choices of simply waiting for colonial justice or buying their freedom as impossible, she argues that "if it were so hard to gain the Liberty of Two, 'twou'd be more difficult to get it that for Three."[6] By becoming more aggressive, Imoinda persuades him to cease viewing himself as a royal accidentally turned slave, and instead to view himself as, in the terms of historian Orlando Patterson, "socially dead" and left with no other option but revolt. In *Slavery and Social Death: A Comparative History*, Patterson differentiates chattel slavery from other forms of domination by focusing on how the slave is a "socially dead person" lacking any "'rights' or claims of birth." One of the chief features of this is "natal alienation":

> not only was the slave denied all claims on, and obligations to, his parents and living blood relations but, by extension, all such claims and obligations on his remote ancestors and on his descendants. He was truly genealogically isolated.[7]

Applied to Oroonoko, slavery should have erased his claims to a royal past as well as his future progeny. No longer a king, he should in theory be like the other slaves; in this chapter, however, I show how Behn's presentation of slavery does not fit this anti-slavery model. Instead of Oroonoko's revolt acting as a sign of awakening to the social realities of his position as a plantocracy slave, it acts to justify the enslavement

---

6 Aphra Behn, *Oroonoko; or, the Royal Slave* (1688), ed. Catherine Gallagher (Boston: Bedford/St. Martin, 2000), 85.

7 Orlando Patterson, *Slavery and Social Death: A Comparative Study* (Cambridge, MA: Harvard University Press, 1982), 5.

of the common African slaves, further distancing the prince from his countrymen.

Continuing this potentially abolitionist reading, Oroonoko's next step toward self-realization involves examining the condition of the other slaves—those not lucky enough to spend their days being distracted by the Behn-like narrator's stories. With pity, he begins "counting up their Toyls and Sufferings, under such Loads, Burdens, and Drudgeries, as were fitter for Beasts than Men; Senseless Brutes than Humane Souls," and after recognizing the moral ills of the situation, Oroonoko progresses to the stage of inciting them to rebel. He informs them that "they had lost the Divine Quality of Men, and were become insensible Asses, fit only to bear; nay worse." In his speech, he appears to specifically show why chattel slavery in the Caribbean is worse than the enslavement of war prisoners in Africa:

> And why, said he, my dear Friends and Fellow-sufferers, shou'd we be Slaves to an unknown People? Have they Vanquish'd us Nobly in Fight?...[being captured in war] wou'd not anger a Noble Heart...but we are Bought and Sold like Apes, or Monkeys to be the Sport of Women, Fools and Cowards; and the Support of Rogues, Runagades, that have abandon'd their own Countries, for Rapin, Murders, Thefts and Villaines.[8]

Here his speech seems to directly attack the institution of slavery in the colonies: in war, there exists an understanding that defeat leads to temporary slavery, but it does not involve the base labor they experience here nor does this 'noble' form of bondage dehumanize its subjects. In chattel slavery, they are no longer people but commodities in the colonial market bought like animals to labor under colonists unfit for European society. The plantation owners are not representative of European society. Instead, they represent the worst elements of society: those that Behn's English readers should wish to disassociate themselves with by not supporting either colonial products—such as exotic luxuries like the pets mentioned—or the institution of slavery that props them up.[9]

This potentially anti-slavery reading, however, is undercut not only by the narrative as a whole but the events that directly follow it. Oroo-

---

[8] Behn, *Oroonoko*, 86.
[9] This gendered attack does little to address more dominant colonial staples such as sugar, the addition of which would have placed blame on both sexes.

noko's ability to observe his fellow slaves actually aligns him with the colonists. Because it is Sunday, the white inhabitants of Surinam that he normally socializes with are "overtaken in Drink" (85) during their day off, as are the indentured servants who usually spy on Oroonoko. As an educated slave accustomed to being in power along with his apparent lack of assigned labor to perform, Oroonoko is seen as a threat to the slavers, planters, and provisional government from his time on the slave ship until his death. The only ones working are the slaves, making Oroonoko's leisure as an outside observer more acute. Another sign of his alienation from the other slaves lies in his uncontested statement that "they had lost the Divine Quality of Men" (86). In his eyes, they have allowed slavery to dehumanize them, while only he possesses the vision necessary to reveal and correct their position.

Their passivity is further emphasized by their hesitancy to follow him; while constantly bowing and deferring to him as their superior, they express concern that a rebellion would endanger their wives and children. Throughout their dialogue, it is clear that the slaves and Oroonoko represent two very different perspectives. The former see the dangers presented by rebellion as making them potentially even more vulnerable to the violent reprimands of their owners. Oroonoko, on the other hand, has not experienced the punishments and tortures set aside each week for "Black Friday" nor does he view himself as a slave leader. He still views himself as a royal general leading an army: they will follow the example of "one *Hannibal* a great Captain, [who] had Cut his Way through Mountains of solid Rocks" (86) and "Plant a New Colony, and Defend it by their Valour" until they can seize a ship to their countries of origin or live as his subjects in Coramantien (87). This mismatched pairing of passive slaves and martial prince leads to the revolt's failure. Rather than mirroring the discipline of a Carthaginian army, the slaves quickly surrender: while attacking the English, they "observ'd no Order...and the Women and Children...being of Cowardly Dispositions, and hearing the *English* cry out, *Yield and Live, Yield and Live, Yield and be Pardon'd*" (89) persuade their husbands to betray their leader. Despite their coming from the same part of the world as he, Oroonoko finds their cowardice culturally alien and chastises himself for having ever grouped himself with them: "he was asham'd of what he had done, in endeavoring to make those Free, who were by Nature Slaves, poor wretched Rogues, fit to be us'd as *Christians* Tools" (90). Not only do their actions distance them from Oroonoko, but they also justify slavery in general by presenting the common Africans as natural slaves. Within the noble race ideology, Oroonoko should be free because he possesses an innate need for freedom that the common slaves lack. By clearly differentiating Oroonoko from the mass of slaves, Behn does not present an argument against slavery. Instead, it becomes clear that what the text finds fault with is not slavery but the enslavement of this royal person in particular.

Further countering the abolitionist argument is the relatively benign depiction Behn gives of life in Surinam. Mr. Trefry, for example, is an ideal colonial slave master. He treats Oroonoko as a guest rather than a slave since he has promised to return the prince to his country. On his plantation, the narrative does not observe any abuse of power. Unlike the colonial "*Rogues…that have abandon'd their own Countries, for Rapin…and Villaines*" (86) that Oroonoko later decries, Trefry poses no physical or sexual threat to his slaves, as is demonstrated by his chaste love for Imoinda. Having been bought earlier and renamed Clemene, Imoinda has bewitched him as "all the white Beautys he had seen, never charm'd him" (70), but he gallantly recognizes Oroonoko's prior claim to her and is "not little satisfied, that Heaven was so kind to the *Prince*, as to sweeten his fortunes by so lucky an Accident" (72). This view of a benevolent plantation owner can also be found in Behn's other works. For example, a year before *Oroonoko*'s publication, her poem "To the Most Illustrious Prince Christopher Duke of Albemarle, on his Voyage to his Government of Jamaica" praises the young colonist for choosing to "more Renown His Name,/ And still maintain aloft His spreading Fame" (ll. 9–10) over "the Confinement of a Home-Retreat" before "soft Repose, that Court-Disease,/ Infectious to the Great and Young,/ Subdu'd His Martial Mind to Ease" (ll. 12, 13–15). The colonies provide royal youths the chance to obtain the martial greatness their titles deserve. Ideally, Behn sees the colonies as a means of encouraging noble traits among the aristocracy.

Interestingly, the poem also draws a favorable comparison between Prince Christopher and Caesar, which also happens to be the name Oroonoko is given in Surinam:

> Well did Great *Cæsar* know,
>
> His Grandeur and Magnificence
>
> To New-found Worlds He cou'd not shew
>
> So greatly to His Fame, as now. (ll. 36–39)

Both men are positively linked to the figure of a leader who usurped Rome's republican principles in favor of what would become an imperial system. Given the royalist politics of both poem and novel, it becomes difficult not to associate *Caesar*'s conflicts with and assassination by members of the Senate with the Stuarts' contentions and bloody dealings with Parliament. In both cases, it is clear with whom Behn's texts political align.

The critique the novel makes is not against colonization and slavery, but against their mismanagement. Behn's text was written before the abolitionist movement truly gained momentum. In 1688, the main debate at hand was over monarchial rights and representative government. After the collapse of the Commonwealth and Protectorate, Charles II restored the monarchy in 1660 and attempted to balance the preservation of his divine authority as king with keeping the parliament and populace satisfied. Fearing a return to Catholicism as the national religion, Parliament attempted to pass a bill forbidding any Catholic from succeeding to the throne, which would have prevented his openly Catholic brother, James II, from becoming king, but Charles blocked this. Upon Charles's death in 1685, however, James, like their father, chose to rule without Parliament and to promote the Roman Catholic religion.

Behn's pro-Stuart stance comes out in much of her work, often timed to counter criticisms launched by political detractors of the throne. Her earlier work, *Love-Letters Between a Nobleman and his Sister* (1684, 1685, 1687), for example, is largely a critique of attacks on the Stuarts, especially those who opposed James II as his brother's successor. In this narrative, Philander's (modeled after Monmouth supporter Lord Grey of Werke) betrayal of his wife through his legally incestuous affair with his sister-in-law, Sylvia, parallels his betrayal of his king when he joins the ranks of the rebellious Prince Cesario. In the logic of the narrative, to betray one's monarch is as unnatural a crime as bedding one's sister.

Behn's *Oroonoko* should be seen as another in a long list of examples in which Behn uses her work to voice an overtly political stance. As Janet Todd points out in *The Critical Fortunes of Aphra Behn*, Behn's support of the crown was not simply a matter of following popular opinion: Stuart support reached its nadir when James's second wife became pregnant, since if a son was born the crown would pass to a Catholic king rather than to Mary, his Protestant daughter from his first marriage. Behn's poem celebrating the Queen's pregnancy not only eagerly anticipates the birth of a future Stuart prince, she is so insistent on her support and adamant that others make similar declarations, even other Royalists felt it was inappropriate:

A court poet, John Baber, thought that a remark—in her poem [on the queen's pregnancy]—that very few poets were writing loyal verses was aimed in part at him, and he countered with an attack on her when he finally did produce his royal poem at the time of the actual birth of a boy.[10]

By the time Behn wrote *Oroonoko*, James's rule was severely threatened. I argue that Behn used the story of a royal slave to contest what she viewed as a barbarous representative government that threatened the noble race of divinely appointed kings.

Behn introduces Oroonoko as set apart from the other slaves of Surinam, in fact apart from the majority of humanity, in order to make an argument for the divine rights of kings based on the universal rights of nobles found in romance. In order to link an African character to the nobles of romance, the novel must provide narrative cues to its readers that present its hero as civilized; to accomplish this, the African kingdom of Coramantien is distanced from what English readers perceived as the undeveloped, savagery of pagan Africa and is drawn closer to the North African, Islamic culture found in medieval romances.

Behn's narrative opens with an argument for her hero's worthiness as a noble from a culture its readers would recognize as civilized. Like the heroes of romance, Oroonoko's story needs to be recorded because aristocrats are the proper subjects of history: Oroonoko is, to her, "deserving an immortal Fame." In the narrative's preface, Behn addresses fellow Stuart supporter Lord Maitland and aligns the threat to the current English king with the unfortunate royal slave. First, she refers to the current political state in England in her praise of Maitland for serving his "Religion and Country...[which] both want such Supporters...[with Maitland's] noble Principles of Loyalty and Religion this Nation Sighs for" (35). For Behn, the nation is in a state of crisis and lacks heroes willing to defend country and faith—figures that are abundant in romance, especially medieval crusade and grail literature. The present does not, in her eyes, live up to the history offered in romance. Maitland, she contends, could be the figure the "Nation Sighs for," and following this line of thought, she offers this story to him. She presents Oroonoko as "a Man Gallant enough to merit

---

[10] Janet Todd, *The Critical Fortunes of Aphra Behn* (Columbia: Camden House, 1998), 16.

your [Maitland's] Protection" (97) if he had survived. In other words, Oroonoko represents a lost opportunity to defend the institutions she sees threatened—a hint that Maitland should not neglect to act when future opportunities occur. By having her opening letter progress from Maitland's greatness to the threats to England to Oroonoko's situation, Behn frames the narrative within English politics. With this in mind, her use of romance tropes serves to present Oroonoko not as a slave but as a member of a noble race, akin to the Stuarts. Oroonoko lacked an adequate champion to define his position as a king; Behn is urging Maitland and other Stuart supporters not to fail to champion their own embattled James II.

As the divinely appointed kings were threatened by the cry for a more representative form of government, Behn presents Oroonoko as an ideal romance ruler in a less than ideal age. Her choice to place this narrative in the form of a novel rather than a play allows her to include details that clearly place her hero in the romance tradition without producing a conventional romance; this evocation of the past is not emphasized in the plays, which instead incorporate the emerging trend of sentimentalism more and more throughout the century. By the time of Ferriar's 1788 adaptation, the narrative was seen as primarily a sentimental attack on the brutality of the plantation slave system.

Behn aligns Oroonoko with the Stuart kings rather than the common slaves. She accomplishes this by using romance tropes in three ways: first, by establishing him as a romance figure and member of a noble race; second, through his wife Imoinda's passive subjection of herself, representing an ideal body politic; last, by comparing Oroonoko's aptness as a leader with the barbarism of the provisional government. As a Royalist, Behn perceived the loss of the Stuart line as a fall from lawful governance to mob rule. Basing her defense of Oroonoko and his Stuart counterpart in an older model of race found in the romance tradition, she critiques what she sees as an unfeeling, unrefined, and unfit new government.

Within the larger context of the genre, romance provides an ideal vehicle for *Oroonoko* to advocate the rights of the aristocracy. Drawing on a tradition that goes back to Ancient Greece and Rome, the romance genre in England originates in twelfth-century translations of Latin epics and histories into French. Roberta L. Krueger describes these early texts as "tales of love and adventures" told by clerks "to aristocratic audiences in the francophone circles of England and

France."[11] These texts were part of a transcultural literary movement that crossed geographical and linguistic boundaries: "As early as the 1170s, the taste for Anglo-Norman and French romances migrated... [;] refashioning of matters French soon became a hallmark of elite culture at the great German courts" (4), and Italian and Spanish territories also adopted the genre. Contrasting the theories of novels that present romance as a homogenized genre, "no single social agenda pervades European romance" (4). Rather than "a panel for the advertisement of social ideals," Krueger makes the case that romances act "as a forum for the construction and contestation of social identities and values" (5). Behn's *Oroonoko* uses this genre to contest the shift in "social identities and values" that occurred during the Stuart dynasty illustrated by the challenges to monarchial authority represented by the Civil Wars, Commonwealth, Exclusion Crisis, and 1688 coup.

The common plot line for many romances closely resembles the *Oroonoko* narrative outlined in the introduction: young lovers, eligible to marry one another, are separated by some misadventure, forced to travel long distances, and sold into slavery, where their lives and chastity are endangered until they are reunited and restored to their rightful social position. These tropes act as a political stance against the changes threatened by the anti-Stuart movement. By placing in an idealized past the right to rule based on the belief in a noble race, the novel conflates James's claim to the throne with a naturalized stability and any challenge to him as a sign of corruption in a deteriorating contemporary moment. The violation of the noble race hierarchy represents in *Oroonoko* a rejection of a better, more orderly past that makes the royal slave's plight lamentable on a larger scale.

From this standpoint, the generic roots of *Oroonoko* should be viewed as a continuation of the romance tradition as much—or even more so—as it is viewed as a starting place for the novel. The romance tradition, when examined separately from the eighteenth-century English novel, emerges as one concerned with unstable national identities and a tradition of social critique. Examining the medieval roots of the romance in the British Isles, Patria Clare Ingham's *Sovereign Fantasies: Arthurian Romance and the Making of Britain* presents romances as reflecting England's initial attempts at colonialism in

---

[11] Roberta L. Krueger, introduction to *The Cambridge Companion to Medieval Romance*, ed. Roberta L. Krueger (Cambridge: Cambridge University Press, 2000), 2.

Wales and its often adversarial (yet linguistically, politically, and culturally intertwined) relations with France, as well as its history as a colony of an old Mediterranean empire, Rome. Romances, she argues, are often tales of the disunity and fragmentation of cultural identity: "when romance stories of King Arthur narrate the mutability, failures, and infidelities surrounding the sovereign, they raise doubts about an unwavering united British past. Such doubts allude to a contested history of Britain, to other desires and lost dreams."[12] Ingham argues that "medieval community [in its pre-nation-state setting] is imagined not through homogeneous stories of a singular 'people,' but through narratives of sovereignty as negation of differences, of ethnicity, region, language, class, and gender" (9). It was a means not of reflecting an existing sense of cultural unity, but a means for "an increasingly literate public…to learn to desire a unified future by delighting in the imagined glories of a unified past" (17). This lack of unity, although coupled with a desire for a unified future, characterizes the medieval romances that Behn's work employs.

This lack of cultural unity leads to porous boundaries between what are frequently seen as discrete national boundaries today. Medieval romances reflected this reality, allowing their literary descendants a means of promoting a transnational view of humanity as national boundaries became firmer. In *Medieval Boundaries: Rethinking Difference in Old French Literature*, Sharon Kinoshita uses these unstable geographical and cultural boundaries to show "that medieval French speakers [including those in England] had a much greater degree of involvement in and knowledge of the cultures of the Iberian peninsula and the Mediterranean than modern readers generally credit."[13] This fluidity between cultures grants romances an interpretative fluidity as well. Rather than romances simply reflecting the ideology of the nobility, they were capable of "delivering different messages to different audiences"; they could offer satisfying endings to those "fired by an ideology of crusade and conquest" while at the same time "gesture toward another kind of civilizational history—one that replaces…the exclusionary history of discrete national traditions with narratives of deviances and transgression" (104). Romance as a means of an

---

[12] Patricia Clare Ingham, *Sovereign Fantasies: Arthurian romance and the making of Britain* (Philadelphia: University of Pennsylvania Press, 2001), 3.

[13] Sharon Kinoshita, *Medieval Boundaries: Rethinking Difference in Old French Literature* (Philadelphia: University of Pennsylvania Press, 2006), 3.

alternative narrative of "deviances and transgressions" becomes an important factor in viewing it as a form of social critique, as I believe it is in *Oroonoko*.

Behn's narrative emphasizes the cultural sophistication of Oroonoko's kingdom by interweaving Islamic imagery throughout, creating a cultural equality between the protagonist and the Europeans of Surinam. Rather than belonging to the simple, innocent lifestyle of Surinam's native Caribs, the royal slave comes from a sophisticated culture aligned with Muslim culture. Behn separates the Caribs from her view of contemporary European politics by aligning them with animals and pre-civilization humans. The description of the native headdress Behn acquired in Surinam follows a listing of Surinam's wildlife (39); by ending this passage with the image of natives covered in feathers, the boundary between dress and wearer blurs. These passive natives become bird-like when tied to the romance imagery that follows, making them into tractable, idealized subjects. Their innocence is a means for the narrator to separate them from the European settlers and align them with the naturalistic descriptions preceding them. They resemble Adam and Eve because of their lack of shame regarding their nakedness, continuing the casual linking of them with animals that also feel no need for clothing.

Whereas the natives are compared to Adam and Eve, innocent and without hierarchy or need for the rule of law, Oroonoko's native Coramantien represents an oriental civilization comparable to any in England. In his African kingdom filled with battles and court intrigues, Oroonoko is captured while inspecting a slave ship he helped to stock. Like a European monarch, the prince faces dangers not only to his person but also to his power to govern. Other elements such as the king's harem, citrus groves, and Persian terms such as 'Otan' mark Coramantien as possessing a history intertwined with Europe's; it depicts this land as a developed nation, leaning on the Orientalist notions of a highly cultured, even decadent world outside Europe. By creating a version of an African kingdom with Islamic overtones, the text separates Oroonoko from other African slaves and inserts him into nostalgia for romantic tropes of nobility.

By drawing the romance model of a race of nobles that transcends geographic and religious differences, Behn uses romance motifs to turn the story of the enslaved African prince into a critique of anti-Stuart movements. As an era of absolute rule by divine right was giving way to more contractual, democratic institutions, the weakening of the crown also lent itself to a weakening of the aristocracy's claims of innate nobility as the basis of its right to rule. In response, *Oroonoko* presents ideas of race that transcend nations, presenting a noble race that alone can control the barbaric tendencies in all commoners, particularly the English. The title of Royal Slave embodies this notion: Oroonoko's kingship is innate within him, regardless of status, because he comes from a noble race. His position as a king is as immutable as his jet-black skin.

The narrator argues that unlike common slaves, Oroonoko clearly belongs to a different stock by aligning him more with European nobles than with Surinam's Africans, allowing the parallels between his fate and that of the Stuart kings to emerge. He is, for all intents and purposes, a European aristocrat. He behaves "in all Points...as if his Education had been in some *European* Court." The text intertwines this demonstration of his worthiness as ruler with a discussion of England's failure to follow its own kings. It serves two purposes for the Royal Slave to have "heard of the late Civil Wars in *England*, and the deplorable Death of our great Monarch [Charles I]" (43). It shows his intellectual equality to his Western counterparts, setting him up as a true noble, while reminding the reader that the common English mob had rejected their own natural rulers of the House of Stuart. The "late king" becomes a way of describing the Royal Slave as well as foreshadowing Oroonoko's own violent death (30). The text's references to the Civil Wars and the execution of Charles I connect its fears of anarchy in Surinam with the political upheavals leading up to the Restoration.

The desire for an absolute ruler is tied not just to a belief in a noble race but also to seventeenth-century political theories aimed at preventing the chaos and bloodshed of wars. Though Thomas Hobbes did not present sovereigns as racially noble and argued that all men were essentially equal, he advocated absolute rule as the best means of preserving life. During times of war, "every man is Enemy to every man... And the life of man, solitary, poore, nasty, brutish, and short"; to prevent this, a sovereign is appointed, from whom "none of his Subjects, by any pretence or forfeiture, can be freed from his Subjection."[14] The sovereign's actions cannot be deemed unjust nor can he be punished by any subject. All this is "because the End of this

---

[14] Thomas Hobbes, *Leviathan*, 1651 (New York: W.W. Norton, 1997), 70, 97.

Institution [the sovereign], is the Peace and Defense of them all [the Subjects]."[15] The need for a strong sovereign to protect his subjects from themselves is compatible with Behn's depiction of the disintegration of Surinam after the provisional government executes Oroonoko. The African Prince represents the rightful sovereign, whose authority should remain unchallenged, while the provisional government is a common mob unable to correctly rule itself or the colony.

Within the political logic of the narrative, Oroonoko's case is tragic, not because slavery is morally wrong but because his nobility is obvious and should make him untouchable. When an English captain captures Oroonoko, the narrative presents his own enslavement as different from the masses of slaves he had sold to this slave trader. Instead, the past slave dealings demonstrate a bond of trust that the captain is criticized for violating. He is ungrateful "for the Favour and Esteem" Oroonoko has shown him. The captain's duplicity is shown by the difference between his outward and inward appearances: "the Captain seem'd to take as a very great Honour" all the luxuries and attention the prince gave him, but internally he plotted to enslave his host. The narrator sarcastically comments that "Some have commended this Act, as brave, in the Captain," while her emphasis on the trust Oroonoko placed in him shows the event to be treacherous and cowardly, as the Captain made sure to separate the prince from his companions and get him drunk. In addition, the characters on the ship agree that the act of imprisoning Oroonoko is starkly different from that of the other slaves: unlike the rest of the cargo, Oroonoko is kept under tight security, because "Valour [was] natural to him" as a prince.[16] Implicit is the idea that the other slaves lack this valor and ultimately do not see their enslavement as a great offense. Oroonoko's situation on the ship poses a unique problem because he is naturally a king, not a slave, and lives by a different set of rules.

Further separating him from the slaves, the Royal Slave's body is invested with symbolic value. Like a true romance hero, his nobility is seen in his outward appearance. The European nobility he shows through his education also manifests through his body. Not only does he know Roman history, his "Nose was rising and *Roman*, instead of *African* and flat." While this does point to a tradition of Eurocentric

---

15 Ibid., 98.
16 Behn, *Oroonoko*, 64.

racism that will emerge in later justifications of nineteenth-century colonial rule, this description also serves an alternative purpose of linking him to a literary tradition that extends back to the Classical era. Differentiating him racially from the common slaves that follow him serves to show that he is from a noble race. While his subjects' skins are "of that brown, rusty Black," his is "a perfect Ebony, or polish'd Jett." His ideal of blackness complements European aristocratic ideals of whiteness. The comparison between his skin color and a polished stone objectifies him, making him seem more like the idea of a body than one in reality. This treatment of Oroonoko continues as his idealization comes through his aestheticization. That "the most famous Statuary cou'd not form the Figure of a Man more admirably turn'd from head to Foot" (43) draws attention to his place as an aesthetic object. As an object of art, Oroonoko distinguishes himself as a true ruler. A king is a permanent entity that manifests itself in the bodies of a noble line of men. Oroonoko and the Stuarts' bodies transcend the biological and enter the realm of the symbolic. They are objects that embody the idea of king, encompassing nation, law, and natural rule. As in romance, his outward appearance represents his inward virtues, and as a king he serves as both a man and a divinely appointed symbol. The erasure of Oroonoko's status as a natural sovereign is one of the chief changes made by the stage adaptations; Southerne, Hawkesworth, and Ferriar attempted to make the story more in step with their current political moments.

In Behn's novel, Oroonoko's body transcends the corporeal, creating a connection between vision and truth. A royal body visibly demonstrates its superiority to others through its beauty, and its gaze forces submission from its subjects. His appearance inspires loyalty in the other slaves, his natural subjects. Even without his princely robes, the "Royal Youth appear'd in spight [sic] of the Slave, and People cou'd not help treating him after a different manner, without designing it" (68). Because kingship is understood as an innate racial trait, Oroonoko can never appear as anything other than the noble he is; consequently, common races instinctually respond to him. Keeping with the romance tradition, his very gaze carries power. First, it naturalizes his ability to create order: though bound, he shames the slave ship captain "with a Look all fierce and disdainful, unbraiding him with Eyes, that forc'd Blushes from his guilty Cheeks" (67). His power to pass judgment is defined in bodily terms: the gaze from his noble form forces the captain's body into submission through the power of the blush.

The strength of his gaze attaches his power directly to his body, making his position as a monarch a natural part of him.

His relationship with Imoinda further establishes his position as a romance hero. His gaze plays on the sensibility of romance, in which the feelings of the noble race are refined to such an extent that they can communicate their heart without the mediation of language. His ability to tell Imoinda he loves her through his eyes with "that silent Language of new-born Love" (45) demonstrates how his nobility manifests itself on his body. What he is (including how he feels) is visible to all. This trait directly contrasts with the duplicity of ignoble characters such as the English captain and, later, the provisional government. His love, like his nobility, defines him and is integrated into his entire being. Neither Oroonoko, nor any other king, can cease being noble and therefore, even if betrayed by foreign or domestic factions, his rightful place as a ruler cannot be challenged.

Behn's use of the concepts of noble races and divine right carries the implication that enslavement is the natural state of those without the authority of rank. The idea of nobles and commoners extends into a more intricate alignment of power. While all nobles share certain traits and rights, they are not equal in practice. A king commanded the loyalty of lesser nobles, just as medieval knights ideally obey their monarchs. This chain of being is further nuanced by differences between the sexes, with women subordinated to the men of their class, such as their husbands and male guardians. Behn complements her notion of the perfect king with the ideal subject—one that cannot rebel.

The initial love triangle between Oroonoko, his grandfather, and Imoinda creates a parallel system by which to judge the provisional government. The conflict takes place within and ideally should be resolved by the old system of kingship where the monarch stands in for the divine. As in romance narratives, Imoinda owes her complete loyalty to the monarch. When Oroonoko's grandfather sends her the Royal Veil signaling her induction into the old man's harem, she goes instantly, despite her secret marriage to the young prince, because "Delays in these Cases are dangerous, and Pleading worse than Treason." After obeying this decree, her attempts to avoid violating her marriage vows by entering the harem emphasize her position as a subject: "she believ'd she shou'd be the Occasion of making him commit a great Sin, if she did not reveal her State and Condition, and tell him, she was anothers, and cou'd not be happy to be his" (47).

Within her argument, the king's needs remain central and Imoinda remains passive: she is not a person, but an 'Occasion' or circumstance that could cause the king to commit a harmful act. Also, her own desire is supplanted: that she "cou'd not be happy to be his" does not refer to her own preference in men, but to her belief that, if she was not already owned, she would obediently become his property. However, youth and virility are privileged over old age, so once the king cannot exert his power—conjugal rights—over Imoinda, he has lost his authority as a king.[17] In this story, Imoinda remains a passive test of kingship: in his failure to rule her sexually the king loses his right to rule, and ideally Oroonoko should take his rightful place as king and husband. Like the power of Surinam's provisional government, the king's continued insistence on his right to Imoinda—therefore to the throne—signals a break in the natural order of rule.

This attitude continues in Surinam, as she is the 'Occasion' that prompts Oroonoko's rebellion without being an active agent. The sight of her crying over their unborn child's future slavery inspires Oroonoko to act on her behalf; however, Imoinda never directly tells him to rebel nor does she initiate any acts of rebellion. Her potential as a source of an anti-slavery or anti-colonial critique is hindered by her focus on only the captivity of her family, not the general condition of slavery. Her position is further undermined by the failure of the rebellion Oroonoko leads because of her passive urgings. Taking it a step further, by listening to his wife instead of the narrator, Oroonoko enters a politically limited role: by siding with the common slaves against the Europeans, he loses his ability to negotiate for the freedom of his family alone. The provisional government, initially wary of his authority, gains the evidence they need to show he holds too much influence over the other slaves. His death becomes due to his misplaced alliance with the common slaves instead of the more noble members of the colony. In this way, the possibility of an anti-slavery position for Imoinda becomes Oroonoko's downfall.

---

[17] This pattern of youthful virility rightfully supplanting the authoritarian claims of men past their prime can be seen throughout romances such as the Lais of Marie de France, as well as Renaissance texts such as Geoffrey Chaucer's *Canterbury Tales* and Giovanni Boccaccio's *Decameròn*. Another prominent example is Solomon's ascension to the throne when his father, David, can no longer perform sexually (1 Kings 1:1–4).

Instead of acting as a space of resistance to the colonial plantocracy, Imoinda functions on the whole more as a model for subjecthood. Her valor in battle and willing acceptance of death reinforce her idealized subjection to her husband. When the common slaves abandon the battle, she and one other slave stay with him out of their devotion to their leader. Her refusal to abandon her husband can be connected to Behn's preface expressing the need for people not to turn against the natural rulers of England—the Stuart kings and the Roman Catholic Church. In the end, when Imoinda faces slavery and rape, her death continues her pattern of obedience to her lord and husband. While she accepts the impossibility of their situation and desires death, she does not possess the agency either to kill herself or to initiate the subject with Oroonoko, two acts of which, in the stage versions, she will be capable. Instead, she waits until he informs "her his Design first of Killing her, and then his Enemies, and next himself";[18] her eager acceptance where she is "faster pleading for Death than he was to propose it" implies that this is not a new thought to her, but that she has patiently waited for him to address the situation and that she obeys him instantaneously. Without him, her husband and ruler, Imoinda argues, she would be unprotected against his enemies, since she is not able to act in her own defense.

As her husband-king, Oroonoko not only decides her fate, but since she is his subject, she is also his property and must be defended. The idea of husbands acting as kings and kings acting as divine representatives is mirrored in her joyful acceptance that he will kill her: "while Tears trickl'd down his Cheeks, hers were Smiling with Joy she shou'd dye by so noble a Hand...for Wives have a respect for their Husbands equal to what other People pay to a Deity."[19] As his subject, she cannot exist without his rule, so she gladly welcomes death. By investing him with a godlike authority, Behn presents Oroonoko as more than a husband—rather a divinely appointed ruler. While she does become the 'Occasion' that leads to his expulsion from Coramantien and his alliance with the common slaves, Imoinda also offers a model of ideal subjecthood in the novel's defense of the Stuarts. Together, she and Oroonoko embody a vision of society where divine right and absolute rule are answered by unquestioning loyalty and obedience.

---

[18] Behn, *Oroonoko*, 95.
[19] Ibid., 95.

The colonial situation in Surinam represents a threat to the natural order of rule established in Coramantien. The problems of the African court scenes can be rectified within the system. Following the format of the romance, Oroonoko remains the rightful heir to the throne even if he must await his grandfather's death. The provisional government thwarts this destiny in two ways. First, it literally prevents him from returning, as it is assumed the royally appointed Governor would have restored his liberty instead of executing him. Second, it menaces the system of noble rule in general by placing commoners in power over the colony. The corruption of the Coramantien throne is due only to an old king outliving his usefulness as a bodily representation of the state; the provisional government poses the possibility of entirely over-turning the system of nobles ruling by divine right.

Behn voices her opposition to this possibility by repeatedly con-trasting Oroonoko's natural aptitude as a leader in Surinam against the barbarism and corruption of the provisional government. Like the stability imagined in the arrival of the Surinam Governor, Oroo-noko represents the possibility for lawful rule that is thwarted by an unnatural and barbaric mob. Lord Willoughby, the crown-appointed Governor, dies in a violent hurricane; Oroonoko falls to an equally violent force, populist politics. In the 'natural' hierarchy, the com-moners see the aestheticization of their noble ruler's body as a right of the crown's power; in this vision of colonial tragedy, the unruly mob governing Surinam sees only its monetary and not its symbolic value. Since power is justified by the need for a noble race to control the common masses, the provisional government in Surinam repre-sents a rejection of law and order in favor of uncontrolled mob rule. In Elliot Visconsi's reading of *Oroonoko*, the text illustrates Behn's position that the English revolutions give evidence "of a barbarous national character [among the commoners] which prefers violence and personal independence to the mercy and moral prudence of a moral government."[20] The members of the governing council embody the barbaric elements, which need to be suppressed through the rule of the noble Norman race. The council's unfitness is shown through its members: it consists "of such notorious Villains as *Newgate* never transported and possibly originally were such, who understood neither

---

[20] Visconsi, "A Degenerate Race" (2002), 673.

the Laws of *God* or *Man*".[21] These men do not represent order, but are the criminals that undermine it. Comparing them to criminals also highlights the unlawfulness of their rule. Visconsi's argument that Behn sees the general populace as uncivilized becomes explicit in reference to her description of Banister, the council member sent out to capture Oroonoko: he is "a wild *Irish* Man, and one of the council; a Fellow of absolute Barbarity, and fit to execute any Villainy."[22] Epitomizing the text's idea of a barbarous common race, Banister's position as Irishman and villain become interchangeable signs of his unfitness to hold power. Instead of virtue, the council practices vice, and they may flourish in a culture that values the wealth of a common colonist over the noble birth of a true king. For Behn, those who call for a more representative government and the removal or limitation of the monarchy are arguing for "the ignorant democratic tyranny of the common people."[23]

As the text plays itself out, Surinam—like England—engages in a power struggle between nobles and commoners. In the absence of the royally appointed Governor of the colony, the barbarism kept down by noble rule emerges and seizes control. Whether he leads a slave rebellion or brokers peace between the Caribs and colonists, Oroonoko's natural ability to rule contrasts to the bloodthirsty policies of Surinam's governing council. In the text, they are unfit to rule because they lack the qualities found in the noble races. They are as duplicitous as the English ship captain who captures Oroonoko: the provisional Governor offers pardon in exchange for surrender, and then withdraws it, instead choosing to torture the rebel leader, Oroonoko. Behn contrasts the non-appointed government with the noble Oroonoko by showing the latter's ability to pass judgment, even when denied the power to punish: Oroonoko

> was not perceiv'd to make any Mone [sic], or alter his Face, only to roul his Eyes on the Faithless *Governor*, and those he believ'd Guilty...he pronounced a Woe and Revenge from his Eyes, that darted Fire, that 'twas at once both Awful and Terrible to behold. (91)

Like his arrival in Surinam where his gaze caused the guilty to blush, Oroonoko maintains his position of authority even while being

---

[21] Behn, *Oroonoko*, 93.
[22] Ibid., 99.
[23] Visconsi, "A Degenerate Race," 676.

punished. His moral superiority also serves to condemn the behavior of the Christian settlers. In Behn's novel, this points to the anti-Stuart movement's threat to both James II and his Catholic faith. Just as the provisional government refuses to recognize Oroonoko's innate superiority, so also do they abandon the Christian values of honesty, integrity, and obedience. The inability to suppress the outward signs of guilt shown by the blush underlines the provisional Governor's untrustworthiness as a leader: the king's word is law, but this man's word cannot be relied upon. Whereas Oroonoko had helped bring order to the colony before the rebellion, the mismanagement of the provisional government leads to a slave revolt, an execution, and eventually such disarray that the colony is lost to the Dutch in 1667.

In his stage adaptation, Thomas Southerne would expand on this theme in another way: the unchristian behavior of the antagonists heightens the tragic heroism of Oroonoko as well as the moral worth of the Welldon sisters, who represent the new colonial order at the end of the play. The theme of pagan honor against Christian hypocrisy would endure and help incorporate later abolitionist readings that sought to condemn slavery on religious grounds. The political agenda of Behn's novel consists of defending the monarchial rights of James II by turning toward the literary past. Her use of tropes from romances, especially the medieval representations of Islam, not only allows the African prince Oroonoko to become interchangeable with the Stuart kings but also reinforces an older model of race that divides people by rank. By extension, the belief in a noble race innately fit to rule justifies the ideology of colonialism. The failure of Surinam is due to the wrong race of people holding power. Under a natural king such as Oroonoko or James II, the text argues, national and colonial holdings would not be lost to foreign interests.

The stage adaptations of the text, however, show a different ideological bent. As the next section shows, Behn's use of romance, her evocation of an Ottoman empire, and her royalist politics would gradually be effaced during the eighteenth century. Changes in England's government and its expanding empire altered its self-image in transnational politics. This is illustrated by the changes in the adaptations as its depictions of Africa move from that of an Ottoman-like power to a site of European exploitation. Through these changes, Oroonoko transforms from an equal—if not superior—oriental prince standing in for monarchial power to a representation of universal manhood that serves to critique African slavery.

Oroonoko after Behn

Because she died in April 1689, Aphra Behn did not face any repercussions for her political actions when James II was ousted in 1688 and replaced in 1689 by the joint rule of his Protestant daughter Mary and Holland's William of Orange. The acceptance of Parliament's Declaration of Rights (later the Bill of Rights), designed to ensure Parliament could function free from royal interference, represented a radical shift from the idea of divine right or a noble race.[24] Ostensibly, this new government was designed around the protection of individual liberties regardless of rank. One of the major proponents of this new constitutional monarchy, John Locke, argued in his *Two Treatises of Government* directly against the divine authority of kings.[25] Locke holds that an individual (if he is a property-owning European male) possesses the right to protect his life, liberty, and property; if these rights were violated, these free subjects would be justified in dissolving the government in power.

This shift presented all men as essentially equal, no longer divided between nobles and commoners. This idea of universal humanity (though still defined as European men) would become one of the major tenets of the Enlightenment in the eighteenth century. However, though Locke considered the loss of these rights to be slavery and the worst state for man, he also participated in the Royal Africa Company and did not see the enslavement of Africans as contradictory to his political arguments. Servants are divided into two categories: those such as he who "gives the Master but a Temporary Power

---

[24] This bill limited the Sovereign's power; reaffirmed Parliament's control of taxation and legislation; provided guarantees against the abuses of power the Stuart Kings had committed; excluded James II, his heirs, and all Catholics from the throne; required the Sovereign to swear to maintain the Protestant religion; forbade the Sovereign from suspending or dispensing with laws passed by Parliament; insisted that the Sovereign summon Parliament frequently; allowed Parliament to further control the King's spending; and, lastly, forbade the King from keeping a standing army in peacetime without the consent of Parliament. It did, however, allow the Sovereign to keep the right to summon and dissolve Parliament, appoint and dismiss Ministers, veto legislation, and declare war (http://www.royal.gov.uk).

[25] Though published anonymously in 1690, there is some debate over whether this text was written prior to 1688, calling for revolution, or afterwards, to justify the coup. I favor Peter Laslett's argument that given the number of texts Locke published after the coup, it is unlikely that he researched, wrote, and drafted all of them prior to his return to England. See Laslett's introduction to *Two Treatises of Government* (New York: The New American Library, 1960), 59.

over him…no greater than is contained in the Contract between 'em"
in exchange for wages and those "which by a particular name we call
Slaves…[who] by Right of Nature subjected to the Absolute Dominion and Arbitrary Power of their Masters."[26] Their loss of liberty is
justified because they are "not escapable of any Property, [and] cannot by the state be considered as any part of *Civil Society*."[27] In other
words, membership in a free society requires the ability to own property; those who cannot accomplish this—unable to gain the status of
free subjects—become the commodities of those who can.

A slave then functions as a means of increasing the state's wealth: he
is the property of freemen. Within this context, *Oroonoko* re-emerges
on the post-1688 English stage as neither a defense of absolute monarchy nor a condemnation of slavery, but as a portrayal of an unjust
reversal of fortunes for a free property-owning subject. The universalism of the romance racial model that linked a noble Oriental Africa
to Europe is supplanted by a different but still limited view of universal manhood: rather than linking Oroonoko to the Stuart kings
through romance, playwright Thomas Southerne connects the hero to
the property-owning citizens behind the 1688 coup, transforming the
Royal Slave into the enslaved property owner in need of liberation
from a corrupt government.

Southerne offered the first stage adaptation of Behn's *Oroonoko*
in 1696, and it reflected the changes brought about by the Revolution. Behn's pro-monarchy message lent itself to a pro-slavery position: nobles naturally ruled and commoners naturally belonged to the
nobles, a hierarchy that included kings and subjects, husbands and
wives, plantation owners and slaves. After the fall of James II, this
political message needed to be subdued. Southerne removed the pro-
monarchy aspects of the story—his Oroonoko views himself more as
part of a universal humanity, while still maintaining his noble heritage. Just as the Revolution's leading apologist, Locke, condemned
the enslavement of freemen but endorsed African enslavement, the
play treats slavery as both a reality and an abstract concept. Slavery

---

[26] John Locke, *Two Treatises of Government* (1688), ed. Peter Laslett (New York:
The New American Library, 1963), 365.
    Within the *Two Treatises of Government*, 'slave' does not refer exclusively to the
African slave trade, but can be applied both to it and to some of the poorer laboring
classes of England.
    [27] Ibid., 366.

is deemed immoral when it involves those the text views as free sub-jects, such as Oroonoko and Southerne's additions, the Welldon sis-ters. This adaptation generalizes slavery into an ambiguous condition affecting women and lovers in a more negative way than it does com-mon African slaves. However, by removing the pro-monarchy stance that justified slavery in Behn, Southerne set the groundwork for the increasingly abolitionist reading that future adaptations provided as the eighteenth century progressed.

In explaining his motivations for adapting the narrative, South-erne praised Behn as a writer and remained mute on her politics: "She had a great Command of the Stage; and I have often wonder'd that she would bury her Favourite Hero in a *Novel*, when she might have reviv'd him in the *Scene*."[28] However, Behn's choice of the novel facilitates her Tory message. The unspoken power his royal body con-veys, for example, becomes obscured in a stage adaptation: his fierce gaze, finely etched jet-black skin, roman nose, and their significance become lost when transferred to a white actor in blackface. The Euro-peanization would be there but in a different way. In place of Behn's black man who naturally lends himself to artificial values, the audience would be more aware of the artifice. For the plays, it would not be that the character had a roman nose but that the white actor playing him did. One could argue that blackface would draw more attention to the hero's racial difference, since the man portraying him must resort to burnt cork to bridge the gap between English and African.

Mediation through stage directions and dialogue is needed to convey these elements. Oroonoko must now explain the connection between his appearance and the reactions of his captors. Responding to the honest planter Blanford—Trefry's counterpart in the play—who had questioned why the other planters stare at the prince, he declares: "Let 'em stare on. / . . . let the guilty blush" (I.ii.240–242). In the novel, the unspoken authority is part of the racial ideology where authority is visible on the body; in the play, the need for this speech shifts the scene's emphasis from Oroonoko's body to the planters' actions. Their guilty blush comes from their knowledge of their own immorality, a fault originating not from their rank as commoners but from their inhumanity toward their fellow man.

---

[28] Thomas Southerne, *Oroonoko* (Lincoln: University of Nebraska Press, 1976), 2–3.

With its universalistic leanings, Southerne's play does not present the prince's enslavement as wrong because of his royalty but because it has deprived him of his natural liberty as a property owner. Without critiquing the colonial system as a whole, this Oroonoko repudiates many of his noble rights in favor of a less hierarchical view of the world. For example, Behn chooses for Oroonoko to express surprise that a common slave could incite romantic sensibilities in anyone: "how they came to be so Unhappy, as to be all Undone for one fair *Slave*?" (70). In the Southerne version, however, Oroonoko argues that noble virtues can exist in anyone regardless of rank: "What though she be a slave, / She may deserve him [the Lieutenant Governor]" (II.ii.124–125). Here, worthiness and respect are based on the individual and not on her position in society. By presenting individual slaves with the potential to carry laudable traits, Southerne takes the story of Oroonoko away from its pro-monarchy roots toward an idea of humanity not naturally divided into aristocrats and commoners.

Critical treatments of the play versions of the novel focus primarily on the first adaptation by Thomas Southerne. Reflecting the concern with intersections of race and gender in the novel's scholarship, analytical work done on this first stage adaptation frequently focuses on Southerne's choice to present Imoinda as a white European instead of African. Jennifer Elmore interprets the heroine's color change as a sign of her sentimentalization and domestication in order to prompt audience sympathy both with Imoinda herself and with what Elmore reads as an abolitionist agenda in this first play version. This shift, she argues, represents a silencing of black women in the British public. Joseph Roach incorporates the first stage version into his reading of performativity across the Atlantic world, citing it as a "disclosure of how these distinctively circum-Atlantic relationships—reproduction and abundance, surrogation and memory, miscegenation and violence—emerge out of the performance of Behn's narrative through the staging of Southerne's dramatic adaptation."[29] For him, the staging of the play allows these issues to emerge out of Behn's original plot in a way unavailable to the novel. Felicity Nussbaum also focuses on the blanching of Imoinda, linking it to the disappearance of the narrator and the emergence of the comic plot's female characters. Combined, she argues, these changes point to the play's desire to rein in women

---

[29] Roach, *Cities of the Dead*, 154.

in general, and in particular the changes are interpreted as a mode of chastising Behn for the independence she displayed throughout her life. While drawing on this scholarship, I take the position that the changes made by the early stage production points to wider transnational implications. The changes reflect England's growing position as an imperial power that no longer needed to imitate or fear more established empires, such as the Ottoman.

Southerne begins to distance the story of Oroonoko from its original author in his Prologue, which looks at conflicts between governments, not classes. Replacing Behn's prefatory remarks on the threats to Stuart power, Southerne places emphasis on the recent conflict between England and France. The internal struggle of the past is projected onto an external one. Southerne further deflects from the previous text's political concerns by turning the war into an allegory for the much more mundane competition between theaters, referring to their vying for audience patronage as "hostile times [between] two neighboring states."[30] The Civil War and multiple dethronements of kings over the past sixty years are replaced by the image of a unified country whose only domestic problems are the surplus of single women found in the new comic plot line.

Continuing this pattern of removing Behn from the story, her narrator persona is replaced by the comic plot's husband-hunting English women. The Welldon sisters and the Widow Lackitt are all outspoken women eventually subdued by marriage. Instead of beginning the narrative in Behn's Moorish kingdom, Southerne opens his play on a ship as Lucy Welldon asks her cross-dressed sister Charlotte, "What will this come to? What can it end in? You have/persuaded me to leave dear England, and dearer London, / the place of the world most worth living in, to follow you a-husband-hunting into America" (I.i.1–4). By beginning with their plot and not introducing Oroonoko until the end of the first act, Southerne radically shifts the story away from Behn's preoccupation with maintaining hierarchical order. Without depicting the African episodes, the play is no longer about an older order, represented by the romanticized Coramantien, with a new one, represented by the provisional government of Surinam.[31] Instead, the two principal

---

[30] Southerne, *Oroonoko*, 1.
[31] In fact, Coramantien is replaced with Angola as Oroonoko's country of origin and the court intrigues are mentioned only briefly in a dialogue to set up Imoinda's introduction into the plot.

places become England as center of all civilization and Surinam as a green space like Shakespeare's forest in *A Midsummer's Night Dream*, where the plot's disorder eventually leads to a new, better organization. At the end of the play, Oroonoko's death is presented as unfortunate but due in part to his own complicity as a slave trader; the women, on the other hand, are "all agreed and all provided for" (V.i.159–160). They represent a new, better order that emerges for Surinam out of the disordered inversions of the play.

The comic narrative adds a positive foil to each of the Royal Slave's predicaments: while reflecting many of Oroonoko's experiences, the women emerge unscathed due to their ability to function in the inverted world of Surinam. For instance, both experience an inversion of circumstances as they arrive on ships as commodities. Oroonoko has been transformed from a slave-trading noble to a chattel slave; the need for a husband has transformed the women into commodities "like the rich silks; they are out of fashion a great while/ before they wear out" (I.i.24–25). To increase their value on the marriage market, they travel to a place where they are not in surplus like London; in Surinam, their labor is needed, so England sends these "decaying beauties/ for breeders into the country to make room for new/ faces to appear" (I.i.44–46). The fates of the Welldons and Oroonoko continue running parallel to one another as they simultaneously reject the slave ship captain and the planters' involvement in the slave trade as immoral (I.ii.188–206); both find a means to undo the inversions that run through both plots.

By killing himself and the Lieutenant Governor, Oroonoko sets aright his contradictory position as both royal and slave, property owner turned property. As a prisoner after the revolt, Oroonoko has not yet re-entered his state of slavery. Finding him in chains as punishment, his English allies free him and from then until the end of the play Oroonoko does not possess a set position in society. He is no longer a rebel leader, nor is he a slave. A man free of any social contract, he enters what Locke refers to as a State of War. Earlier he awaited the civil arbitration that the true Governor would bring, but now he acts on his natural right to kill those who wish to deprive him of his freedom. According to Locke, "he that makes an *attempt to enslave* me, thereby puts himself in a State of War with me," making it "Lawful...[to] kill him if I can."[32] Through violence at the play's end,

---

[32] Locke, *Two Treatises*, 17.15–16, 18.10, 18.16.

Oroonoko avoids his own re-enslavement and avenges the government's abuses of power by killing the Lieutenant Governor and then himself. As he dies, he expresses his satisfaction with this resolution, judging that it "'Tis as it should be now" (V.v.302). He has defended himself not as a king, but as a free man.

Whereas Behn presents Oroonoko's death as the fault of a barbarous provisional government, Southerne's message becomes more ambiguous. That Oroonoko dies free in order to preserve his freedom is clear, but the play suggests the possibility of his demise being, if not a result of, at least ironically linked to, his involvement in the slave trade. Instead of passive slaves needing him to incite them, Oroonoko's own his former slave turned companion, Aboan, challenges pro-slavery views. Responding to the prince's justification of slavery as "an honest way of trade" where the "load [is] so light, so little to be felt" (III.ii.110, 116), Aboan must educate him about the "bloody Cruelties" of slavery (III.ii.124) and remind him that even though Blanford did not treat him like a slave, his children would still legally be slaves. Oroonoko's own complicity in the cruelties of Surinam makes his death a necessary resolution to the play. His unjust enslavement is avenged by his killing the Lieutenant Governor, while his past as a royal slave trader is atoned for by his suicide. This is the reading future adaptations would highlight as England's plantation holdings lost public favor. For Southerne, it is the inversion of roles carried over from Behn that places Oroonoko's enslavement in a special category. By retaining the novel's stance that the revolt fails because the other insurgents are naturally slaves,[33] Southerne's play does not take a stance against either slavery or the colonial system.

Continuing the theme of restoring order to inverted roles, the highly independent women from the comic plot are reinscribed into the traditional social order through marriage without critiquing the social order they briefly rebel against. Successfully arranging marriages for the female characters, including herself,[34] Charlotte puts away her breeches and independence in favor of petticoats and subordination.

---

[33] "To think I could design to make those free/ Who were by nature slaves—wretches designed/ To be their masters' dogs and lick their feet" (IV.ii.60–62).

[34] To accomplish this, a cross-dressed Charlotte woos and marries the widow. On the wedding night, our heroine takes a page from Shakespeare's *As You Like It*, and the less genteel widow is tricked into marrying her appropriate spouse when another character takes Charlotte's place. By the time all is revealed, Charlotte has gained a husband for a sister, and a sizable amount of the widow's money; out of fear of social

She changes from Stanmore's "old friend in breeches that was and now your humble servant in petticoats" (V.i.44–45). While the phrase "your humble servant" was a common form of address even between social equals, in this context it serves to underscore how Charlotte willingly gives up the freedom she has enjoyed throughout the play in favor of a heteronormative ending. In *The Limits of the Human*, Felicity A. Nussbaum sees this reining in of women as a potential critique of Behn for her own independence: "In the final act Charlotte Welldon reveals that Stanmore 'has persuaded me into a woman again' (V.i). Charlotte, once an 'arrant woman' like Behn (V.i), rejoins the feminine sphere by dressing in petticoats, promising to marry Stanmore and preserving the play's other romantic relationship by becoming Oroonoko's go-between to Imoinda."[35] Giving up her breeches undermines the potential political critique of her plot. The early acts consist of an inversion of sexual power where Charlotte possesses both economic and marital control. In the last acts, Charlotte no longer performs as the center of her own plot, one that takes up almost half of the play, and subordinates herself to the tragic, male-centered narrative by becoming no more than a barely active supporter of Oroonoko.

Though she intercedes on the royal slave's behalf, Charlotte's plot helps to justify Oroonoko's demise. Both have upset the conventional social order, Oroonoko by his contradictory positions as royal slave/trader and Charlotte Welldon as a cross-dressed woman enjoying male privileges. Oroonoko's multiple inversions of royal turned slave trader turned slave can only be resolved through his death. Charlotte, however, can easily shed her masculine woman persona with a costume change. With her happily married and living near the other now-married women from her plot, the future of Surinam is not bleak. True, Oroonoko's torture and betrayals are condemned, but they are resolved with the Lieutenant Governor's death. The Welldon sisters successfully free themselves from slavery and emerge as worthy managers of colonial property.

The similarities that Southerne creates between their situation on the marriage market and that of the slaves during the Welldons' marriage negotiations reinforces the Lockean disdain for enslaving free subjects

---

censure, the widow repents her initial rejection of a suitor, gives up her stubborn resistance, and submits to him as her lawful husband.

[35] Felicity A. Nussbaum, *The Limits of the Human* (Cambridge: Publisher, 2003), 174.

while downplaying any potential critique of the African slave trade. When the slave ship captain announces that he has "money enough" to purchase Lucy (I.ii.123), Charlotte attempts to distance this transaction from that of the slaves: "This is your market for slaves; my sister is a free woman / and must not be disposed of in public" (126–27). The fact that she must articulate her sister's status as a free woman shows that their whiteness does not preclude them from slavery—an idea reinforced by Southerne's depiction of Imoinda—and that the process of men arranging marriages is a financial exchange of commodities like the African slaves. By Charlotte successfully navigating the marriage market she gives her sister an easily dominated husband and provides herself with a spouse of her own choosing: rather than being sold by male realities, Charlotte's cross-dressing allows her to manipulate the system and emerge owning herself. Planning to remain in Surinam, the couples of the comic plot point to a new future for the colony where princes are not enslaved and the dissolute Lieutenant Governor is no longer in power. Contrasting Behn's bleak image of a Surinam overrun by corruption and eventually lost to the Dutch, Southerne offers a colony purged of its undesirable elements: a violent Governor, Oroonoko, and an element absent in the novel—the interracial marriage between Oroonoko and a now-white Imoinda.

Imoinda as Black Moor Washed White[36]

One of the major changes Southerne makes involves the transformation of Oroonoko's wife Imoinda from the daughter of a fellow Coramantien to that of a French man who immigrated to the African kingdom. While the reason behind this change remains unknown, the play's Imoinda gains a degree of agency that her predecessor lacks, which in turn undermines Behn's idealization of the ruler/subject relationship. In the novel, Imoinda's loyalty to her husband is mediated by her viewing Oroonoko as both her natural ruler and a divine authority; in the play, she acts as the moral center, and she must defend herself when Oroonoko fails to protect her. By positioning her as a moral

---

[36] See Ania Loomba, *Shakespeare, Race, and Colonialism,* 56–57: "There was a long tradition of speculating about the depth of skin colour. In the eleventh of Aesop's *fables,* a man buys an 'Aethiopian slave' and attempts to wash him white, thinking that the dark colour indicates bodily filth."

agent in her own right, Southerne further disassociates the narrative from Behn's noble hierarchy and leads to a Lockean universalism that lends itself to an anti-slavery reading later in the eighteenth century.

This critical change of skin color makes slavery a non-racialized event. At first glance, it seems to remain compatible with the romance tradition of nobles being able to marry across cultural divisions, but the way the play changes her actions moves away from the argument that Behn uses romance to support—the innate right of nobles to rule—by erasing the novel's presentation of their marriage as a symbol of the sovereign-subject relationship. Instead, the new representation of Imoinda lays the foundation for the abolitionist reading that would eventually dominate the narrative. The idea that anyone could be in danger of enslavement would repeatedly emerge as a theme in abolitionist writing such as William Wells Brown's appeal to British anti-slavery groups in his nineteenth-century novel *Clotel*.[37] Joseph Roach argues that this serves to "radically condense the circum-Atlantic crucible of sex and race into an imagined community of the disposed."[38] Imoinda, like her husband and the Welldon sisters, arrives in Surinam as a result of global economic and political concerns. They are all international drifters lacking a nation and reacting to various markets: Imoinda's father as a French-born general in Angola's army, herself as a commodity that can be sold into slavery due to a domestic dispute in her adopted country, Oroonoko as a prince without a throne and slave-trader turned slave, and the Welldon sisters as women traveling to increase their value as potential spouses.

Through Imoinda, slavery ceases to be a matter of European imperialists enslaving Africans, but a cross-cultural condition. She sees herself as "tossed" about the world by "tempestuous fate" (II.iii.149). Regardless of who controls the colony, her condition would remain the same: "Indians or English! / Whoever has me, I am still a slave" (II.iii.150–151). Her ambivalence echoes Southerne's presentation of the concept of slavery as harmful, but separates this from the actual

---

[37] This novel not only carries the theme of the tragic mulatta who, despite her light skin and white ancestry (the heroine, Clotel, is Thomas Jefferson's daughter), cannot escape the evils of slavery. One chapter diverts from the main plots to describe the fate of an enslaved German immigrant, who is treated in the same brutal fashion as the slaves of African descent.

[38] Roach, *Cities of the Dead*, 155.

institution of slavery in the colonies. She, like Oroonoko and the Well-dons, remains a victim of fate and international trade.

As a moral instructor, the Imoinda of the play alters Oroonoko's world view that values martial might, a hallmark of medieval romance. In his relationship with her, Oroonoko comes to dissociate himself from the power he holds as a prince in favor of a relationship based on equality. Before their courtship, Oroonoko initially feels he can lessen Imoinda's grief when her father dies by giving her slaves he captured in battle; however, once they meet, he realizes that she does not want property or a display of dominance and instead needs an interpersonal relationship to deal with her grief. She needs a husband to replace her father. With this, Oroonoko shifts from a vocabulary of power, where military victory and domination of other hold sway, to one that values internal characteristics, such as sympathy: "But when I saw her face/ And heard her speak, I offered up myself" (II.ii.89–90). Where Behn centers their courtship on silent, meaningful gazes, Southerne emphasizes the exchange of ideas in conversation. The two lovers must enter a complementary relationship that functions as a partnership.[39] Imoinda becomes the domestic voice of morality that guides Oroonoko's public actions.

The action in Surinam sees this pattern continue, with Imoinda acting as a moral voice as she insistently rejects the Lieutenant Governor's advances. Not only does she verbally rebuke him, she physically resists him as well: "*She struggles and gets her hand from him*" and when he threatens to rape her—"if you struggle with me, I must take"—she remains defiant—"You may [take something from me], my life, that I can part with freely" (II.iii. 23–24). At this point in the play, Blanford has yet to intervene to protect her as he does in the last act, and Oroonoko is not present to aid her. In her first scenes on stage, Southerne shows her articulate, bodily resistance. That she repeatedly succeeds in avoiding rape highlights her ability to act independently, though, unlike Charlotte, she behaves within the bounds of conventional femininity.

---

[39] This coincides with Locke's analogy of marriage and state: rule "naturally falls to the Man's share, as the abler and stronger. But this reaching but to the things of their common Interest and Property, leaves the Wife in the full and free possession of what by Contract is her peculiar Right, and gives the Husband no more power over her Life, than she has over his" (*Two Treatises*, 364). This relationship is then mirrored in society, with the state protecting the people's "Interest and Property" as long as the social contract remains unviolated.

Her suicide in the final act shows her as Oroonoko's and the audience's moral superior. Southerne picks up on the novel's themes of pagan virtue opposed to Christian vice, and positions Imoinda as a lesson in feminine virtue for the London spectators. While the novel's Imoinda waits for her husband to decide her fate, the play requires her to act for herself when Oroonoko finds he cannot kill her. After his repeated failures to work up the courage to stab her, Imoinda alone masters her emotions and comes to his aid: "Nay then I must assist you. / And since it is the common cause of both, / 'Tis just that both should be employed in it" (V.v.274–76). This changes what, for Behn, was the enactment of monarchial obligation and authority to a scene of mutuality and consent. While the novel certainly does demonstrate Imoinda's desire to die at her husband's hand, the play invests her with much more agency in the act. Instead of awaiting her husband's blow, Imoinda stabs herself by moving Oroonoko's hand that holds the dagger; she emphasizes the mutuality of their marriage by turning her death into a "common cause" for which they should carry equal responsibility. Though her husband and the Epilogue later rewrite Oroonoko as the sole actor, the play positions her as both initiating and completing the act.[40] In place of Behn's image of a docile subject gladly accepting death by her king's hand before the provisional government can execute him, Southerne steps away from this imagery that could evoke the execution of Charles I or the recent coup. Instead their deaths become a double suicide pact: the sentimental notion of two lovers unable to live without each other covers over the novel's now unpopular politics.

Imoinda moves from moral instructor of the characters to moral instructor of the audience. In line with the general trend toward sentimentality that would flourish on the eighteenth-century English stage, the play praises her decision to kill herself as an ideal of wifely devotion, using her to critique the immorality of London women. Describing Imoinda's willingness to die with her husband, a no longer unruly Charlotte denounces the sexual freeness of town ladies:

She wanted some of our town breeding.

Forgive this Indian's fondness of her spouse;

---

[40] "Governor: Who did the bloody deed [killing Imoinda]? / Oroonoko: The deed was mine" (V.v.294–95). Imoinda "thought her husband killed her out of kindness" (Epilogue 23–25). Both instances contradict the actual staging of her death scene.

Their law no Christian liberty allows.

Alas! They make a consequence of their vows!

If virtue in a heathen be a fault,

Then damn the heathen school where she was taught.

She might have learned to cuckold, jilt, and sham

Had Covent Garden been in Surinam. (Epilogue 28–335)

This sarcastic portrayal of 'town breeding' perhaps stands as a general condemnation of the libertinism of the Stuart Restoration; it certainly contradicts the sexuality found in Behn's own plays as well as the reputation she would garner after her death.[41] During her lifetime, she defended herself against charges that her plays were too bawdy. In 1673, she prefaced *The Dutch Lover* with a pre-emptive attack on would-be critics: "if such as these durst profane their Chast [*sic*] ears with hearing it over again, or taking it into their serious Consideration in their Cabinets; they would find nothing that the most innocent Virgins can have cause to blush at."[42] However, charges of indecency in her plays as well as her personal life continued throughout the eighteenth century. Todd points out that her proponents' "effort[s] to give Behn respectability through critical praise and genteel biographical claim tended to fade as the age became increasingly clear about what it thought of the Restoration period, with its anathematized politics and its lewd culture."[43] Ending with Imoinda as a model of feminine chastity not only reflects the play's distancing from Behn's Stuart politics but also the image of Behn as a licentious woman who wrote steamy plays.

Southerne's play deflects attention from the novel's original political ideology by supplanting the romance tropes with the sentimentalism of Oroonoko and Imoinda's marriage and the courtship comedy of the Welldon sisters. Behn's novel ends with the ultimate deterioration of the English colony through Surinam's loss to the Dutch. This final loss connects to her pro-Stuart argument that without the natural king, governments cannot be legitimate or successful. Surinam acts as

---

[41] Once again, Southerne takes a less overtly political, secondary theme from the novel and develops it into a major portion of the play. Behn does use her *Oroonoko* as a platform for feminine modesty that differs from her more bawdy plays.

[42] Qtd. Todd, *Critical Fortunes*, 8.

[43] Ibid., 28.

a warning to her audience about the potential danger of losing England itself due to the rule of a barbaric mob. However, by allowing the tragic plot line to run its course, the Southerne play purges Surinam of its corrupt government, leaving the colony safely in the English hands of Charlotte and her companions. They offer the possibility of a bright future for English interests in the Caribbean.

Oroonoko *in the Eighteenth Century*

Despite the lack of critique on slavery as an institution and its positive portrayal of colonialism, the Southerne play and subsequent adaptations increasingly became read as anti-slavery as the eighteenth century progressed. This changing view, however, was tied not so much to a growing abolitionism within the plays, but to the declining economic and political status of the British West Indies. The 1759 version by John Hawkesworth points to a growing public dislike of the Caribbean holdings, but not necessarily of the slave systems found there. Hawkesworth continues Southerne's trend toward the sentimental by focusing on the tragic elements of the play.[44] Cutting the comic elements and having every character speak in blank verse, this adaptation eliminates Southerne's differentiation between high and low characters as well as increasing the tragic heroism of the story. Despite Southerne's attempt to create a morally centered play, Hawkesworth finds fault mainly with his predecessor's balance of comedic and tragic elements. The women's courtship plot needed to be cut because it

> degraded [Oroonoko and Imoinda's story] by a Connexion with some of the most loose and contemptible [scenes] that have ever disgraced our Language and our Theatre...its Immorality ought to prevent its Exhibition; but as it is connected with the tragic, it is in a still higher Degree preposterous, absurd, and pernicious.[45]

The plot dominated by women comes to represent the corruption of the Restoration. Since Southerne's addition of the breeches plot filled in for the absence of Behn as narrator, this new adaptation's erasure

---

[44] There is also a 1760 Glasgow adaption by Francis Gentleman that though noted I did not perceive as different enough from Hawkesworth's work to merit inclusion.

[45] John Hawkesworth, *Oroonoko, A Tragedy, As it is now Acted at the Theatre-Royal In Drury-Lane. By His Majesty's Servants. By Thomas Southern. With Alterations* (1759), (Cambridge: Chadwyck-Healey, 1994), v.

of all female parts—with the exception of Imoinda and an unnamed woman—points to yet another degree of separation between the Oroonoko legend and its originator. With her libertinism and pro-Stuart politics, Behn becomes an undesirable within her own narrative. Her use of romance and the Oriental gloss she places upon her African kingdom become associated in later adaptations with Restoration decadence and political tyranny. It is not until the romance and Islamic elements are removed that an abolitionist reading—in which Africans are powerless before English colonial slavery—can emerge.

Continuing the shift in focus away from Behn's pro-Stuart rhetoric of divine right and noble races toward a sentimental and potentially abolitionist reading, Hawkesworth credits Southerne the adaptor, not Behn the author, for the popular narrative. Despite his objections to its immoral comic scenes, Hawkesworth presents the earlier play rather than the novel as what will draw the audience to the production: "This Night your tributary Tears we claim, / For Scenes that *Southern* drew; a fav'rite Name!" (Prologue l. 1–2). Even though the play has delighted the previous generations by touching "your [the 1759 audience's] Fathers' Hearts with gen'rous Woe" and teaching "your Mothers' youthful Eyes to flow" (l. 3, 4), Hawkesworth insists that the original play is morally flawed and blames Southerne's comedic courtship scenes on a corrupt era still tainted by Restoration rule that made the playwright "Slave to Custom in a laughing Age" (l. 7). Just as Southerne felt he was correcting Behn's failure to place her protagonist on the stage, Hawkesworth presents himself as a moral corrector who while "[h]e bows with Rev'rence to the hoary Sire: / With honest Zeal, a Father's Shame he veils" (l. 16–17). Part of his addition to the Oroonoko legend is his creation of a new history surrounding its authorship. Rather than acknowledging it was authored by a female playwright famous for her licentious plays, Hawkesworth writes a new patrilineal lineage of the story that ignores the novel and acknowledges only its theatrical versions.

Besides his removal of the comic female voices of the play, Hawkesworth also bolsters the role of the other principal slave characters, *Aboan* and *Hotman*. By emphasizing Aboan's role, this version lessens Oroonoko's uniqueness among his fellow slaves. Whereas in the Southerne version Aboan plays a significant role in convincing his prince to lead the rebellion, the new version introduces him through a soliloquy. It also brings to the forefront a more anti-slavery stance as Aboan relates the anguish of his situation before turning his thoughts toward insurrection: "'Tis all Regret, Oppression, and Despair.—/Yet why Despair!—something may yet be done" (I.iii.5–6). While Southerne does present Aboan as the initiator of the slave revolt, his version does not grant Aboan the interiority of the Hawkesworth. In the 1759 production, the audience witnesses the call to action first in Aboan's musing and rousing of other slaves before he approaches his former ruler. He is presented as possessing just as much intellect and sensibility as Oroonoko. Rather than performing the part of a subject still loyal to the sovereign who sold him into slavery, he emerges more as an equal, disrupting the novel's depiction of a noble sovereign and his naturally subordinate subjects.[46]

Despite these changes, it is unclear that Hawkesworth possessed any more abolitionist sentiment than either Southerne or Behn. The 1759 adaptation still retains Oroonoko's speeches defending the plantation owners' right to buy slaves and his condemnation of the other slaves as fit only for chains. Hawkesworth's removal of the Welldon sisters' success as colonialists points to a cultural environment less enthusiastic about a British presence in that part of the world. At the same time, these audiences appeared more open to seeing the plight of slaves in general, and not just misplaced princes, as appropriately tragic. Hence, characters such as Aboan receive a greater degree of interiority while the comic plots seem out of place.

These changes in the *Oroonoko* narrative correspond to the economic and political shifts occurring in eighteenth-century Britain. After the fall of James II, the idea of the natural right of a noble race and the divine authority of a king lost ground. Without this privileging of nobles as possessing a nearly exclusive hold on virtues, other characters gain more of an inner life. Parliament in actuality ruled while the monarchy acted as a symbol of national power. This government celebrated the equality and liberty of freeborn English men while leaving the slave plantations of the colonies relatively unchallenged.

---

[46] The changes made to Hotman's part also lend the play a more egalitarian view of the other slaves. In Southerne's play, Hotman's treachery seems due largely to his display of fear and his failure to follow the Royal Slave. As long as Hotman's betrayal is linked to his own lack of bravery, the emphasis on nobility over a criticism of slavery exists as an ideological link between Behn's novel and the play. By making Hotman a spy for the colonial government from the beginning, however, Hawkesworth shows that the slaves posed a threat to the plantations even without Oroonoko, and, unlike in the previous versions, the revolt fails because of an individual's subterfuge rather than the common slaves' lack of valor.

As Robin Blackburn points out in his comparative history *The Over-throw of Colonial Slavery*, in "the period 1630–1750 the British Empire witnessed an increasingly clamorous, and even obsessive 'egotistical' revulsion against 'slavery' side by side with an almost uncontested exploitation of African Bondage."[47] John Locke opens his *Treatises* by declaring that "Slavery is so vile and miserable an Estate of Man and so directly opposite to the Generous Temper and Spirit of Our nation; that 'tis hardly to be conceived, that an *Englishman,* much less a *Gentleman*, should plead for 't."[48] However, as a stockholder in the Royal Africa Company he did not extend this call to the literality of chattel slavery occurring in the colonies. At the time, England's Caribbean holdings stimulated and created new industries and markets in England. Southerne's adaptation coincides with the coup's paradoxical belief in individual liberty and plantation slavery. England's power in the Caribbean was just beginning to grow, so the comic optimism of the Welldon sisters finding marriage and financial stability in Surinam still carried ideological validity with audiences. However, as Britain's relationship with the Caribbean changed, the popular opinion of it and slavery became radically altered.

As Britain's imperial interests began their 'Eastern Swing' toward India and other locations, Caribbean monopolies on goods such as sugar began to stifle the financial interest of England-based capitalists.[49] Alongside these economic changes, abolitionist sentiments began to

---

[47] Robin Blackburn, *The Overthrow of Colonial Slavery* (New York: Verso, 1988), 42.

[48] Locke, *Two Treatises*, 175.

[49] For Eric Williams in *Capitalism and Slavery* (London: André Deutsch Limited, 1989), industries in England eventually outgrew the need for the monopolies of their Caribbean colonies: "When British capitalism depended on the West Indies, they ignored slavery or defended it. When British capitalism found the West Indian monopoly a nuisance, they destroyed West Indian slavery as the first step in the destruction of West Indian monopoly" (169). While industrialists were becoming increasingly disenchanted with their forced reliance upon their Caribbean colonies, Britain was also losing its dominance in the region, as illustrated in *The Problem of Slavery in the Age of Revolution* by David Brion Davis (Ithaca: Cornell University Press, 1975.): "In 1700, British planters had supplied nearly half the sugar consumed in Western Europe; by 1789, St. Domingue alone was exporting more than all the British colonies combined" (53).
This change was brought about by the fragility of the sugar industry, competition from India, and the U.S. Revolution that broke the British West Indies' hold on the industry. While retaining speeches defending slavery, Hawkesworth's omission of the comedic happy ending disallows a positive portrayal of the colony. Instead, it becomes a space of corruption and loss, which in turn mirrors the deterioration of Britain's position among the Caribbean plantation economies.

grow. Evangelicalism and the sentimental valuation of the 'man of feeling' also contributed to the anti-slavery movement.[50] For much of Western Europe, Surinam in particular became synonymous with the abuses of the slave plantation. In 1759, Voltaire used it as the setting where his protagonist Candide abandons his optimism when confronted with slavery. In 1796, John Gabriel Stedman published his *Narrative of Five Years Expedition against the Revolted Negroes of Surinam*, which became a source for the abolitionist movement in England.[51] By the time John Ferriar produced his version of *Oroonoko* in 1787, public sentiment toward slavery, in the British Empire in general as well as the Caribbean and Surinam in particular, had changed. As Catherine Gallagher points out in her edition of Behn's novel, Ferriar

> accused Hawkesworth of weakening the antislavery implications of the story by adhering too closely to Southerne's original design: 'Although the incidents appeared even to invite sentiments adverse to slavery... [Southerne] delivered by the medium of his Hero, a groveling apology for slave-holders.[52]

Over a century after Behn's original, a cultural assumption had emerged that any story dealing with plantation slavery must involve a condemnation of that institution.

At the time of Ferriar's *Oroonoko* adaptation, entitled *The Prince of Angola*, France had surpassed Britain in economic success in the Caribbean, and the British public was becoming increasingly disenchanted not just with these Atlantic colonies but also with the institution of slavery.[53] A Unitarian physician and active abolitionist, Ferriar

---

[50] See David Brion Davis, "Chapter Ten: Religious Sources of Antislavery Thought: Quakers and the Sectarian Tradition" and "Chapter Eleven: Religious Sources of Antislavery Thought: The 'Man of Feeling' in the Best of World," in *The Problem of Slavery*, 291–364.

[51] Richard Price and Sally Price, introduction to *Narrative of Five Years Expedition against the Revolted Negroes of Surinam*, by John Gabriel Stedman (Baltimore: John Hopkins University Press, 1992), xiii.

[52] Behn, *Oroonoko*, ii.

[53] Hawkesworth relocates Oroonoko's kingdom to Angola, and Susan B. Iwanisziw sees the move to Angola as an attempt to make the characters more sympathetic to English audiences: it "changed Oroonoko from Akan to Bantu but, more importantly, deflected attention from violent Coramantien slaves who, as a cultural group, had in 1675 fomented a rebellion in Barbados" ("The Eighteenth-Century Marketing of *Oroonoko*: Contending Constructions of Maeceanas, the Author and the Slave," in *Troping Oroonoko from Behn to Bandele*, Eds. Susan B. Iwanisziw (Burlington: Ashgate, 2004) 162). Interestingly, according to Douglas B. Chambers, the presence of a Coramantien nation seems to come largely from Behn's own text: "Her account of the noble slave Oroonoko...may have had a germinal role in constructing, for literate Englishmen

deliberately staged his version as an attack upon the slave trade. His Manchester production positioned Oroonoko not as an extraordinary example of one man wrongfully enslaved, but as a symbol of the suffering of all slaves regardless of rank. Following its debut, the *Manchester Mercury* reprinted the prologue as part of the local abolitionists' campaign. The new version emphasizes a universal humanity that differs from even the Hawkesworth version. In it, "sad Oroonoko pleases, / For each poor African that toils and bleeds" and the "MIND has no COLOUR—ev'ry Heart can feel" (Prologue l. 5–6, 26). Along with its later advertisements for the printed versions of the play, the *Mercury* expresses its hopes that Ferriar's play will help influence the anti-slavery legislation soon to come before the British Parliament.

This version represents the solidification of Behn's original narrative's position in the public imagination as an abolitionist text. Staying close to the Hawkesworth version, Ferriar introduces speeches that directly address the slave debate. Oroonoko is no longer a slave trader; in fact, the prince no longer retains the speech from the Behn novel that argues that those that buy slaves lawfully are not responsible for how the sellers obtain their cargo. Ferriar also removes Oroonoko's concern over only the liberty of his family and not the other slaves:

> No private sufferings urge me to your side—
>
> You've know me honour'd, courted here, and soon
>
> Would see me publicly restored to freedom,
>
> And royal rights. But never should my ear

---

at least, the master recursive metaphor of Coramantee as a 'very warlike and brave' nation of noble savages.... In 1701, Christopher Cordrington, in a letter to the Board of Trade about a recent Coramantee-led uprising in Antigua, expanded this metaphor, nearly plagiarizing Behn" ("Ethnicity and Diaspora: The Slave Trade and Creation of African 'Nations' in the Americas," in *Slavery and Abolition*. 22.3, 2001, 31).

In a paper given at American Society of Eighteenth Century Studens annual meeting, however, Adam Beach gave a convincing argument that the image of a rebellious Coramantien such as Oroonoko could be based upon slaves from that geographical region who acted as go-betweens between African suppliers of slaves and their European counterparts. The multilingual skills of these slaves, their knowledge of European practices, and their sense of superiority to enslavement made them the most likely to resist enslavement and therefore, the least desirable slaves to purchase. Beach suggests that this may be the reason why an educated, ex-slave-trading slave such as Oroonoko would end up at one of the least productive colonies, Surinam, instead of a more lucrative one such as Jamaica, which possessed the finances to purchases the 'best' slaves. See Adam Beach,"Behn's Oroonoko, Atlantic Creoles, and the Early Modern Gold Coast," *ASECS Annual Meeting*, Richmond, VA, 26 March 2009.

Forget the bondman's cry; still should I droop,

For my sad brethren left in slavery.

Let us be jointly free or jointly perish. (III.iii)

As Spencer points out in *Afterlife*, this claim to a universal humanity and transcendence of rank creates a potential bond between Oroonoko and the audience in their shared concern for the suffering slaves.

However, like the universalism expressed in Behn's racial model and Southerne's Lockean principles, Ferriar's version does not necessary represent a claim of complete equality between all people. Ferriar's version emphasizes a cultural gap between Africa and Europe not found in the romance tropes of the Behn novel. In his preface, Ferriar demonstrates a disdain for non-Christian cultures, calling "an African's highest religious mystery" nothing but "Mumbo Jumbo."[54] Jane Spencer presents this as a small detraction from an otherwise egalitarian play, arguing that "on the whole it is remarkable how thoughtfully this version of *Oroonoko* deals with the transformation of a heroic tragedy into a piece of political theater."[55] While it does present a laudable attack on colonial slavery, the play also illustrates a Christian bias against the cultural status of those it sought to help.

Conclusion

Although as an author and critics Ferriar has fallen into near obscurity, his vision of an abolitionist *Oroonoko* persists to the present day. Transitioning from the Ottoman gloss of Behn's African kingdom to a its current association with European enslavement of Africans, the ideology of the 1787 production of *Oroonoko* dominates nineteenth century. Due to an adaptation nearly a century after her death, Behn's prose narrative gained a reputation as an unquestioned attack on slavery. Victorian poet Algernon Charles Swinburne championed not her more scandalous poems and plays that would seem to connect his work with hers; instead he suggests that *Oroonoko* be reprinted alongside Harriet Beecher Stowe's abolitionist novel, *Uncle Tom's Cabin*.[56] Swin-

---

[54] Ferriar, *The Prince of Angola* (Manchester: J. Harrop, 1788), v.
[55] Spencer, *Afterlife*, 259.
[56] Janet Todd, *The Critical Fortunes of Aphra Behn* (Columbia: Camden House, 1998), 56.

burne's contemporaries also connect the two authors. Wilbur L. Cross, for example, refers to the novel as "the first humanitarian novel in English...[meant] to awaken Christendom to the horrors of slavery."[57] The insertion of Behn into a political tradition different from the one she participated in during her lifetime enabled *Oroonoko* to remain a politically viable and actively read text for over three centuries.

Behn's use of romance—though containing its own ethnical conundrums—lends itself to a different image of Africa within Christian Europe's culture. Within that generic tradition and Europe's long history of Islamic influence, at least some of those enslaved are presented as the cultural equals of those seeking to free them. From Behn's conflation of European and African nobility to Southerne's and Hawkesworth's critique of Christian hypocrisy to Ferriar's religious call to arms, the novel and the plays trace the cultural attitudes toward Caribbean plantocracy, illuminating the interconnectivity of economics and religious forces driving Britain's political choices.

---

[57] Qtd. ibid., 55.

THE CONTINUED ANXIETIES OF EMPIRE:
AFTER THE OTTOMAN INFLUENCE

By the end of the eighteenth century, the decline of the Ottoman Empire was obvious to its internal government and the rest of Europe. Long-standing internal inefficiencies as well as the rise of European empires were the primary factors of its loss of dominance. As Kemal H. Karpat points out that during this time, the infrastructure of the vast Ottoman Empire had become critically compromised: "The conflict between the central authority and the provinces, which had brought down many of the Muslim empires in the past and which the Ottomans success-fully avoided for centuries, dealt them ultimately a fatal blow."[1] Yet, even in this lower status, the memory of its past influence framed the discussion of newly ascendant nations. Tsar Nikolai I, for example, framed his discussion of Anglo-Russian security within the context of the Ottomans. According to the British ambassador's letters, the Tsar felt that Russia and England could rise in the world because the Ottoman Empire was now the 'sick man' of Europe.[2] Meanwhile, as the center of the British Empire, England was becoming more pow-erful and would dominate global politics in the nineteenth century. Despite some loss of transatlantic clout due to territorial losses in the American War and the financial inefficacies of its Caribbean plutoc-racies, Britain had begun its 'swing to the East,' which would prove much more successful, culminating in the Victorian Empire on which the sun never set. The disparate imperial power between England and the Ottoman Empire of the beginning of the eighteenth century had reversed.

Evidence that this transition period of Ottoman decline and British rise had entered the English public consciousness begins to appear at the eighteenth century draws to a close. In the autobiography

---

[1] Kemal H. Karpat, *Studies on Ottoman Social and Political History: Selected Arti-cles and Essays* (Leiden: E.J. Brill, 2002), 37–38.
[2] Candan Badem, *The Ottoman Crimean War (1853–1856)* (Leiden: E.J. Brill, 2010), 68.

The Life of Olaudah Equiano, or Gustavus Vassa, the African (1789), ex-slave Olaudah Equiano's narrative charts not just his enslavement and emancipation, but his global travels in search of social and financial elevation, as well as a search for a new homeland.[3] Towards the end of *The Life*, Equiano debates where to settle himself physically and spiritually. Located outside of the transatlantic triangle of the British slave trade, the Ottoman Empire offers a possible new start for Equiano. The 'New' World of the Americas harbors the old dangers of a return to slavery if he is captured and limited legal protection if he remains free. The older empire offers an escape from those dangers. Tempted, Equiano presents the inhabitants as generally "fond of black people" and kind to him despite the fact that they keep other Christians "separate, and do not suffer them to dwell immediately amongst them."[4] Ottoman Turkey is presented as a sophisticated culture where he would be physically and legally secure. There, he could have an identity that severed him from a slave identity.

Despite these enticements, *The Life* ultimately presents the British Empire in general and England in particular as the superior option. Although life under Ottoman rule would ensure Equiano's physical safety, it would also require an apolitical stance towards religion and slavery. Just as he presumably would ignore the segregation of other Christians in the country, so would he ignore the plight of other slaves: "I was surprised to see how the Greeks are, in some measure, kept under by the Turks, as the negroes are in the West Indies by the white people." The link between the Turkish enslavement of the Greeks and the British enslavement of Africans is brought out further by the cultural affiliation he constructs: "The less refined Greeks, as I have already hinted, dance here in the same manner as we do in my nation." Although he intellectually links his past enslavement and the present situation in Turkey, he declares, "I liked the place and the Turks extremely well."[5] For him to become politically engaged, he must find national and spiritual identities that reflect a sense of the present and future rather than the past. England is presented as the empire of the future, while the Ottoman Empire is presented as

---

[3] I expand upon and discuss the pedagogical implications of this argument in my contribution to *Teaching The Interesting Narrative of Olaudah Equiano*, edited by Eric D. Lamore and forthcoming from the University of Tennessee Press.

[4] Olaudah Equiano, *The Life* (Mineola: Dover Publications, 1999), 125.

[5] Ibid., 126.

belonging to an admirable past that is slowly fading from the transnational stage.

The shift Equiano observes can also be observed in documents from the Ottoman perspective. But there is a distinct difference. In their attempts to reaffirm their role as a global power, the Ottomans did not look to the rising power of England's British Empire. The Ottomans may have loomed large in the cultural imaginations of the English, but as an imperial center, England was still too newly established for the declining empire to take seriously. France, however, was a major trading partner in the Ottoman territories. According to Edhem Eldem, "[b]etween 1726 and 1789, the volume of this trade represented an annual average of some 22.5 million *livres tournois,* with exports (from the Levant) reaching 19 million and imports 13.5 million."[6] In the seventeenth century, the English and Dutch traded more with the Ottomans, but during the eighteenth century this changed, so that by "mid-century, French trade in the Ottoman capital had developed to the point of representing nearly two-thirds of all western trade."[7]

France and other European nations, often geographically closer to Ottoman territories, perceived the Ottoman decline sooner than more distant and less established ones such as England. When examining the shifting representations of the Ottomans in the mid-eighteenth century, I interpret the changes as resulting from alternations in how the English viewed their own empire. If this study were extended to other nations, such as France, Prussia, or the Polish-Lithuanian Commonwealth, the sense of the Ottoman's fading power would likely appear earlier than it does in English texts. France, especially, with their "particular and privileged position in this new balance of power," noted this change, and had begun renegotiating their relationship with the Ottomans as early as the 1720s.[8] By "the last two decades of the century, Frenchmen had gained enough self-assurance to label the Ottoman Empire a 'colony of France,' to speak of the Ottoman 'tribute paid to [French] national industry,' and to deplore—somewhat hypocritically—the unheeding 'passiveness' of Ottomans in the face

---

[6] Edhem Eldem, *French Trade in Istanbul in the Eighteenth Century* (Leiden: E.J. Brill, 1999), 13.

[7] Ibid., 28.

[8] Ibid., 277.

of foreign exploitation."[9] The colonial attitude the French adopt fits with Said's Orientalism, but it is important to note that it occurs in a specific historical moment and only after they perceive the Ottomans are in decline.

It should not be surprising then that Ottoman attempts to reassert their former position as a dominant power would occur in states such as France rather than in England. In 1786, Sultan Selim III turned to France's Louis XVI—even when revolutionaries imprisoned him—help modernize the Ottoman military in order to regain lost territories.[10] In her work on Mouradgea d'Ohsson's 1790 *Tableau générale de l'Empire Othoman*, Elizabeth Fraser argues that the text was conceived and marketed to French audiences in order to re-establish the Ottomans as a culturally relevant force in Europe.[11] Similarly, Ali Uzay Peker's examination of Western influences on Ottoman architecture describes a shift into Occidentalism that corresponds with a decline in Ottoman influence:

> Only at the end of the eighteenth century did the Ottoman elite recognize the importance of having information on European lands and civilization.... [Amidst other "information-gathering missions" in Europe, in] 1789 Mahmud Raif Efendi referred to this reformist era as a *Nizam-i cedid* (new order/new civilization) in a book printed in French by the engineering school of the Ottoman army *Tableau des nouveaux règlements de l'Empire Ottoman*. The administrative reforms of the nineteenth century developed out of the acculturation that took place during the eighteenth.[12]

By the end of the nineteenth century, "the Ottoman intelligentsia maintained that civilization was centered in Europe (for many, in Paris). During the eighteenth century, by contrast, general knowledge about Europe was much more limited."[13] Although the actual political and economic circumstances leading to a shift from Ottoman to

---

[9] Ibid., 285. Edlem's conclusion covers the disruption the French Revolution caused in trade relations. See 293–94.

[10] Stanford J. Shaw, *History of the Ottoman Empire and Modern Turkey* (1976), Volume 1 (Cambridge: Cambridge University Press, 1997), 260.

[11] Elisabeth Fraser, "Print Culture from Constantinople to Paris: An Ottoman Dragoman between Two Empires" (paper presented the annual meeting for the American Society for Eighteenth-Century Studies, Albuquerque, New Mexico, March 17–20, 2010).

[12] Ali Uzay Peker, "Western Influences on the Ottoman Empire and Occidentalism in the Architecture of Istanbul" in *Eighteenth-Century Life* 26.3 (2002), 144–45.

[13] Ibid., 157.

European dominance occurred earlier over a lengthy period, the realization of this by either side was often delayed and uneven. Even as the Ottomans recognized and tried to remedy their decline, the nation to which they often measured themselves was already being eclipsed by the rising British Empire.

England's Imperial Identity

Although the Ottomans looked to France to validate their importance in international relations, France grew to view England as its chief rival. Their military conflicts between the 1756 commencement of the Seven Years War to the 1815 Battle of Waterloo preoccupied both nations. The outcome of these conflicts resulted in the solidification of Britain as the dominant power of the nineteenth century. As Maya Jasanoff explains in her study of Britain imperial rise in the East: "In France, war with Britain had catastrophic consequence for the state, the economy, and ultimately, the monarchy. It was global war. Fought on multiple continents, in defense of imperial interest, it decisively affected the pace, motives, and direction of British and French imperial expansion."[14] England, as the center of the British Empire, became the force that shaped the domestic and foreign policies of other nations.

My book argues England was imperially insecure during the seventeenth and into the early eighteenth century. Its representations of the more established Ottoman Empire reflect an envious desire to emulate the Ottoman's influence alongside a fear of being overtaken by it. The first three chapters illustrate these anxieties through the discourses surrounding apostasy—the fear of 'losing' ones Englishness to a more culturally powerful and desirable Ottoman world. The two main texts examined in this book's first section, *Hayy Ibn Yaqzan* and *Robinson Crusoe*, illustrate this shift through alteration in their popularity and interpretations. Ibn Tufayal's philosophical narrative falls out of the public sphere, never again experiencing in England the multiple translation projects and debate it spurred in the late seventeenth and early eighteenth century. Arabic studies would continue to grow, but as Edward Said argues, it was now largely part of an imperial endeavor:

---

[14] Maya Jasanoff, *Edge of Empire: Lives, Culture, and Conquest in the East, 1750–1850* (New York: Knopf, 2005), 9.

The main issue for them [i.e., the scholars] was preserving the Orient and Islam under the control of the White Man.... What is required of the Oriental expert is no longer simply 'understanding': now the Orient must be made to perform, its power must be enlisted on the side of 'our' values, civilization, interests, goals.[15]

Britain's expansion to the East changed its perception of the Orient. Rather than the Ottoman Empire, the Orient was increasingly defined in British minds as Egypt and India, with whom it relationships differed greatly from that of England and the Ottomans at the beginning of the eighteenth century. Only in recent years has *Hayy Ibn Yaqzan* generated interest outside of Arabic studies. Even then, it is often is relationship to a more globally known narrative: Daniel Defoe's *Robinson Crusoe*.[16]

Reinterpretations of *Robinson Crusoe* provide a powerful reflection of Britian's growth as an empire. Robinson Crusoe became an imperial symbol. Soon, Daniel Defoe's novel came to exist as more than a book in the minds of many in England and the rest of Europe: it became a sort of mythical narrative, to explain alternatively, individual, English and European mastery of the self and world.[17] Treating *Robinson Crusoe* almost as an anonymous folk tale, Jean-Jacques Rousseau's *Emile* (1762) placed a heavily abridged version of the text at the heart of his educational program. As Louis James explains:

Rousseau's advocacy placed *Crusoe* at the centre of the rapid expansion of children's literature that followed the Enlightenment in Europe, and influenced the changing concept of the child—particularly of the boy—

---

[15] Edward Said, *Orientalism* (1978) (New York: Vintage Books, 1994), 238.

[16] A prime illustration of this trend to re-examine *Hayy* within the context of *Robinson Crusoe*, the 2010 Broadview Edition, includes an excerpt of the 1708 Simon Ockley translation as an important precursor to Defoe's narrative. See Daniel Defoe, *Robinson Crusoe*, edited by Evan R. Davis (Peterborough, Ontario, Canada: Broadview Press, 2010).

Other examples of include recent scholarship produced by scholars such as Matthew Reilly and Beyazit H. Akman. See Matthew Reilly, "'No eye has seen, or ear heard': Arabic Sources for Quaker Subjectivity in Unca Eliza Winkfield's *The Female American*." *Eighteenth-Century Studies* 44, no. 2 (2010): 261–283. http://0-muse.jhu .edu.library.colby.edu/ (accessed January 25, 2011) and Beyazit H. Akman, "How Novel is the First Novel? Robinson Crusoe and Hayy bin Yaqzan" (paper presented the annual meeting for the American Society for Eighteenth-Century Studies, Richmond, Virginia, March 25–28, 2009).

[17] For a study on the declining publication of the Crusoe sequels see Melissa Free's "Un-erasing Crusoe: Farther Adventures in the Nineteenth Century," *Book History* 9 (2006) 89–130.

during the period. In Germany the term 'Robinsonalter' came to be used to describe the point at which the twelve-year-old boy discovers himself on the island of responsible life.... Through the nineteenth century, the Crusoe story in England developed from practical instruction, to a celebration of colonialism. Leslie Stephen's [1909] essay on Defoe sees Crusoe as the representative of the men who "were building up vast systems of commerce and manufacture; shoving their intrusive persons into every quarter on the globe", from America to Australia and the Far East. The Crusoe myth became inscribed not only in the reading, but in the actual lives of nineteenth-century Britons.[18]

This reading of *Robinson Crusoe* reflects a shift in outward perceptions of Britain, which saw it rising as a culturally and imperially influential power. The empire it came to represent, however, was also the result of a change in Britain's ideas about empire.

Alongside the transition in power relationships between Britain and other empires, such as France and the Ottomans, its own definition of the nature and use of imperial power evolved. In looking at shifting representations of race, especially in the reinterpretations of *Othello* and *Oroonoko*, the last three chapters of this book show England's growing sense of prominence as an international power during the second half of the eighteenth century. Demonstrating this transition on a larger historical scale, Lawrence James, in his analysis of the changing policies and views of empire in *The Rise and Fall of the British Empire*, positions the loss of some of its North American holdings (the newly formed United States) and unprofitable Caribbean holdings (or at least, less profitable than those under French control) coincides with a reassessment of colonial holdings: "[economist, Adam] Smith's theories [that state control over colonial trade 'was an encumbrance to commerce which interfered with natural market forces and raised prices'] and the post-war pattern of British trade undermined the economic arguments which had hitherto justified the empire."[19] As a result, the Canadian colonies received more autonomy, and imperial resources were placed in the East and Pacific. Unlike North American and the Caribbean, these areas proved more profitable in the late

---

[18] Louis James, "Unwrapping Crusoe: Retrospective and Prospective Views," in *Robinson Crusoe: Myths and Metamorphoses*, editors Lieve Spaas and Brian Stimpson (New York: St. Martin Press, 1996), 2–3.

[19] Lawrence James, *The Rise and Fall of the British Empire* (New York: St. Martin's Press, 1994), 120.

eighteenth and nineteenth centuries. India is the principle example of British overseas imperial growth:

> In 1740 the East India Company was purely a commercial enterprise, which imported and exported goods from its factories at Bombay, Madras and Calcutta, unbothered by the internal politics of India. By 1815 the Company owned the most powerful army in India and governed, directly and indirectly, Bengal, much of the upper Ganges basin and extensive areas of eastern and southern India.[20] After overcoming competition with the French as well as with local authorities, British domination in India "was an accepted political fact of life".[21]

India became an imperial power base that allowed the British to extend themselves into much of Asia, and the Indian army provided them with an efficient military force that could be deployed to expand and defend the empire.

England's rise was noted by other imperial powers. The in the late eighteenth and early nineteenth centuries the Ottomans looked to the French for several reasons. Historically, it had a closer relationship with France than it did with England. This relationship was also marked by a greater degree of equality that than between the Ottomans and the English. As discussed in Chapter One, English representations of the Ottoman Empire expressed fears of conquest and loss of identity in part because the Empire was powerful enough to dictate the relationship between them at a national level as well as undermine already unstable concepts of English national and religious identity through the possibility of financial again or the threat of captivity. Another factor influencing the Ottoman's initial preference for France over England was that at turn of the century France arguably was the major power in Europe.[22] Yet, the empire England would rule would not be based primarily in Europe or even in the transatlantic, areas that had been the focus of power struggles prior to the nineteenth century. The eighteenth century began with the Ottoman Levant represented an opportunity for Englishmen to rise financially. By its end, however, "placing a son in the [East India] Company's army had become a valuable source of additional income to many middle-class families in Britain."[23] Even as the East India Company's influence faded to

---

[20] Ibid., 123.
[21] Ibid., 137–38.
[22] Ibid., 138.
[23] Ibid., 131.

be replaced by the British Raj in 1858, many Englishmen sought the economic uplift once found in the Ottoman Empire within Britain's own empire.

Cultural Sway of the British Empire

England's rise in the nineteenth century made it both a center of power as well as a place of safety and stability. The wars and political upheaval in the rest of Europe meant that large numbers of refugees sought shelter in the British Isles.[24] This alongside the exportation of British culture to its nineteenth-century colonies affected the interpretation of existing cultural narratives. Chapter Five of this book references the rise of Shakespeare as national icon as a sign of emerging sense of an English identity culturally equal with, if not superior to, the rest of the world. During the nineteenth century, another shift occurred. As Jane Moody puts it,

> The Victorian period was an age of Shakespearean transcontinental migration. British performer now began to acquire bit parts and starring roles in an international cultural market made possible by empire and by steam. From the 1850s, Britain was exporting leading performers like Charles Kean and William Macready, and indeed entire productions, often for months at a time: the empire, together with America provided British theatre with a new a lucrative cultural market. Shakespeare, the most valuable form of theatrical stock, was being 'blown about the world at a fearful rate.' Yet despite this flourishing trade, dramatic critics continued to lament the relentless commercial dominance of foreign plays on the British stage.[25]

---

[24] "Britain became a leading place of refuge for Jews fleeing religious persecution in Eastern Europe, and for political refugees from the Hapsburg Empire and from Russia." Jane Moody, "Shakespeare and the Immigrants: Nationhood, psychology and Xenophobia on the Nineteenth-century stage," in *Victorian Shakespeare, Volume 1, Theatre, Drama and Performance*, editors Gail Marshall and Adrian Poole (New York: Palgrave MacMillan, 2003), 99.

[25] Ibid., 99. At the same time, the emphasis on free trade that shifted British imperial efforts also affected the theatre: "the final abolition of patent monopoly in 1843 had established the institutional conditions for free dramatic trade. The gradual revival of the metropolitan dramatic economy in the decades which followed led to the arrival of a new generation of theatrical migrants from the European continent and laid the foundations for London's increasingly profitable position on the international stage circuit" (100).

The exportation of Shakespeare abroad and the importation of foreign Shakespearean actors opened up the plays to new interpretations. The Othello of Italian actor Tommaso Salvini, for instance, was praised for its excessive jealousy and passion, but still contrasted the more subdued interpretations of Victorian British actors. Moody contends, "immigrant productions had played a crucial role in liberating Shakespeare from the prison of Englishness."[26]

This 'liberation' allowed other nations to claim Shakespeare as their own national icon. The English national poet became a global figure, and *Othello* became intertwined with new racial paradigms and political contexts. In the 1980s and 1990s, two groundbreaking Shakespearean productions reinterpreted *Titus Andronicus* and *Othello* as narratives of South African apartheid. Commenting on her 1988 production of *Othello* in an interview with Pascale Aebischer, Janet Suzman presents Shakespeare's play as a natural fit to her own nation's history and anxieties surrounding racial difference:

> I looked carefully at Iago's speech in (III.iii lines 232–37) and knew we had a tight case; the speech is as if straight from the mouth of a doctrinaire apartheidist. Iago was a militarist black-uniform-wearing right-winger, causing mayhem and spouting bigotry...I simplify.' In the same letter, she concedes that 'Having been born and brought up in apartheid SA, I fear I am quite unable to see Othello except through the pervasive prism of colour.'[27]

In this context, productions of Shakespearean plays represented a space to contest different forms of South African identity. The imperial history of the nation with British Empire introduced Shakespeare to the populace, but Suzman does not present this past colonial relationship as problematic. Her Shakespeare is neither a foreign export nor part of the European culture that created Apartheid. Instead, they

---

[26] Ibid., 113–14.

[27] Pascale Aebischer, *Shakespeare's Violated Bodies: Stage and Screen Performance* (Cambridge: Cambridge UP, 2004), 139.

Aebischer goes on to argue that despite the productions merits, Suzman conflates her male lead, John Kani, with Othello: "She is dangerously close to collapsing the distance between character and actor in these statements and to subscribing to the naturalization, if not the violence, at least of gullibility as a racial characteristic of black men; however, she courts and even greater danger when talking about the reasons for casting Joanna Weinberg as Desdemona. What she was looking for, she says, was 'chemistry'—but she did not seek it in Weinberg, apparently supposing that he white woman would be able to *act* the requisite passion (and indeed she did)" (142).

present Shakespeare's plays as offering a critique of twentieth-century South African apartheid.

The appropriation of Shakespeare into other countries is found frequently in the United States, as well. In a fascinating U.S. production at the Shakespeare Theater in Washington, D.C. that has yet to receive much scholarly attention, Jude Kelly's 1997 production of *Othello* reversed the perceived racial roles of the play. White British actor Patrick Stewart performed Othello with a predominately African-American cast, with only a few parts such as Cassio's mistress, Bianca, and the servants played by white actors. In a 2010 interview with Robert Llewellyn, Stewart claims much of the credit for the production's origin.[28] His narrative presents Britain as a space of impossibilities. Due to past racism, he cannot perform Othello in the blackface used by Laurence Olivier, and though he does not mention them, the more ambiguous Moorish figure of the twentieth century, such as Orson Welles and Anthony Hopkins, seem as impossibility as well. His proposal to stage a 'photo-negative' production is also rejected in Britain. To stage a production that allows him to perform a role beloved since his childhood and avoid the racial masquerade of past British performances, he needs to invent a new way of framing questions of race within the play. To move into this imagined future of Shakespeare performance, he moves to a new center of cultural innovation: the United States. Echoing the way Equiano's autobiography positions the Ottomans as a space bound by the past and England as one of a potentially progressive future, Stewart's account of the production emphasizes the unwillingness of British theatres to embrace change and the exciting dynamism of U.S. theatre.[29]

His account climaxes in a special matinee performance "full of inner-city kids." The children refuse to accept Othello as the play's hero. Instead they cheer loudly for Iago to the point Stewart claims he was afraid to take his final bow. To them, Othello represents the institutionalized racism so visible in the U.S. capital. Iago is then a

---

[28] Patrick Stewart, "Sir Patrick Stewart," *Car Pool* [Video] Retrieved 22 January 2011, from http://www.youtube.com/watch?v=zvNMYqWZ4BM.

[29] For a solid overview of the ways *Othello* in particular has influenced U.S. representations of race, see Celia R. Daileader, *Racism, Misogyny, and the 'Othello' Myth.* (Cambridge: Cambridge University Press, 2005). An excellent discussion of racial depictions of Othello in the US and Europe in the nineteenth and twentieth centuries can be found in Pascale Aebischer's *Shakespeare's Violated Bodies: Stage and Screen Performance.*

hero who rises up to challenge the powerful. Like Suzman, they read
Othello through their own national narratives of race. Yet, that there
was a special performance for these students points to the idea that
students in the troubled school district of D.C. somehow need Shakespeare. The idea that lower-income children will benefit from expo-
sure to the playwright is one common in the history of the U.S. and
extends beyond theatrical productions. In the United States, generations of government workers and educators have incorporated Shakespeare's works into college placement exams, community projects, and
the acculturation of immigrants. In her analysis of the twenty-first
century US National Endowment of the Arts (NEA) "Shakespeare in
American Communities" program, Denise Albanese notes that

> as part of its legitimatization narrative, the NEA's associated pamphlet
> provides a capsule overview of Shakespeare's theatrical pervasiveness in
> America, especially in the nineteenth century. [Former NEA chairman
> Dana] Gioia makes clear what's at stake in this return when he avers that
> a genealogical relation exists between national formations and Shake-
> spearean ones: 'I think it's impossible to understand American culture
> or American theater without understanding Shakespeare.'[30]

The globalization of Shakespeare originates from a rising British
Empire whose colonial efforts included the indoctrination into the
ideology that English culture was superior and deserved imitation.
Yet, this twentieth-century cooption of Shakespeare by countries once
ruled by the British Empire also points to its deterioration.

Another Transition of Power: The Decline of the British Empire

After a century of imperial stability and dominance, the British Empire
began to decline. Like that of the Ottomans, this decent was gradual.

---

[30] Denise Albanese, *Extramural Shakespeare* (New York: Palgrave Macmillan,
2010), 14.
   "When [in 2003] 'Shakespeare in American Communities' was first announced by
[former chairman of the NEA] Dana Gioia, it was designed to send noted regional
theater companies across the country to perform a limited repertory of Shakespeare
plays: *Romeo and Juliet, A Midsummer's Night's Dream, Richard III*, and *Othello*. Thus
its twin aims: the reinvigoration of a touring theater-company tradition and the introduction of 'a new generation of audiences to the greatest writer in the English language'" (ibid., 14). Despite this initial focus on local theater, the program soon shifted
its emphasis more to incorporating Shakespeare into classrooms.

Some historians such as Lawrence James point to the World Wars as key moments during which external pressures severally compromised the Empire's integrity. The First World War fulfilled "the late-Victorian and Edwardian dream of the various parts of the empire joining together to form one solid battleline," and won the Empire new territories in the Middle East.[31] Yet, in the aftermath, the English imperial center could not address the demands of the colonial periphery. Long held colonies such as India were demanding self-rule. Newly acquired ones such as Egypt were gained in part through alliances with Arab nationalist groups formed in response to the final dismantling of the Ottoman Empire. These groups "argued that the region could not be treated as Africa had been in the last century, as a backward area which could be partitioned and conquered without reference to the wishes of its people."[32] In a way, the Levant maintained some of its past authority. The historical view of the region as culturally and political sophisticated. In the past, it influenced English anxieties about the Ottomans. In the twentieth century, a former Ottoman-ruled North Africa invokes this position in order to gain more authority within the British Empire.

In the seventeenth and eighteenth century, England overestimated Ottoman power, missing the signs of decline the France exploited. Conversely, in the early twentieth century, those holding power in the British Empire underestimated the nationalist unrest found throughout its own colonies. Instead, blame for "all expressions of popular discontent in Britain and throughout the empire...[on] convert Communist agitation."[33] In his study of the domestic political factors that lead to imperial decline, *Britain's Declining Empire: The Road to Decolonisation, 1918–1868,* Ronald Hyam outlines the changing public and government attitudes within the United Kingdom towards the far-reaching Empire. As Britain gained global dominance, it was portrayed as an empire of ideals: "according to Lord Macauly in 1833, [the empire] was 'a pacific triumph of reason over barbarism,' and there would be 'an empire exempt from all natural causes of decay.'"[34] A global empire, its subjects spread out throughout world, their diasporic

---

[31] James, *Rise and Fall of the British Empire*, 370.
[32] Ibid., 398.
[33] Ibid., 372.
[34] Ronald Hyam, *Britain's Declining Empire: The Road to Decolonisation, 1918–1868* (Cambridge: Cambridge University Press, 2006), 7.

communities adapting to while altering their new communities. True, English subjects traveled to English colonial holdings in the prior to the shifts of the eighteenth century, but much of the world was held by other nations. Reflecting this shift, consider the limited vision of empire found in texts at the beginning of the eighteenth century. Defoe places Crusoe plantation in Spain's Brazil, and the provisional government of Surinam that execute Behn's Oroonoko are supplanted by Dutch colonists. But in the late eighteenth through the first half of the twentieth centuries, British subjects—whether English, Scottish, Sikh, or Chinese—could wander the globe without leaving the empire.

In the twentieth century, however, the stability of Britain as the central power began to falter. Hyam places much on the blame on poor governance:

> in the twentieth century the essential characteristic [of the British Empire] was to be dysfunctional, as responsibilities simply overwhelmed it.... Almost none of the plans and policies developed after 1918 were without flaws, and several were seriously embarrassing failures.[35]

The Second World War exacerbated these fault lines comprising the stability of the British Empire. In addition to demands for more autonomy in India, Ireland, and the Middle East, the United States now held a more dominant position than Britain. The financial burden of running an empire and participating in two global wars led to a large British debt to the U.S. Despite America's own imperial

---

[35] Ibid., 8–9.

Hyam argues that five programs were the chief causes of the decline. One was a turn to Indirect Rule as "the preferred method of imperial administration" that "had to be abandoned in the 1940s for failing to meet modern requirements" (12–13). Another Hyam cites was the desire for a "white man's country," in which white British subjects would hold a higher position in the colonies. This policy failed in the early 1920s when Indians used a campaign for greater rights in Kenya, where they were the second largest population, as "as testing-ground for imperial policy towards all Indians overseas" (20). Third, the move of the capital of the Raj from Calcutta to Delhi, that resulted in an extravagant new palace for the viceroy controversial both in London and India (22). Fourth, a mismanaged program to make English the international language through the invention "British American Scientific Industrial Commercial" (Basic) English, a simplified version of English, meant to be promoted and implemented by the British Ministry of Education in 1947, only to have funding cease in 1953. Although English emerged as a dominant global language, Basic English was costly, mismanaged, and ill-received within and outside of the Empire (26). Lastly, the "Special Relationship" between Britain and the U.S. led "makers of British external policy had the possible reactions of the United States always at the back of their mind" (26).

endeavors, its professed ideology was anti-imperialist: the "general line was that all empires, including the British, were parasitic tyrannies which were fast becoming obsolete."[36] The loss of the Indian army due to India's 1947 independence also made it more difficult to control its remaining colonies. But most of all, as James points out, "there was the new, multi-racial Commonwealth."[37] It did not provide a hoped-for "surrogate empire" by all the former colonies joining and supporting British influence in world affairs.[38] As a result, the Britain of the mid-twentieth century looked to alliances with the more powerful U.S. as well as attempted to create a source of shared power joining European alliances.

Ironically, this decline had a liberating effect upon English domestic culture. Chapter Six argued that the lack of profitability bolstered the argument of abolitionists and others critical of Britain's transatlantic plantation economies. The cost and turmoil of the remaining colonies also made a retreat from imperialism more attractive. At the end of the eighteenth century, Britain turned its colonial focus away from the Americas towards India. The move to the East, restructuring of colonial policy, and abolition of slavery were facilitated by the low cost and possible high profit they offered to those in England. In the mid-twentieth century, finding Africa a poor replacement for its loss of India, Britain forged a new international identity. As at the start of the nineteenth century, the lack of upheaval felt in England facilitated the change. Living standards rose in the 1950s. Lawrence James argues there was little need for England to mourn the loss of imperial status: "No jobs were lost, factories closed or investment opportunities frustrated as a result of the loss of the colonies. Britain's exports to the Commonwealth grew fitfully…[but those] to the countries of the European Economic Community (EEC) were increasing."[39] Many Britons distanced themselves from the Victorian conventions once used to establish English superiority and justify their imperial rule.

> At the same time Britain was shedding its empire it shed many of its inhibitions. In 1960 gambling was legalized and the crown lost its case against the publication of D.H. Lawrence's *Lady Chatterley's Lover*; in

---

[36] James, *Rise and Fall of the British Empire*, 511.
[37] Ibid., 533.
[38] Ibid., 534.
[39] Ibid., 595.

1965 official censorship of the theatre was ended; in 1967 homosexual
acts and abortion became legal; and in 1969 divorce became easier to
obtain. Britain appeared suddenly to have relaxed and the old imperial
capital, London, became a byword for novelty, stylishness and, like the
1960s as a whole, sexual permissiveness.[40]

Yet at the same time, there were attempts to cling to the moral and
political authority claimed during the height of empire. British Prime
Minister Harold Wilson, according to Hyam, "believed in a beneficent
British imperial and global role, as a unique and distinctive function,
'an influence'" based upon relationships rather than military might,
that alongside its allies and the Commonwealth would fight "'oppression and radicalism.'"[41]

In a production reflecting these dual desires to escape the restrictions
of the past but retain some form of moral authority, the Royal Shakespeare Company (RSC) commissioned reinterpreting Behn's narrative
for yet another generation's worldview at the end of the twentieth
century. Like its predecessors by Southerne, Hawkesworth, and Ferriar, playwright Biyi Bandele's 1999 *Aphra Behn's Oroonoko in a New
Adaptation* actively seeks to make amends for the political stances of
past productions. It attempts to combine the cultural equality found
in Behn's use of Romance with the decidedly anti-slavery stance of
Ferriar, while inserting a non-European female agency lacking in the
other versions. The first production's director Gregory Doran had
experience placing old narratives within new cultural contexts. Like
Suzman's *Othello*, his 1995 *Titus Andronicus* placed the Shakespearean
play in a South African context, and "deliberately raised expectations
of a critical engagement with the immediate cultural surrounding of
the production and especially with attitudes towards race, claiming
that the production was 'localising [sic] the play by highlighting its
themes of racial tension and cycles of violence.'"[42] In the introduction to the published version of Bandele's *Oroonoko*, Doran touts the

---

[40] Ibid., 596.
[41] Hyam, *Britain's Declining Empire*, 332.
[42] Aebicher, *Shakespeare's Violated Bodies*, 113. She also points to an earlier example *Titus* being used to explore South Africa's domestic issues: "When, in 1970, Dieter
Reible had directed *Titus Andronicus* at the Hofmeyr theatre (Cape Town) as a challenge to the Apartheid government's racial politics, he had significantly cast a white
Afrikaans actor as Aaron, allowing for a reading of the part as a projection of racist
stereotypes onto the black 'Other'" (113).

play as a recuperation of Behn's original work: "In this version for the RSC, Biyi Bandele brings both halves of his hero's story together, from warrior and prince in the West African Kingdom of Coramantien to slave in Surinam. This is the first time, therefore, that Oroonoko's entire story has been presented on the stage."[43] However, the alterations made by the new production center more on the RSC's vision of British liberalism than on a revival of Behn's efforts or a criticism of slavery and the imperialism that drove it.

Part of the appeal of this new production for contemporary audiences is tied into the British abolitionist movement that emerged sooner than its counterparts in the U.S. or South America. It plays into a vision of a tolerant, progressive Britain, augmented by its new playwright, Biyi Bandele, a British national of Nigerian birth. The play's popularity also came in part because of its original author. Considered the first English woman to earn her living by writing, Aphra Behn and her text have gained advocates for being perhaps the originator of the English novel. In both subject and authorship, it presents a vision of a liberal, multiculturally tolerant Britain. It restores Behn's African court scenes, which Jessica Munns describes as a "mixture of the ornate and the familiar [in the language of the court scenes that]...finds an equivalent to Behn's Romance Africa."[44] It fleshes out underdeveloped African characters. For example, Onahal is a minor character in Behn's narrative. She is one of the king's former wives, now in charge of his younger wives and mistresses, who reluctantly helps Oroonoko and Imoinda when the king separates them. In the new interpretation she becomes the outspoken Lady Onola, who loudly challenges the sexism of Coramantien's men and acts as Imoinda's foster mother. These changes seem to point to a desire to present a more feminist, anti-racist production, but the reality is a little more complicated.

This production also rests on the assumption that a secular, European figure is needed to successfully manage a non-white, potentially violent populace. The play's recuperation of the African scenes, though perhaps unconsciously, takes a decidedly politicized stance on the

---

[43] Biyi Bandele, *Aphra Behn's Oroonoko in a New Adaptation* (Oxford: Amber Land Press, 1999), 9.

[44] Jessica Munns, "Reviving *Oroonoko* 'In the Scene'" (Burlington: Ashgate, 2004), 187.

role of religious diversity. Though still set in Coramantien (today's Ghana), Bandele writes in his preface to the play that he "re-imagined *Oroonoko* in a Yoruba—which is to say Nigerian—setting."[45] In his native country today, the population is roughly half Muslim.[46] Given the Orientalist mode of the Behn text, a return to the source material could arguably have incorporated these original details into its depiction of the court and of its hero. The new production takes a contrary stance by placing the court in direct conflict with its Muslim neighbors. The stage directions make it clear that the emissaries, Ibn Saeed and Ibn Sule, should be seen as outsiders: "they are dressed in turbans and other such accoutrements of the desert-farer: clothing that immediately marks them apart from the people of Coramantien, who are dressed in the coastal Yoruba style of 'Agbada' and 'dashiki'" (Bandele, I.1.i). The play opens with a military threat issued by I. Saeed, and the scene closes with him carrying away the head of his companion. The quick execution of the emissary is meant to set up the kingdom in the English audience's eyes as strong, proud, and politically savvy. Behn makes a similar move in her text, but does so through descriptions of courtly behavior. The scene of the violent expulsion of the Muslim characters from the kingdom is never critiqued in the play, even though its government will be. King, counselors, and Oroonoko look at it in solidarity and approval.

In Behn's text, the hero's lack of remorse for his past as a slave trader signals the absence of an abolitionist stance in the work as a whole. This political stance shifted in the versions of the play as audience preferences changed, culminating in Ferriar's explicitly abolitionist adaptation. What then should be made of audience preferences for the Bandele text? The execution of the Muslim emissaries in the new version points to an accepted view of Muslims as a threat whose elimination needs little justification. That Bandele's stage directions make a point of portraying the Muslims as outsiders also points to the potential critique of present-day Nigeria's own ethnic-religious conflicts. It certainly represents a departure from the Behn version's vision of an Africa predominantly dominated by Muslim culture.

---

[45] Bandele, *Aphra Behn's Oroonoko in a New Adaptation,* 5.
[46] The religion of the Nigerian population is 50% Muslim 40% Christian, and 10% indigenous beliefs 10% ("World Fact Book," Central Intelligence Agency, 2007).

While the portrayal of the Muslim emissaries can be seen as a stance on Islamic aggression, the court of Coramantien also reflects the play's stance on the non-Muslim factions of African governments. The king and his counselor are corrupt, as shown in their dealings in the slave trade and the rapes of Imoinda. In the Behn version, Oroonoko stands in as a younger, better alternative to his grandfather the king, but in the Bandele, he is re-envisioned into a child needing to be led and not as a warrior-prince fit to rule. His mentor chides him for lacking the "responsibility" to be a good leader when he takes "part in a childish game" and then tries to blame it on his servants (I.1.ii). He is not the aggressor in his marriage to Imoinda; instead, her foster-mother, Onola, arranges it out of the belief that unlike the other male characters in the Africa scenes, Oroonoko poses no sexual threat to her charge. Throughout the rest of the play, the stage directions and dialogue demonstrate the affection within the marriage without touching on the erotic. The nonsexual nature of their relationship is reinforced by Bandele's omission of Imoinda's pregnancy, which in earlier versions acted as the impetus for Oroonoko's revolt.[47] Through the early reprimands by a more mature man and Onola's view of him as nonsexual, Oroonoko emerges as a child swept away by events, while those ruling the kingdom are corrupt rapists; it is they, not Oroonoko, who are involved in the slave trade. The first half ends with an image of an African country in need of proper leadership, but without any legitimate internal options for reform.

When Jessica Munns interviewed Simon Reade, an RSC member who worked with Doran and Bandele on the play, she asked about Bandele's depiction of Surinam and the play's reliance on the Hawkesworth adaptation for its second act. Reade responded that "after Bandele had written the African part…he did not produce a second part and explained that he was not interested in writing the Surinam section."[48] As a result, Doran and Reade "edited [the Hawkesworth

---

[47] This disturbing lack of marital contact mirrors some productions of *Othello* that use the lack of a bedroom scene prior to Desdemona's murder to imply their marriage was unconsummated. Southerne's version of *Oroonoko* heavily borrows from Shakespeare, and the transformation of Imoinda into a white European reinforces the connection between playwrights. In the case of Bandele's adaptation, the connection to *Othello* colors Imoinda's death scene. If he is like Othello, is Oroonoko then a misguided murderer rather than a clear-sighted husband protecting his wife from physical and sexual abuse by the colonial government?

[48] Munns, "Reviving *Oroonoko*," 190.

adaptation] down and Bandele added link passages" to the new first
act. Reade added that he felt the stylistic contrast between the two acts
worked to make the African scenes more vibrant, while the second half
reflected "the drab world of slavery," making the "audience register
that they had left Africa and entered the world of a Restoration play"
(190). In doing so, Reade hoped they reversed what he implied was
the Orientalism of the original novel, making it the "Surinams that are
sordid, unjust and cruel, but which are also polished by the glamour
of the exotic and the gloss of heroism" (190). Of note is the way the
Restoration and romance values that Behn uses are seen as archaic and
corrupt, which in a way, mirrors Hawkesworth's assessment of Southerne. Ironically, though Hawkesworth sought to separate the play from
its late seventeenth-century roots, his version emerges in twentieth-
century adaptation as representative of those Restoration values. Also
relevant is the implicit argument made the RSC production that the
African scenes are more realistic than the ones in Surinam. Considering Bandele's association of the first act with his vision of Nigeria, the
killing of the Muslim messengers becomes a more central and, in my
opinion, disturbing aspect of this representation of Africa. It sends a
clear signal that this iteration of the *Oroonoko* narrative rejects any
past associations with the Ottoman Empire and Islamic culture. Its
Royal Slave is no oriental prince.

By comparison, the English colony at Surinam is largely portrayed
as egalitarian space. The man in charge of the Lord Governor's estate,
Trefry, opens Act Two with a critique of slavery and acts as a more
effective protector of Imoinda than her husband is able to be. He, and
not Oroonoko, is the one who fights with the villain of the play, Byam,
to protect Imoinda. Oroonoko, on the other hand, leads the slave revolt
as he does in the older versions, but lacks the grand speeches to incite
the slaves to follow him. They have been already convinced by his former servant to join. The failure of the uprising, his killing of Imoinda,
and his own death lose much of their original meaning, since by doing
so, he—in Bandele's version—thwarts his own freedom. Too emotionally broken by the events, Oroonoko cannot comprehend the fact that,
in the end, Trefry has saved him. Preventing the local authorities from
prosecuting Oroonoko for either the revolt or Imoinda's death, Trefry
arranges with the newly arrived Lord Governor for the slave to be
freed. Realizing that if he had not killed his wife she would no longer
be in danger, Oroonoko charges at Trefry with a knife, forcing Trefry

to shoot. This is quite different from Behn's narrative. In her *Oroonoko*, Imoinda's death is justified because the Lord Governor has died and the lovers will not be freed. Instead, the colony has fallen into irredeemably corrupt hands and after Oroonoko's grisly public execution, Imoinda, if left alive, would most certainly face retaliation for her role in the rebellion. Trefry does in fact receive "gloss of heroism" to which Reade refers, but at the expense of the presumed hero of the play, Oroonoko.

In Bandele's version, Imoinda's death necessitates Oroonoko's. Without her, he does not need his freedom. In a play where the women are oppressed and victimized, the majority of the men are corrupt sexual predators, and the hero is largely a nonsexual child, it is oddly Oroonoko's killer who emerges as the play's moral center. The stage directions in Bandele clear Trefry of culpability in the killing: "*Oroonoko charges towards Mr. Trefry with every intention of stabbing him. Mr. Trefry hesitates, then he shoots Oroonoko. Oroonoko falls down. Mr. Trefry runs over to him*" (II.2.1). The Englishman's hesitation, even when his life is in danger, and his immediate concern for his potential killer mark him as a sympathetic character and justify this final action. This—along with his early speeches against slavery, his protection of Imoinda and Oroonoko, and his alliance with the new colonial government—shows that Trefry represents a character to whom the English audience may relate.

But what are the implications of these choices? How do they fit into end of a century that witnessed the decline of Britain as a world power and the dismantling of its empire? One thing they demonstrate is a great deal of comfort with the legacy of slavery. The need to be abolitionist has passed. Instead, characters are caught up in a tragic train of events where well-meaning liberals are forced to kill their non-white friends, but order is restored in the end by the return of the Lord Governor and the political triumph of Trefry. This may largely be owed to the early moves toward British emancipation, which predate many of its contemporaries in Europe and the Americas. Yet, in celebrating this nineteenth-century imperial accomplishment, it disregards any culpability in the fates of its former colonies.

An echo the ideology of English superiority used to justify the occupation of other countries, Trefry as an English colonizer is morally superior to Oroonoko and his subjects. The play contrasts the liberalism of the English colony with the violence and oppression found in other cultures. Observe the opening scene: Bandele's fantasy of former British-ruled Nigeria depicts Muslims as a threat to be quickly dispatched while non-Muslim governments are corrupt and oppressively patriarchal. Its one hope of a legitimate ruler, Oroonoko, is represented as childlike. In contrast, the English colony is only under a temporary bad rule, which is solved by the end. This, along with the de-emphasis on slavery, makes Oroonoko, in many ways, to blame for his own demise; his inability to endure what fate gives him, not his enslavement—and certainly not Trefry's act of self-defense—becomes the culprit for his death. If anything, the liberal, white, non-royal Englishman is portrayed as the ideal ruler: Trefry can critique the situation but still 'puts down' insurgents even if he may sympathize with them.

Conclusion

Like its predecessors, the Bandele version finds in the *Oroonoko* narrative elements that fit its own ideologies. Southerne's recuperation of Surinam through the comic plot, Hawkesworth's colonial decline, and Ferriar's abolitionist activism each found something in Behn's story that resonated with their particular audience. The issues of Behn's importance as a female author and her role in the development of the novel, as well as her choice to center her final work around the tragic execution of a slave in the colonies, continues to provoke debate over not only what she intended her text to mean but also how each generation of readers attempts to come to terms with it within their own political and historical moments.

The tendency to efface past associations in new interpretations of old narratives, as in the case of the obscuration of Ottoman influence in the eighteenth-century narratives discussed here, offers an opportunity see how shifts in popular culture reflect changes in historical relationships between nations. It also offers a model for examining national identities and political actions today. By looking at how audiences and authors reinterpret past narratives, we can see what anxieties influence our own identities today.

In many ways this book is a starting place for asking new questions rather than an answer to old ones of empire and Orientalism. It seeks to bridge what I see as a gap between medieval/early modern and nineteenth-century scholarship on England's representations of with the Ottoman Empire. The majority of this work challenges concepts of an ahistorically powerful England and shows both that the intermingling of Islamic and English Protestant identity was a recurring theme of the century, and that this cultural mixing was a topic of debate and anxiety in the English cultural imagination. These representations were not always entirely accurate in their portrayal of the political reality of either England or the Ottoman Empire, but demonstrate a gradually shifting worldview through the anxieties surrounding domestic tensions, foreign influence, and the idea of empire.

BIBLIOGRAPHY

Aebischer, Pascale. *Shakespeare's Violated Bodies: Stage and Screen Performance.* Cambridge: Cambridge University Press, 2004.

Akman, Beyazit H. "How Novel is the First Novel? Robinson Crusoe and Hayy bin Yaqzan." Paper presented the annual meeting for the American Society for Eighteenth-Century Studies, Richmond, Virginia, March 25–28, 2009.

Allen, Ned B. "The Two Parts of *Othello*." *Aspects of Othello: Shakespeare Survey* 21 (1977): 75–91.

Anon. *The City-Wifes Petition Against Coffee Presented to the Publick Consideration, the Grand Inconveniencies that Accrue to Their Sex, From the Excessive Drinking of that Drying And Enfeebling Liquor: To the Right Honourable, the Worshipful Court of Female Assistants, the Humble Petition and Address of Several Thousand of Buxome Good Women, Languishing in Extremity of Want.* London (Printed for A.W.) 1700. Early English Books Online. Gale Group. http://galenet.galegroup.com/servlet/EBBO.

——. *A Broadside Against Coffee; Or, the Marriage of the Turk,* London: 1672. Early English Books Online. Gale Group. http://galenet.galegroup.com/servlet/EBBO.

——. *A Companion to the Theatre: or, the Usefulness of the Stage to Religion, Government, and the Conduct of Life.* London, 1736. Eighteenth Century Collections Online. Gale Group. http://galenet.galegroup.com/servlet/ECCO.

——. *The Maidens complain[t] against coffee, or, The coffee-house discovered beseiged, stormed, taken, untyled and lai[d] open to publick view…* London: Printed for J. Jones, 1663. Early English Books Online. Gale Group. http://galenet.galegroup.com/servlet/EBBO.

Ashwell, George. Introduction to *The History of Hai Eb'n Yockdan* by Muhammad ibn 'Abd al-Malik ibn Tufayl. London: Richard Chiswell and William Thorp, 1686. Early English Books Online. Gale Group. http://galenet.galegroup.com/servlet/EBBO.

Aravamudan, Srinivas. *Tropicopolitans: Colonialism and Agency, 1688–1804.* Durham, NC: Duke University Press, 1999.

Archibald, Elizabeth. "Ancient Romance." In *A Companion to Romance from Classical to Contemporary,* edited by Corinne Saunders, 10–25. Malden, MA: Blackwell Publishing, 2004.

Armitage, David. "The Scottish Vision of Empire: Intellectual Origins of the Darien Venture." In *A Union for Empire: Political Thought and the British Union of 1707,* edited by J. Robertson, 97–119. Cambridge: Cambridge University Press, 1995.

Backscheider, Paula. *Daniel Defoe: His Life.* Baltimore: John Hopkins Press, 1992.

Ballaster, Ros. *Fabulous Orients: Fictions of the East in England 1662–1785.* Oxford: Oxford University Press, 2005.

Bandele, 'Biyi. *Aphra Behn's Oroonoko in a New Adaptation.* Oxford: Amber Land Press, 1999.

Barbour, Richmond. *Before Orientalism: London's Theatre of the East, 1576–1626.* Cambridge: Cambridge University Press, 2003.

Bartolomeo, Joseph F. *A New Species of Criticism: eighteenth-century discourse on the novel.* Cranbury, NJ: Associated University Presses, 1994.

Basker, James G. "Intimations of Abolitionism in 1759: Johnson, Hawkesworth, and *Oroonoko*." *Age of Johnson: A Scholarly Annual* 12 (2001): 47–66.

Beach, Adam. "Behn's Oroonoko, Atlantic Creoles, and the Early Modern Gold Coast," Paper presented the annual meeting for the American Society for Eighteenth-Century Studies, Richmond, Virginia, March 25–28, 2009.

Behn, Aphra. *Oroonoko; or, the Royal Slave* (1688), edited by Catherine Gallagher Boston: Bedford/St. Martin, 2000.

——, "To Mr. Creech (under the Name of Daphnis) on his Excellent Translation of Lucretius." Cambridge: Chadwyck-Healey, *1992. Literature Online.* UCSD Libraries. http://lion.chadwyck.com.

——, "To the Most Illustrious Prince Christopher Duke Of Albemarle, On His Voyage O His Government Of *Jamaica.*" Cambridge: Chadwyck-Healey, 1992. *Literature Online.* UCSD Libraries. http://lion.chadwyck.com.

Bell, Sandra. "Writing the Monarch: King James VI and *Lepanto.*" In *Other Voices, Other Views: Expanding the Canon in English Renaissance Studies,* edited by Helen Ostovich, Mary V. Silcox, and Graham Roebuck, 193–208. Cranbury, NJ; Associated University Presses, 1999.

Black, William. *A Short View Of Our Present Trade and Taxes, Compared With What These Taxes May Amount to After The Union.* [Edingburgh?], [1706?]. Eighteenth Century Collections Online. Gale Group. http://galenet.galegroup.com/servlet/ECCO.

Blackburn, Robin. *The Overthrow of Colonial Slavery 1776–1848.* New York: Verso, 1988.

Braddick, Michael J. "Civility and Authority." In *The British Atlantic World, 1500–1800,* edited by David Armitage and Michael J. Braddick, 93–112. New York: Palgrave Macmillan, 2002.

Badem, Candan. *The Ottoman Crimean War (1853–1856).* Leiden: E.J. Brill, 2010.

Brown, Laura. "The Romance of Empire: *Oroonoko* and the Trade in Slaves." In *The New Eighteenth Century: Theory, Politics, English Literature,* edited by Laura Brown and Felicity Nussbaum, 41–61. New York: Methuen, 1987.

Burgess, Glyn, translator. *The Song of Roland.* London: Penguin, 1990.

Burgh, James. *The Art of Speaking, . . .* (1761). 2nd Edition. Dublin, 1763.

Capell, Edward. *Notes and Various Readings to Shakespeare, . . .* Vol. 1. London, 1779–80. Eighteenth Century Collections Online. Gale Group. http://galenet.galegroup.com/servlet/ECCO.

Carretta, Vincent. *Equiano, the African: Biography of a Self-made Man.* Athens, GA: University of Georgia Press, 2005.

Chambers, Douglas B. "Ethnicity and Diaspora: The Slave Trade and Creation of African 'Nations' in the Americas." In *Slavery and Abolition.* 22.3 (2001): 25–39.

Chejne, Anwar G. *Islam and the West: The Moriscos, A Cultural and Social History.* Albany: State University of New York Press, 1983.

Cholakian, Patricia. "Signs of the 'Feminine': The Unshaping of Narrative in Marguerite de Navarre's *Heptameron,* Novellas 2, 4, and 10." In *Reconsidering the Renaissance,* edited by Mario A. Di Cesare, 229–244. Albany: SUNY Press, 1992.

Conrad, Lawrence I. "Resources on Ibn Tufayl and Hayy Ibn Yaqzan." In *The World of Ibn Tufayl: Interdisciplinary Perspectives on Hayy Ibn Yaqzan,* edited by Lawrence I. Conrad, 267–293. Leiden: E.J. Brill, 1996.

Daileader, Celia R. *Racism, Misogyny, and the 'Othello' Myth.* Cambridge: Cambridge University Press, 2005.

Davis, David Brion. *The Problem of Slavery in the Age of Revolution, 1770–1823.* Ithaca: Cornell University Press, 1975.

Davis, Natalie Zemon. *Trickster Travels: A Sixteenth-Century Muslim Between Worlds.* New York: Hill and Wang, 2006.

Defoe, Daniel. *The Advantages of Scotland by an Incorporate Union with England, compar'd with these [sic] of a coalition with the Dutch, or league with France. In answer to a pamphlet, call'd, The advantages of the Act of security, &c. . . .* [Edinburgh?], 1706. Eighteenth Century Collections Online. Gale Group. http://galenet.galegroup.com/servlet/ECCO.

——. *An Appeal to Honour and Justice, tho' it be of his worst enemies. By daniel de foe. Being a true account of his conduct in publick affairs.* London, 1715. Eighteenth Century Collections Online. Gale Group. http://galenet.galegroup.com/servlet/ECCO.

——. *An Essay at Removing National Prejudices Against a Union With Scotland.* London, 1706. Eighteenth Century Collections Online. Gale Group. http://galenet.galegroup.com/servlet/ECCO.

—— *A Review of the Affairs of France.* July 1, 1704 to January 6, 1705. Facsimile Book 2 of Volume 1. New York: Columbia University Press, 1938.

——. *Robinson Crusoe* (1719), edited by John Richetti. London: Penguin Books, 2001.

——. *Roxana* (1724), edited by Melissa Mowry. Peterborough, Ontario, Canada: Broadview Press, 2009.

De Krey, Gary. *A Fractured Society: The Politics of London in the First Age of Party 1688–1715.* Oxford: Oxford University Press, 1985.

——. *Restoration and Revolution in Britain: A Political History of the Era of Charles II and the Glorious Revolution.* New York: Palgrave Macmillan, 2007.

Dirks Nicolas B., *The Scandal of Empire: India and the Creation of Imperial Britain* Cambridge, MA, USA: Belknap Press of Harvard University Press, 2006.

Dixon, Philip. "Ashwell, George (1612–1694)." In *Oxford Dictionary of National Biography*, online ed., edited by Lawrence Goldman. Oxford: Oxford University Press. http://0-www.oxforddnb.com.library.colby.edu/view/article/788.

Dobson, Michael. *The Making of the National Poet: Shakespeare, Adaptation, and Authorship, 1660–1769.* Oxford: Claredon Press. 1992.

Doyle, Laura. "The Folk, the Nobles and the Novel: The Racial Subtext of Sentimentality." *Narrative* 3.2 (May 1995): 161–187.

Eldem, Edhem. *French Trade in Istanbul in the Eighteenth Century.* Leiden: E.J. Brill, 1999.

Elmore, Jenifer B. "'The Fair Imoinda': Domestic Ideology and Anti-Slavery on the Eighteenth-Century Stage." In *Troping* Oroonoko *from Behn to Bandele*, edited by Susan B. Iwanisziw, 35–58. Burlington: Ashgate Publishing Company, 2004.

Equiano, Olaudah. *The Life of Olaudah Equiano, or Gustavus Vassa, the African* (1789). Mineola, NY: Dover Publications, 1999.

Eschenbach, Wolfram V. *Parzival: A Romance of the Middle Ages*, translated by Helen M. Mustard and Charles E. Passage. New York: Vintage Books, 1961.

Ferguson, Moira. "Juggling Categories of Race, Class and Gender: Aphra Behn's *Oroonoko*." In *Aphra Behn*, edited by Janet Todd, 209–233. New York: St. Martin's Press, 1999.

Ferriar, John. *The Prince of Angola, A Tragedy, altered from the play of Oroonoko and adapted to the circumstances of the present times.* Manchester: J. Harrop, 1788.

Fielding, Henry. *Tom Jones*, edited by Sheridan Baker. New York: W.W. Norton and Co., 1995.

Fraser, Elisabeth. "Print Culture from Constantinople to Paris: An Ottoman Dragoman between Two Empires." Paper presented the annual meeting for the American Society for Eighteenth-Century Studies, Albuquerque, New Mexico, March 17–20, 2010.

Free Melissa. "Un-erasing Crusoe: Farther Adventures in the Nineteenth Century." *Book History* 9 (2006): 89–130.

Fulton, A.S. Introduction to *The History of Hayy ibn Yaqzan*, by Muhammad ibn 'Abd al-Malik ibn Tufayl. London: Chapman and Hall, 1929.

Gildon, Charles. *The life and strange surprizing adventures of Mr. D---- de F--, of London, hosier, who has liv'd above fifty years by himself, in the Kingdoms of North and South Britain....* London: J. Roberts, 1719.

Hankey, Julie. Introduction in *Othello*, by William Shakespeare. Cambridge: Cambridge University Press, 1987.

Hadfield, Andrew, editor. *A Routledge Literary Sourcebook on William Shakespeare's Othello*. New York: Routledge, 2003.

Hall, Kim F. *Things of Darkness: Economies of Race and Gender in Early Modern England*. Ithaca, NY: Cornell University Press, 1996.

Harlow. Vincent T. *The Founding of the Second British Empire 1763–1793: Volume I: Discover and Revolution*. London: Longman, 1952.

Harris, Walter. *A Short Vindication of Phil. Scot's Defence of the Scots Abdicating Darien*. Edingburgh, 1700. Early English Books Online. Gale Group. http://galenet .galegroup.com/servlet/EBBO.

———. *An Enquiry into the Caledonian Project* Edingburgh, 1701. Early English Books Online. Gale Group. http://galenet.galegroup.com/servlet/EBBO.

Hawkesworth, John. *Oroonoko, A Tragedy, As it is now Acted at the Theatre-Royal In Drury-Lane. By His Majesty's Servants. By Thomas Southern. With Alterations*. 1759. Cambridge: Chadwyck-Healey, *1994. Literature Online*. UCSD Libraries. http://lion .chadwyck.com.

Hakluyt, Richard. *The Interpretation of the letters in Hakluyt's The Principal Navigations, Voyages, Traffiques and Discoveries of the English Nation*. Glasgow: Glasgow University Press, 1904.

Hobbes, Thomas. *Leviathan, or The Matter, Forme and Power of a Common-Wealth Ecclesiasticall and Civill*. (1651), edited by Richard E. Flathman and David Johnston. New York: W.W. Norton, 1997.

Hochschild, Adam. *Bury the Chains: Prophets and Rebels in the Fight to Free an Empire's Slaves*. Boston: Houghton Mifflin Company, 2005.

Hunter, J. Paul. *The Reluctant Pilgrim: Defoe's Emblematic Method and Quest for Form in Robinson Crusoe*. Baltimore: John Hopkins Press, 1966.

Hyam, Ronald. *Britain's Declining Empire: The Road to Decolonisation, 1918–1868*. Cambridge: Cambridge University Press, 2006.

Ingham, Patricia Clare. *Sovereign Fantasies: Arthurian Romance and the Making of Britain*. Philadelphia: University of Pennsylvania Press, 2001.

Iwanisziw, Susan. "The Eighteenth-Century Marketing of *Oroonoko*: Contending Constructions of Maeceanas, the Author and the Slave." In *Troping* Oroonoko *from Behn to Bandele*, edited by Susan B. Iwanisziw, 140–173. Burlington: Ashgate, 2004.

James, Lawrence. *The Rise and Fall of the British Empire*. New York: Saint Martin's Press, 1996.

James, Louis. "Unwrapping Crusoe: Retrospective and Prospective Views." In *Robinson Crusoe: Myths and Metamorphoses*, edited by Lieve Spaas and Brian Stimpson, 1–9. New York: St. Martin Press, 1996.

Jasanoff, Maya. *Edge of Empire: Lives, Culture, and Conquest in the East, 1750–1850*. New York: Knopf, 2005.

Johnson, Lemuel A. *Shakespeare in Africa (and Other Venues): Import and Appropriation of Culture*. Trenton, NJ: Africa World Press, Inc., 1998.

Jones, Emrys. "*Othello, Lepanto* and the Cyprus Wars." In *Aspects of Othello: Shakespeare Survey* 21 (1977): 61–66.

Jones, J. R. *Country and Court: England, 1658–1714*. London: E. Arnold, 1978.

Karpat, Kemal H. *Studies on Ottoman Social and Political History: Selected Articles and Essays*. Leiden: E.J. Brill, 2002.

Keith, George. Advertisement to the Reader in *An Account of Oriental Philosophy* by Muhammad ibn 'Abd al-Malik ibn Tufayl. London: s.n, 1674.

Kinoshita, Sharon. *Medieval Boundaries: Rethinking Difference in Old French Literature*. Philadelphia: University of Pennsylvania Press, 2006.

Knolles, Richard. *The Generall Historie of the Turkes*. London: Adam Islip, 1603.

Krueger, Roberta L. Introduction to *The Cambridge Companion to Medieval Romance*, edited by Roberta L. Krueger, 1–9. Cambridge: Cambridge University Press, 2000.

Kugler, Taduesz and Siddharth Swaminathan, "The Politics of Population: India, China, and the Future of the World." *International Studies Review* 8 (2006): 581–596.

La Fayette, Marie-Madeleine de. *La Princesse de Clèves* (1678) In *Romans et Nourvelles*, edited by Émile Magne, 240–412. Paris: Garnier Frères, 1970.

——. *Zaîde: Histoire Espagnole* (1670–1671). In *Romans et Nourvelles*, edited by Émile Magne. 37–235. Paris: Garnier Frères, 1970.

Laslett, Peter. Introduction to *Two Treatises of Government*, by John Locke. New York: The New American Library, 1963.

Levin, Richard. "The Indian/Iudean Crux in Othello." *Shakespeare Quarterly* 33.1 (Spring, 1982): 60–67.

Lennox, Charlotte. *Shakespear Illustrated: or the Novels and Histories, on which the Plays of Shakespear are Founded, Collected and Translated from the Original Authors. With Critical Remarks. In Two Volumes. By the Author of The Female Quixote.* Vol. 1. London, 1753. Eighteenth Century Collections Online. Gale Group. http://galenet.galegroup.com/servlet/ECCO.

Locke, John. *An Essay Concerning Human Understanding* (1690), edited by Raymond Wilburn. London: J.M. Dent & Sons, 1959.

——. *Two Treatises of Government* (1688), edited by Peter Laslett. New York: The New American Library, 1963.

Long, Edward, *The History of Jamaica. Or, General Survey of the Antient And Modern State Of That Island: With Reflections on its Situation, Settlements,...* Vol. 2. London, 1774.

Loomba, Ania. *Shakespeare, Race, and Colonialism.* Oxford: Oxford University Press, 2002.

Loomie, Albert J. "King James I's Catholic Consort." *The Huntington Library Quarterly* 34.4 (1971): 303–316.

McJannet, Linda. *The Sultan Speaks: Dialogue in English Plays and Histories about the Ottoman Turks.* New York: Palgrave Macmillan, 2006.

MacLean, Gerald. *Looking East: English Writing and the Ottoman Empire Before 1800.* New York: Palgrave Macmillan, 2007.

——. *The Rise of Oriental Travel: English Visitors to the Ottoman Empire, 1580–1720.* New York: Palgrave Macmillan, 2004.

Mason, Virginia. "Race Mattered: Othello in Late Eighteenth-Century England." *Shakespeare in the Eighteenth Century: Shakespeare Survey* 51 (1998): 57–66.

Matar, Nabil. *Britain and Barbary, 1589–1689.* Gainesville: University Press Florida, 2005.

——. *Europe through Arab Eyes, 1578–1727.* New York: Columbia University Press, 2009.

——. *In the Lands of the Christians: Arabic Travel Writing in the 17th Century.* New York: Routledge, 2003.

——. *Islam in Britian, 1558–1685.* Cambridge: Cambridge University Press, 1998.

——. *Turks, Moors, and Englishmen in the Age of Discovery.* New York: Columbia University Press, 1999.

McCail, Ronald. Introduction to *Daphnis and Chloe*, by Longus, vii–xxix. Oxford: Oxford University Press, 2002.

Moody, Jane. "Shakespeare and the Immigrants: Nationhood, Psychology and Xenophobia on the Nineteenth-Century Stage." In *Victorian Shakespeare, Volume 1: Theatre, Drama and Performance*, edited by Gail Marshall and Adrian Poole, 99–118. New York: Palgrave Macmillan, 2003.

Munns, Jessica. "Reviving *Oroonoko* 'in the scene': From Thomas Southerne to 'Biyi Bandele.'" In *Troping* Oroonoko *from Behn to Bandele*, edited by Susan B. Iwanisziw, 174–194. Burlington: Ashgate, 2004.

Murdoch, Alex. "Scotland, the Caribbean and the Atlantic World." *Journal of Scottish Historical Studies* 25.2 (2005): 149–151.

Novak, Maximillian. "Robinson Crusoe's 'Original Sin.'" *Studies in English Literature, 1500–1900*, I (1961): 19–29.

Nussbaum, Felicity A. *The Limits of the Human: Fictions of Anomaly, Race and Gender in the Long Eighteenth Century*. Cambridge: Cambridge University Press, 2003.

Ockley, Simon. Preface and Appendix to *The Improvement of Human Reason, Exhibited in the Life of Hai ebn Yokdhan*, by Muhammad ibn 'Abd al-Malik ibn Tufayl. London, 1708. Eighteenth Century Collections Online. Gale Group. http://galenet.galegroup.com/servlet/ECCO.

——. Appendix to *The Improvement of Human Reason, Exhibited in the Life of Hai Ebn Yokdhan*, by Muhammad ibn 'Abd al-Malik ibn Tufayl. London: E. Powell, 1708. Don Cameron Allen Renaissance Collection, Mandeville Special Collections Library, University of California, San Diego.

——. *The History of the Saracens. Containing the lives of Abubeker, Omar, Othman, Ali, Hasan, Moawiyah I. Yezid I. Moawiyah II. Abdolla, Merwan I. and Abdolmelick, the immediate successors of Mahomet. Giving an account of their most remarkable battles, sieges, &c. particularly those of Aleppo, Antioch, Damascus, Alexandria, and Jerusalem. Illustrating the religion, rites, customs, and manner of living of that warlike people....* Vol. 1.3rd edition. Cambridge, [1757]. Eighteenth Century Collections Online. http://galenet.galegroup.com/servlet/ECCO.

Orr, Bridget. *Empire on the English Stage, 1660–1714*. Cambridge: Cambridge University Press, 2001.

Paige, Nicholas D. Introduction to *Zayde: A Spanish Romance*, by Marie-Madeleine de La Fayette. *The Other Voice in Early Modern Europe*. Chicago: University of Chicago Press, 2006.

Parker, G.F. *Johnson's Shakespeare*. Oxford: Clarendon Press, 1989.

Patterson, Orlando. *Slavery and Social Death: A Comparative Study*. Cambridge: Harvard University Press, 1982.

Peker, Ali Uzay. "Western Influences on the Ottoman Empire and Occidentalism in the Architecture of Istanbul." *Eighteenth-Century Life* 26.3 (2002): 139–163.

Pestana, C.G. "Religion." In *The British Atlantic World, 1500–1800*, edited by David Armitage and Michael J. Braddick, 69–89. New York: Palgrave Macmillian, 2002.

Price, Richard and Sally. Introduction to *Stedman's Surinam: Life in an Eighteenth-Century Slave Society*, by John Gabriel Stedman. Baltimore: John Hopkins University Press, 1992.

Reilly, Matthew. "'No eye has seen, or ear heard': Arabic Sources for Quaker Subjectivity in Unca Eliza Winkfield's *The Female American*." *Eighteenth-Century Studies* 44. 2 (2010): 261–283. http://0-muse.jhu.edu.library.colby.edu/ (accessed January 25, 2011).

Roach, Joseph. *Cities of the Dead: Circum-Atlantic Performance*. New York: Columbia University Press, 1996.

Rosenberg, Marvin. *The Masks of Othello: The Search for the Identity of Othello, Iago, and Desdemona by Three Centuries of Actors and Critics*. Cranbury, NJ: Associated University Press, 1992.

Rousseau, Jean-Jacques. *A Discourse on Inequality* (1755), translated by Maurice Cranston. New York: Penguin Books, 1984.

Rowe, Nicolas. "Some Account of the Life" (1709). In *Eighteenth Century Essays on Shakespeare*, edited by D. Nichol Smith. Oxford: Claredon Press, 1963.

"Royal Family." The Offical Site Website of the British Monarchy. Buckingham Palace, 2004. 12 Nov. 2004 <http://www.royal.gov.uk>.

Russell, G.A. "Introduction: The Seventeenth Century: The Age of 'Arabick.'" In *The 'Arabick' Interest of the Natural Philosophers in Seventeenth-Century England*, edited by G.A. Russell, 1–19. *Brill's Studies in Intellectual History*. New York: E.J. Brill, 1994.

——. "The Impact of the *Philosophus autodidactus*: Pocockes, John Locke and the Society of Friends." In *The 'Arabick' Interest of the Natural Philosophers in Seventeenth-Century England*, edited by G.A. Russell, 224–265. *Brill's Studies in Intellectual History*. New York: E.J. Brill, 1994.

Rymer, Thomas. *A Short View of Tragedy It's Original, Excellency and Corruption*. London: Richard Baldwin, 1693.

Said, Edward. *Orientalism*. 1978. New York: Vintage Books, 1994.

Schama, Simon. *Rough Crossings: Britain, the Slaves and the American Revolution*. New York: Harper Collins, 2005.

Scott, Jonathan. *Commonwealth Principles: Republican Writing Of The English Revolution*. Cambridge: Cambridge University Press, 2004.

Shaheen, Naseeb. "Like the Base Judean." *Shakespeare Quarterly* 31, no. 1 (Spring, 1980): 93–95.

Shaw, Stanford J. *History of the Ottoman Empire and modern Turkey*, Volume 1 (1976). Cambridge: Cambridge University Press, 1997.

Shakespeare, William. *Othello, The Moor of Venice* (1603), edited by Julie Hankey. Cambridge: Cambridge University Press, 1987.

Southerne, Thomas. *Oroonoko* (1696), edited by Maximillian E. Novak and David Stuart Rodes. Lincoln: University of Nebraska Press, 1976.

Spencer, Jane. *Aphra Behn's Afterlife*. Oxford: Oxford University Press, 2000.

Stanivukovic, Goran V. "Introduction: Beyond the Olive Trees: Remapping the Mediterranean World in Early Modern English Writings." In *Remapping the Mediterranean World in Early Modern English Writings*, edited by Goran V. Stanivukovic, 1–20. New York: Palgrave Macmilan, 2007.

Stedman, John Gabriel. *Stedman's Surinam: Life in an Eighteenth-Century Slave Society*, edited by Richard and Sally Price. Baltimore: John Hopkins University Press, 1992.

Stewart, Patrick. Interview by Robert Llewellyn. "Sir Patrick Stewart" (2010). *Car Pool* [Video] Retrieved 22 January 2011, from http://www.youtube.com/watch?v=zvNMYqWZ4BM.

Strickland, Debra Higgs. *Saracens, Demons and Jews: Making Monsters in Medieval Art*. Princeton: Princeton University Press, 2003.

Stuart, James I. *His Maiesties Lepanto, or Heroicall Song Being Part of His Poeticall Exercises at Vacant Houres*. London: Simon Stafford and Henry Hooke, 1603.

Taylor, J.E., translator. "Selection from Giraldi Cinthio's *Hecatommithi*." In *The Tragedy of Othello: Moor of Venice*, edited by Alvin B. Kernan, 134–146. New York: Penguin, 1998.

Thomson, Ann. *Barbary and Enlightenment: European Attitudes towards the Maghreb in the 18th Century*. New York: E.J. Brill, 1987.

Todd, Janet. *The Critical Fortunes of Aphra Behn*. Columbia: Camden House, 1998.

Tufayl, Muhammad ibn 'Abd al-Malik ibn. *An Account of Oriental Philosophy,...* translated by George Keith. London: s.n, 1674.

——. *The history of Hai Eb'n Yockdan, an Indian prince, or, The self-taught philosopher...* Translated by George Ashwell. London: Richard Chiswell and William Thorp, 1686. Early English Books Online. Gale Group. http://galenet.galegroup.com/servlet/EBBO.

——. *The Improvement of Human Reason, exhibited in the life of Hai ebn Yokdhan*. Simon Ockley (trans.) London, 1708. Eighteenth Century Collections Online. Gale Group. http://galenet.galegroup.com/servlet/ECCO.

Tutino, Stefania. *Law and Conscience: Catholicism in Early Modern England, 1570–1625*. Burlington: Ashgate, 2007.

Valensi, Lucette. "The Making of a Political Paradigm: The Ottoman state and Oriental Despotism." In *The Transmission of Culture in Early Modern Europe*, edited by

Anthony Grafton and Ann Blair, 173–204. Philadelphia: University of Pennsylvania Press, 1990.

Visconsi, Elliot. "A Degenerate Race: English Barbarism in Aphra Behn's *Oroonoko* and the *Widow Ranter*." *ELH* 69 (2002): 673–701.

Vitkus, Daniel. *Turning Turk: English Theater and the Multicultural Mediterranean, 1570–1630*. New York: Palgrave Macmillan, 2003.

Walker, John. *The Academic Speaker; or, a Selection of Parliamentary Debates, Orations, Odes, Scenes, and Speeches, from the Best Writers. Proper to be Read and Recited by Youth at School*. Dublin, 1796. Eighteenth Century Collections Online. Gale Group. http://galenet.galegroup.com/servlet/ECCO.

Walpole, Michael. *A Briefe Admonition to All English Catholikes*. Saint-Omer: English College Press, 1610.

Watt, Douglas. *The Price of Scotland: Darien, Union and the Wealth of Nations*. Edinburgh: Luath Press, 2007.

Wheeler, Roxann. *The Complexion of Race: Categories of Difference in Eighteenth-Century British culture*. Philadelphia: University of Pennsylvania Press, 2000.

Williams, Eric. *Capitalism and Slavery*. London: André Deutsch Limited, 1989.

Winkler, John J. "The Invention of Romance." In *The Search for the Ancient Novel*, edited by J. Tatum, 23–38. Baltimore: John Hopkins University Press, 1994.

The World Factbook 2009. Washington, DC: Central Intelligence Agency, 2009. http://www.cia.gov/library/publications/the-world-factbook/index.html.

Zhiri, Oumelbanine, *L'Afrique au Miroir de l'Europe: Fortunes de Jean Léon l'Africain à la Renaissance*. Geneva: Droz, 1991.

INDEX